THE
WHITE MAN'S
BURDENS

The material in this anthology, much of it previously uncollected, is drawn from a broad cultural spectrum that includes narrative poetry, heroic verse, patriotic ballads, music hall monologues, and poems from *Punch*. A substantial Introduction sets the Poems in the context of the economic, political and ideological development of British imperial rule, and headnotes historicize the poems themselves, which are presented chronologically—from George Chapman's 'De Guiana, Carmen Epicum' of 1596 to Fred D'Aguiar's 'At the Grave of the Unknown African' of 1993. The result is a poetic summary of the changing attitudes of an imperialist nation to its own imperialism—attitudes which range from jingoism and racism, through religious idealism and liberal anxiety, to outright disgust at the whole enterprise.

THE
WHITE MAN'S
BURDENS

AN ANTHOLOGY
OF BRITISH POETRY
OF THE EMPIRE

EDITED BY
CHRIS BROOKS
AND
PETER FAULKNER

'Take up the White Man's burden ...'
RUDYARD KIPLING, 1898

'The White Man's Burden, Lord, is the burden of his cash'.
WILFRED SCAWEN BLUNT, 1899

UNIVERSITY
of
EXETER
PRESS

First published in 1996 by
University of Exeter Press
Reed Hall, Streatham Drive
Exeter, Devon EX4 4QR
UK

British Library Cataloguing in Publication Data
A catalogue record of this book is
available from the British Library

Hardback ISBN 0 85989 492 4
Paperback ISBN 0 85989 450 9

Typeset in Plantin Light
by Colin Bakké Typesetting, Exeter
Printed and bound in Great Britain
by Short Run Press Ltd, Exeter

CONTENTS

[v]

CONTENTS

CONTENTS

CONTENTS

LIST OF POETS

INTRODUCTION

The White Man's Burdens

BRITAIN, POETRY AND EMPIRE

Anthologizing the Empire

In 1898, notoriously, Kipling urged the imperialist nations to
'Take up the White Man's Burden'; the following year, in *Satan
Absolved*, Wilfrid Scawen Blunt angrily replied, 'The White
Man's Burden, Lord, is the burden of his cash.' Such conflicting
positions—and a whole range of intermediate stances—feature in
much of the poetry British writers produced about the British
Empire over the four centuries of its rise and fall. In recent
years the discourses of postcolonialism have drawn attention to
the major and continuing significance of the cultural products of
the period of Western imperialism. But, so far, they have
concentrated largely upon fiction and upon the writings and
experiences of those parts of the world that were subject to
colonialism and imperialist oppression. This anthology offers
modern readers, for the first time, a cross-section of British
poetry in which the Empire was the burden of the song. We
have drawn our material, much of it previously uncollected,
from a broad cultural spectrum, in itself indicative of the perva-
siveness of the idea—and ideas—of empire: narrative poetry,
heroic verse, patriotic ballads, music-hall monologues, poems
from *Punch*. The context for all these poems was the develop-
ment of British imperial rule, both as an economic and political
system and as a shifting body of ideas: our introductory essay
provides an outline (and it can be no more) of that development.
Headnotes historicize the poems themselves, which are pre-
sented chronologically—from George Chapman's 'De Guiana,
Carmen Epicum' of 1596 to Fred D'Aguiar's 'At the Grave of
the Unknown African' of 1993. The result is a poetic summary

[1]

of the changing attitudes of an imperialist nation to its own imperialism, attitudes which range from jingoism and racism, through religious idealism and liberal anxiety, to outright disgust at the whole enterprise.

In seeking to anthologize the Empire, we have been prompted by a desire to encourage interest in the whole field of study and debate suggested by the title of Edward Said's *Culture and Imperialism* (1993). In this fine book Said asserts the enormous importance of imperialism (particularly as conducted by Britain, France and now the United States) in shaping the modern world, and offers constructive ways of approaching 'the connection between the prolonged and sordid cruelty of such practices as slavery, colonialist and racial oppression, and imperial subjection on the one hand, and the poetry, fiction and philosophy of the society that engages in these practices on the other' (p. xiv). Said offers examples of 'contrapuntal' readings, showing how the numerous histories which constitute imperialism intertwine and overlap, and he attempts 'to formulate an alternative both to a politics of blame and to the even more destructive politics of confrontation and hostility' (p. 19).

A number of valuable studies of the connections between British imperialism and literature have appeared in recent years, as the study of 'English' has moved towards a greater interest in ideology, the whole sphere of cultural practices, and away from the idea of an autonomous arena of the literary. These include Martin Green's pioneering *Dreams of Adventure, Deeds of Empire* (1979), Peter Hulme's *Colonial Encounters* (1986), and Patrick Brantlinger's *The Rule of Darkness* (1988), as well as Said's work. But it is notable that all these works tend to focus on novels, and to a lesser extent on plays; poetry is much less apparent. This is quite understandable as it is in these forms that the most obvious works of the literature of imperialism exist. The various courses that now exist for its study must necessarily draw on Shakespeare's *The Tempest*, Defoe's *Robinson Crusoe*, Rider Haggard's *King Solomon's Mines* and *She*, Conrad's *Heart of Darkness*, Kipling's *Kim*, Forster's *A Passage to India*, Orwell's *Burmese Days* and so on. In these cases we have complete works focusing on the idea and experience of empire. No British poet—with the exception of Kipling—has written so consistently on the subject. What we have are poems from numerous authors, writing for various cultural audiences, which arise from the imperial experience but which do not constitute their author's main commitment. A number of well-known poets appear here, along with others now largely forgotten, but none of these—again with the exception of Kipling—is known primarily as a poet of empire. Nevertheless, the quantity—and sometimes the quality—of these poems show how pervasive for British authors were the issues and experiences of the Empire, from its beginnings in the reign of the first Elizabeth to its dissolution in the reign of the second.

The poems brought together here have been chosen primarily for their subject matter, and we have been largely unconcerned with questions of aesthetic merit. Nevertheless, the vitality that many of these poems still have for the reader shows that the imperial theme was one that engaged many lively minds. Nor was that engagement in any sense monolithic. Indeed, to think of the Empire as a single theme, or of responses to it as homogeneous, is mistaken. Unsurprisingly, over a historical period of some four centuries, the view that British people took of the Empire varied widely. But attitudes could also diverge sharply at almost any given moment during that time, and do so within the work of a single writer. Although readily identified by his contemporaries and since as a proponent of imperialism, Kipling is a case in point, his writings full of complexities, subversive ironies, and—perhaps most frequently—contradictions. In poems that were often written to promote particular beliefs and attitudes, we need to read in the full awareness that few texts, and few beliefs, are without their significant inner tensions.

The poems in this collection present British perspectives on the Empire, not those of either subject peoples or those who became colonists, and later colonials. This is not because the writings of such people are of no account, but on the contrary because they are of so much account (and amount) that they could not be included without enormously over-extending the length of the book. Moreover, excellent anthologies already exist of the poetry of the Empire in this form, and the present anthology should be read alongside such others as Stephen Gray's *Penguin Book of South African Verse* (1989), and Peter Burnett's *Penguin Book of Caribbean Verse in English* (1986). The lines of demarcation are not always obvious: someone initially a traveller, for example, could become a colonist. In general, however, this collection is complementary to such anthologies as those mentioned above because it gives the viewpoint of the people at the centre of the imperial web, the British themselves. We use the term British rather than English advisedly, since it is the adjective invariably attached to the Empire, for the good reasons given in Linda Colley's authoritative *Britons: Forging the Nation 1707–1837* (1992). Significantly, one of the strongest influences Colley sees on the making of an ideology of national unity in this period, apart from a sense of the French as 'an obviously hostile other', is that 'increasingly as the wars went on, they [the British] defined themselves in contrast to the colonial peoples they conquered, peoples who were manifestly alien in terms of culture, religion and colour' (p. 5). The poems of the eighteenth century included here can usefully be viewed in the light of this remark; and of course the repercussions pass through the nineteenth into our own century.

One major problematical area remains, that of Ireland: *England*'s oldest colony, ante-dating the formation of the United Kingdom, into which it was not incorporated until the 1801 Act of Union. The complex history of Anglo-Irish relations, and Anglo-Irish literature, precludes any simple solution. As everyone knows, Irish writers have been major contributors to 'English' literature; many have lived and written in England. Again, the reader is directed to another appropriate anthology, Thomas Kinsell's *New Oxford Book of Irish Verse* (1986), and its informative Introduction. The only 'Irish' poems included here are by poets who lived in England and wrote at least partly from that perspective, like Allingham and Blunt; poems like Yeats's 'Easter 1916' belong to the other side of the story, as discussed by Said in his chapter on 'Resistance and Opposition'.

We have chosen to present the poems, as far as possible, in date order. This means date of publication, except when a poem was unpublished, or there was a long gap between composition and publication, or when the date of composition was particularly important: in all such cases, as indicated in the text, the date when the poem was written has been used. This means, of course, that poems by any one author are distributed between those by others. We have adopted date order in the belief that this gives readers the greatest freedom to create their own patterns of significance from the material: the reader may well wish to put together all the poems by, say, Tennyson or Kipling, or all those that deal with India (see List of Poems and List of Poets at the start of the book). But we have been motivated too by the belief that chronological arrangement encourages us not only to read poems by different writers in direct relationship to one another, but also to read them in the context of the historical moment of their production. Although texts are made by individuals, they are also parts of a larger history and culture, as indeed are the authors themselves. Reading in this way helps to avoid the over-simplifications which often beset discussions of the Empire. The result, we hope, should encourage neither anachronistic flag-waving, nor smugness about our own moral superiority to it all, but rather an analytic scrutiny of these products of a cultural history to which we are all heirs, whether as descendants of the colonizers or of the colonized. We cannot and should not avoid coming to political conclusions as we read, but these need to be based on the fullest understanding that we can achieve—and this must mean a historicized understanding. There is no blinking the fact that the Empire rested upon the systematic imposition of alien authority on subject peoples in order to secure economic and political advantages for Britain. Yet the British Empire also engaged the energies and the imaginations of many honest men and women, and we should try to grasp how, and even why, this was so.

'Frighting the wide heaven': the Beginnings of Colonialism

The British Empire is conventionally thought of as originating in the energies of the later Elizabethan period, with the defeat of the Armada of the great imperial power of Spain in 1588 as its symbolic moment. This is to ignore the earlier colonization of Ireland, alluded to in that most elaborate of Elizabethan poems, Edmund Spenser's *The Faerie Queene* (1590; 1596). In Book Five, the knight Artegall, aided by the iron man Talus with his terrible flail, establishes Justice by defeating various enemies of his queen, Gloriana/Elizabeth. She is presented as a great and, by implication, imperial ruler, but in an allegorical mode that makes no direct allusion to empire. Nevertheless, the account of Artegall and his deeds is often seen as a particularly impassioned defence of Arthur Gray, the Lord Deputy of Ireland, whom Spenser knew and worked under and whom he praised and exonerated in his *View of the Present State of Ireland* (1596). The implied claims for Elizabeth do give *The Faerie Queene* an imperialist sub-text, but it was in the three volumes of the *Principall Navigations, Voyages and Discoveries of the English Nation*, compiled by Richard Hakluyt between 1598 and 1600, that claims for English imperial status became explicit. Hakluyt gives accounts of numerous English seamen and adventurers, including the Cabots, Sir Hugh Willoughby, Sir John Hawkins, Francis Drake, Sir Humphrey Gilbert, Martin Frobisher, John Davy and Sir Walter Raleigh, celebrating their confident claims for their country. No Elizabethan or Jacobean poetry can equal Hakluyt in range or influence, nor match the subtlety of Shakespeare's myth or parable of colonization in *The Tempest* (1611). Among Shakespeare's earlier plays, *Henry V* and *Richard II* both feature set-piece speeches that were often quoted in later patriotic contexts, but that allude only obliquely to empire.

The first significant poems that we have found are by Chapman and Drayton. Chapman's 'De Guiana' of 1596 originally prefaced Kemys's account of his voyage to Guiana, on the north coast of South America, and was republished in Hakluyt. Untroubled in its confidence, the poem's tableau of the (female) figure of Guiana making 'euery signe of all submission' to 'faire England' and her 'most admired Soueraigne' promises an unproblematic colonial future. Nevertheless, it seems that Raleigh, who sponsored Kemys and is directly addressed in the poem, needs forceful encouragement to undertake the proposed new expedition. It was in fact delayed until he was forced to go, disastrously, in 1616: the failure of the expedition led to his execution two years later. A more direct and more paradigmatic imperialist poem is Michael Drayton's 'To the Virginian Voyage' (1606), which briskly encourages Britons—not unflattered by being addressed as 'brave heroique minds'—to set out for the New World. Virginia, described as 'Earth's onely paradise', will fulfil the adventurers' material hopes with its 'pearle and gold' and its bountiful and apparently unlaborious triple harvests. The voyagers are called upon to 'Let cannons roare, Frighting the wide heaven' as they approach. This seems unnecessary, as the 'delicous land' appears uninhabited, but may be seen to suggest the unadmitted aggression of the imperial enterprise. The poem ends peacefully, however, with the hope that poetry will flourish in the New World, its progress unencumbered by any pre-existing culture.

Embarking upon Empire: the Seventeenth Century

From these relatively tentative beginnings, the Empire was developed steadily during the seventeenth century. Virginia, the first permanent colony in North America, was established in 1607 by the voyagers Drayton encouraged on their way. Massachusetts followed in 1629, Maryland in 1632, Rhode Island between 1636 and 1644. By the end of the century colonial settlement extended along most of the eastern seaboard and was already pushing well inland. These American colonies were first established by private enterprise, often by merchant adventurers backed by London money, and came subsequently under the Crown. Private enterprise—much of it in the form of privateering—also led the way in the Caribbean, where colonial ascendancy was hotly contested with Spain. The success of the Virginian tobacco plantations encouraged the establishment of the first permanent British settlement, on Saint Kitts, in 1623, followed by Barbados in 1627, and other islands of the Leeward, Windward, and Virgin groups in the next few decades. In the event their economic success was built on sugar, with plantations developed in the mid-century to serve firstly the Dutch market and then the market that emerged in Britain itself. Meanwhile, British merchants were making the first substantial overtures to India, where the mighty Mogul Empire was at the height of its power. The first royal charter for trading to India was granted to the London Company of Merchants in 1600; British factories were established at Surat in 1612; the first English ambassador to the Mogul court arrived three years later; and in 1640 the first genuinely colonial settlement was founded at Madras.

Very little of all this early imperialist activity is engaged by the poetry of the seventeenth century, though more oblique references are not uncommon. In the great poem of the period, Milton's *Paradise Lost*, for example, God's colonization of the earth, the rival ambitions of Satan, and much of the imagery throughout, carry overtones of the imperial. Andrew Marvell's 'Bermudas' (*c*.1654), however, does address the issue of empire directly. It is a highly urbane and elegant poem in which the emigrants to the Bermudas raise their song to God in thanks for having been led past the peril of the sea to their haven, 'Safe from the Storms, and Prelat's rage'—an escape from the political and religious strife of England to a far more tranquil world. Everything here is provided for human delight, the sensuous pleasures evoked in Marvell's English poems like 'The Garden' transposed to a Caribbean cornucopian with tropical fruits. This Edenic spot is again a virgin land, and its possession by the divinely directed settlers is an act of displaced—and characteristically Marvellian—eroticism. In other poems, like 'The Character of Holland' (1653) and 'On the Victory obtained by Blake over the Spaniards' (1657), Marvell's focus is firmly on Europe, and on immediate political rivalries. So too is Dryden's in *Annus Mirabilis* of 1667, which begins with a celebratory review of the Dutch War of the previous year. But such European concerns were of major importance to Britain's imperial future. Increasingly, England was challenging Dutch economic leadership in Europe, and the mid-century Dutch Wars, which were direct results of this, had significant colonial consequences. Cromwell's navy successfully challenged Dutch and Spanish interests in the Caribbean in the 1650s, acquiring Jamaica in the process, and by the Treaty of Breda, which ended the Second Dutch War in 1667, Holland withdrew from colonial competition in North America. Britain was left in possession of New York and New Jersey as a result.

'Bartering baubles for the souls of men': Colonial Commerce and the Slave Trade

In the later seventeenth and early eighteenth centuries, Britain's economic growth, with its attendant expansion in colonial trade, was conducted, albeit unevenly, under the protectionist system known as mercantilism, which effectively excluded foreign competition from key areas of national commerce. Much of the lucrative trade of the emerging Empire was monopolized by corporations operating under royal charter—the largest, and ultimately most successful being the East India Company. An intrinsic part of this increasing economic activity was slaving. Slavery had been introduced into the Caribbean by the Spanish in the early sixteenth century, and the development of British plantations in North America and the West Indies depended on slave labour. By the end of the seventeenth century, slaving had settled into a regular triangular trade. West Africans, frequently rounded up by native slavers, were shipped across the Atlantic on the terrible 'middle passage' to British possessions in the Caribbean, where they were bought by plantation owners. The slave ships then carried sugar, cotton, and ginger back to Britain. From there they took textiles, metal goods, and arms back down to West Africa, where they were traded for more slaves. The American colonies established their own slave triangle between the ports of the Atlantic seaboard, West Africa, and the West Indies. There was some protest from Dissenters, especially Quakers, but as far as the great majority of whites was concerned, in Britain as well as the colonies, black slaves were mere commodities. Among the few voices raised against slaving was that of Daniel Defoe, whose satiric poem *Reformation of Manners* (1702) contains an attack upon commercial London's greedy support of the trade. Defoe, though, was hardly consistent: very different attitudes are to be found in his far more celebrated work, *Robinson Crusoe* (1719).

'Britannia rule the waves': Conquest and Commerce in the Eighteenth Century

The 1707 Act of Union, formally integrating Scotland with England and Wales, provides the starting point for Linda Colley's account of the development of the British nation. She rightly draws attention to the importance of imperial expansion through the first half of the eighteenth century, culminating in victory in the Seven Years' War (1756–63), 'the most dramatically successful war the British ever fought' (p. 101). The disintegration of the Mogul Empire was exploited by the East India Company at the expense alike of native states and the French, Britain's principal colonial rival. Territorial expansion and consolidation in the years following Clive's victory at Plassey (1757) gave Britain ascendancy among the European powers on the subcontinent; Wolfe's triumph at Quebec (1758) ended direct French colonial involvement in Canada; successful campaigns in the Caribbean brought more islands under the British Crown. Such imperial feats of arms served to boost Britain's relatively new-found sense of nationhood, and were celebrated in contemporary songs like Garrick's 'Heart of Oak' (1759). Even so, the expansion of empire had not been without its earlier eighteenth-century critics. One of the most succinct dismissals of imperialism occurs in Jonathan Swift's ironic answer to *Robinson*

Crusoe—Gulliver's Travels (1726). In the final chapter, Gulliver, having developed some doubts about the justice of colonial acquisition, gives his reasons for not wishing to add further territories to the Empire:

> For Instance, A Crew of Pyrates are driven by a Storm they know not whither; at length a Boy discovers Land from the Top-mast; they go on Shore to rob and plunder; they see an harmless People, are entertained with Kindness, they give the Country a new Name, they take formal Possession of it for the King, they set up a rotten Plank or a Stone for a Memorial, they murder two or three Dozen of the Natives, bring away a Couple more by Force for a Sample, return home, and get their Pardon. Here commences a new Dominion acquired with a Title by *Divine Right*. Ships are sent with the First Opportunity; the Natives driven out or destroyed, the Princes tortured to discover their Gold; a free Licence given to all Acts of Inhumanity and Lust; the Earth reeking with the Blood of its Inhabitants: And this execrable Crew of Butchers employed in so pious an Expedition, is a *modern Colony* sent to convert and civilise an idolatrous and barbarous People.

Nothing in poetry of the period equals this for force of indignation, although Swift's friend Alexander Pope wrote sadly about the destruction of primitive innocence in *Windsor-Forest* (1713) and Frances Seymour retold the story of 'Inkle and Yarico' (1726), in which a young Englishman betrays the black woman who has saved his life. Later in the century, the literary schools of Sentiment and Sensibility were to return to such topics.

But the paramount note in the poetry that addressed Britain's growing imperial role was both self-confident and self-congratulatory. British overseas trade, emerging from beneath the fostering wing of mercantilism, began to expand decisively. In agriculture, the most important sector of the domestic economy, the gradual introduction of capitalist modes of production—the process that came to be called the Agrarian Revolution—began to achieve new levels of output, and new levels of profit for farmers and landowners. At home and abroad Britain could be seen to be assuming a leading economic position among European nations. For much of this the Whigs—dominant in government between 1714 and the 1760s—assumed the credit, by no means always deservedly. In the emerging rhetoric of imperial growth, great emphasis was placed upon commerce, on the

British navy as its protector, and on the combination of the two as the basis for a peaceful and co-operative world. Seeing aggressive economic expansion backed by armed force as a recipe for global harmony is certainly among the more daring paradoxes of the imperialist position. Even so, the 'cult of commerce', to use Colley's phrase (p. 54), went well with Britons' image of themselves, by contrast with all foreigners and particularly the French, as 'under God ... peculiarly free and peculiarly prosperous' (p. 32). Such beliefs were expressed most consistently by the Scots poet James Thomson, who lived and wrote in London and has been well described by James Sambrook as 'a child of the Union, and perhaps the first important poet to write with a British, as distinct from a Scots or English, outlook' (*James Thomson, 1700–1748. A Life*, 1991, p. 53). We find these qualities in *The Seasons* (1730; revised 1744), *Britannia* (1727), *Liberty. A Poem* (1735–6), and even *The Castle of Indolence* (1748). But it is *Alfred. A Masque*, written jointly with David Mallett and first performed in 1740 in the gardens of Cliveden, that includes Thomson's best known poem. At the end of the rather improbable story, the Earl of Devon defeats the Danes on behalf of King Alfred, and a 'venerable Bard, Aged and blind' appears, and intones what was to become the most famous of British patriotic songs, 'Rule, Britannia'. The values of this poem, discussed at the beginning of Colley's book, are consistently Whig: Britain arose 'at heaven's command'; she is entitled to 'rule the waves'; other nations are less blest while she is 'great and free'; commerce will bring riches to her cities while freedom will encourage the writing of poetry; and 'manly hearts' will guard 'the fair'— the sexes will continue in their separately happy spheres. The Hermit's prophecy which follows the song—and is hardly known, not having been set to music—is even more explicit about Britain's right to control the future commerce of the world, and about the role of the British navy in providing the power to achieve it: 'They rule the balanc'd world, who rule the main'.

'An obstinate hill to climb': the Campaign against Slavery

There was, however, one aspect of the commercial empire which Thomson found disturbing, and which was to become of increasing importance as the century moved on: the slave trade.

An unusually powerful section of 'Summer', in *The Seasons*, describes the horrific scene when a slaving ship is approached by a shark seeking 'his share of prey' from 'the partners of that cruel trade,/Which spoils unhappy Guinea of her sons'. Both 'tyrants and slaves' perish as the shark 'dyes the purple seas/ With gore, and riots in the vengeful meal'. In the British consciousness—or even conscience—such scenes long retained their power to shock, as evidenced by the sensational impact of J.M.W. Turner's painting, *Slave Ship [Slavers throwing overboard the Dead and the Dying, Typhoon coming on]*, at the Royal Academy of 1840—even though, as Colley points out (p. 351), both slavery and the slave trade had by then been abolished. The moral problem, not to say flat contradiction, presented by the preeminence of the slave trade in the British Empire of the eighteenth century, with its self-congratulatory emphasis on the idea of freedom ('Britons never shall be slaves'), could not be ignored by writers of any humane sensitivity. William Cowper is a case in point. In 'Boadicea' (1782) he shows that he can prophesy imperial greatness with the best of them, envisaging a future British Empire that will outdo that of Rome: 'Regions Caesar never knew/Thy posterity shall sway', the poem's bard tells the dying queen. Alongside such confident fervour for empire, however, Cowper maintained a sincere loathing for the slave trade upon which so much of it relied, a hatred reinforced by his evangelical Christianity and his friendship with the reformed slaver John Newton.

Opposition to slavery, increasingly widespread but also uncoordinated, was galvanized into an effective campaign by the Society for the Abolition of the Slave Trade, founded in 1786 and led, most prominently, by Thomas Clarkson and William Wilberforce. Cowper was recruited to the cause and in 1788 wrote a group of poems, including 'The Negro's Complaint', to propagandize the Society's campaign. Other evangelicals like Hannah More similarly voiced their support in verse, and Robert Southey, showing few signs of his later conservatism, produced the vigorously angry 'Poems on the Slave Trade' (1795). More radical, both politically and aesthetically, was William Blake's passionate sympathy for the victims of slavery and empire alike. *A Vision of the Daughters of Albion* (1793) includes among its characters the despicable slave-driver, Oothon, and Number 39 of Blake's designs shows 'a slave trying to lift himself from the ground'. In the great harvest festival in Book 9 of the long prophetic poem *The Four Zoas* (1804), the 'New Song' of celebration is composed by an African and sung by all the slaves of the earth. More succinctly, the 'Little Black Boy' of *Songs of Innocence* (1789) not only challenges white feelings of superiority over blacks, but also probes the corrosive effect of racism upon the consciousness of its innocent targets. Despite all such efforts, the campaign was a long one and it was not until 1807 that the slave trade was declared illegal throughout the British dominions: 'it was an obstinate hill to climb', wrote Wordsworth in a congratulatory sonnet to Clarkson. Abolition was greeted by a clutch of poems, among the more remarkable of which was James Montgomery's *The West Indies* (1809), with its panoramic view of the history of slavery in the Caribbean, and its picture of Britannia awaking at last to declare 'Africa, be free!' Freedom actually took rather longer to arrive: it was not until 1834 that slavery itself was abolished in the Empire, and not until 1838 that complete emancipation was achieved.

American Independence, the Second British Empire, and the Abolition of Slavery

The campaign against the slave trade had a vital relationship to the greatest single reverse in British imperial history: defeat in the American War of Independence (1775–83) and the loss of the American colonies. The catalyst for the conflict was the attempt to impose a measure of taxation on the colonies for the first time. Ironically this resulted from the need to pay off the debts the British government had incurred during the Seven Years' War, which had been so very advantageous in terms of territorial acquisition but which had been financed by unprecedented levels of borrowing. There was considerable opposition in Britain to the American War, and poets and politicians alike blamed the intransigence of the government for what was often seen as a conflict with fellow-countrymen—views expressed with bitter clarity in the anonymous 'Boston in Distress' (1776) and in James Freeth's 'Bunker's Hill' (1780). Besides its strategic and economic consequences, defeat gave a sharp check to the self-esteem that the British had enjoyed so complacently only a few years earlier. Linda Colley has seen the intensification of the anti-slavery movement after 1783 as 'a means to redeem the nation, a patriotic act', as well as 'a means whereby the British could impress foreigners with their innate love of liberty and reassure themselves whenever their own faith was in danger of flagging' (p. 354).

There were other, less ideologically motivated reasons as well. The loss of the North American colonies—with the exception of Canada—brought to an end what became known as the First British Empire. But the Second Empire was already in the process of creation, centred on the vast promise of the Indian subcontinent, and on the Pacific, where Cook's voyages of exploration had opened a whole new realm to British expansion and had laid claim *en route* to another subcontinent—Australia. The Caribbean, with its slave-dependent plantations, was still a vital element in the British economic jigsaw, but its importance diminished in the early nineteenth century as the imperial pattern took on a new form. It was not the plight of outraged humanity alone that had inspired the campaign against slavery: *laissez-faire* capitalism, formulated in the pages of Adam Smith's *The Wealth of Nations* (1776), was also opposed to it, for slave-owning constituted a fundamental interference in the freedom of the labour market. The dubious benefits of such freedom were already being experienced by the British working class, and the theories of free market capitalism would soon extend to the global arena that was opening to imperialist expansion. The exploitation of the economic potential of the Second Empire, in contrast to the First, did not need the formal institution of slavery. It would be unjust to campaigners like Clarkson and Wilberforce, and indeed Cowper and Montgomery, to say that slavery was abolished because Britain's new economic gospel and new imperial interests made it redundant: but the campaign, protracted as it was, may have proved even longer had those interests rested, more heavily than they did, upon the backs of black slaves.

The basis of the new Empire was secured during the virtually continuous war that Britain waged against Revolutionary and Napoleonic France, and its allies, between 1793 and 1815. It was a world war, with British forces engaged on every ocean and every continent—as Felicia Hemans proclaimed in her patriotic threnody 'England's Dead' (1813). By the time it was all over and Napoleon was aboard the *Bellerophon* bound for permanent exile on the tiny British colony of St Helena, the 'nation of shopkeepers' had substantially enlarged its premises. Further tracts of India had been added to the possessions of the East India Company; Ceylon (now Sri Lanka) and Cape Colony had been wrested from Dutch control; Britain was firmly established as the dominant imperialist power in the West Indies; colonial settlement was beginning to push forward in Canada, Australia, and New Zealand; nearer home, unhappy Ireland had lost the last semblance of independence and been absorbed into the British realm by the 1801 Act of Union. More important than territorial acquisition, perhaps, was the emergence of the British fleet into a position of unchallenged supremacy. Thomas Campbell's 'Ye Mariners of England' (1801; 1805) carried the sentiments of 'Rule Britannia' forward into a new age in which Trafalgar, The Nelson Touch, and The Wooden Walls of England became the talismans of a whole mythology of naval invincibility. Thus guarded, commerce and colonialism could flourish: as early as 1828 Campbell's 'Lines on the Departure of Emigrants for New South Wales' advertised the alluring prospects of life in Britain's most distant domain. Thomas Hood's 'I'm Going to Bombay' (1832) offered an equally peaceable, but distinctly less elevated view of the utility of empire. And by 1834, to return to the point made earlier, it was an empire in which slavery had been legislated away, an empire that could feel morally superior—particularly to the Americans, who had retained slavery despite the democratic rhetoric of the Declaration of Independence. In 'O Mother Britain Lift Thou Up' (1833–4) the young Tennyson greeted abolition with an ardour that blithely ignored the preceding centuries of bloody exploitation: 'What other people old or young/Had done so just a thing?' For the veteran poet Samuel Rogers, no less smug but politically more worldly in his lines 'Written in 1834', abolition vindicated both the martial triumphs of the Napoleonic War and the commercial triumphs of imperial trade.

'The heathen in his blindness': Empire and the Christian Mission

For many people in Britain watching the spread of the early nineteenth-century Empire, the abolition of slavery was proof that imperialism could be the agent of moral and religious enlightenment—such enlightenment always perceived, of course, from the standpoint of the European Christian tradition. The most dynamic articulation of this was the missionary campaign that now began to gather momentum. The evangelical passion that had transformed the Hanoverian church could be exported, and the commercial energies driving the Empire harnessed to a religious crusade. With an imperial domain beckoning in the dawn of the nineteenth century, the British churches could Christianize the world. Earlier efforts had been far more modest. Although organizations like the Society for the Promotion of Christian Knowledge (1696) and the Society for the Promulgation of the Gospel (1701) had been established with a missionary agenda, their work had been largely confined to the British inhabitants of the Empire: the East India Company, indeed, discouraged missionary activity because its disruptive impact was a threat to trade. Even so, the Moravian Brethren, centred in Germany, had established permanent missions to the West Indies and—extraordinarily—to the Inuit peoples of Greenland, a Danish colony, as early as the 1730s, and their example impressed Wesley and influenced the evangelical movement generally. In 1795 the interdenominational London Missionary Society was established, followed in 1799 by the Church Missionary Society, which became 'the first effective organ of the Church of England for missions to the heathen'. Thomson's belief that the rise of Britain took place 'at Heaven's command' was extended to embrace the growth of the Empire.

The missionaries who embarked for heathen shores did so with the conviction that Christianity was morally and spiritually superior to all other religions. Their aspirations found voice in missionary hymns, among which Reginald Heber's 'From Greenland's Icy Mountains' (1811) is both one of the earliest and one of the best known. Having been vouchsafed 'the lamp of life', true Christians must carry it to 'men benighted' who have never heard 'Messiah's name'. The intention is concerned and generous, but narrowly determined by Heber's dismissal of all native religions. 'Error's chain' binds the whole non-Christian world, represented by Greenland, the focus of the Moravians' efforts; by India, where Heber was to become Bishop of Calcutta in 1822; and by Africa, which Europeans then scarcely knew beyond its coasts. Although God is bountiful and kind, 'The heathen in his blindness/Bows down to wood and stone', and only Christianity can deliver him from his idolatry. Such a belief informed the whole thrust of missionary activity, though hymns rarely expressed it so explicitly. Its basis in a stark cultural and racial antithesis between Christian civilization and pagan savagery is evident in Montgomery's long poem *The Pelican Island* (1827), where the unredeemed state of the peoples of the Pacific is represented with a sensationalism that verges on the hysterical. Such overheated fantasies contrast with Montgomery's own attitudes towards missionary work in the West Indies —about which he knew much more than he did about the South Seas—and with the warm personal sympathy evident in George Beard's record of Wesleyan missions to the Caribbean in his twelve-book epic *The History of Methodism* (1840). A more specialized, Anglican version of the relationship between Christianity and the Empire is provided by Wordsworth's three ecclesiastical sonnets 'Aspects of Christianity in America' (1842). Proponents of mission remained unvaryingly Eurocentric throughout the nineteenth century, though missionary rhetoric, particularly in hymns, often cloaked religious imperialism in metaphorical oppositions between light and dark. Sarah Stock's 'Let the Song Go Round the Earth' (*c.*1890), for example, manages to suggest a freer commitment by the happy converts of Africa and Asia— 'Where the daylight has its birth'—but is overtly hostile to Islam, which 'darkly broods' over the domestic hearths of its followers.

The 'vast domain': Enterprise and Annexation in the Early Victorian Empire

As missionary activity began to intensify in the early 1840s, the Empire itself was on the threshold of its greatest period of expansion. Powering this were the dramatic changes taking place in the domestic economy of the United Kingdom. From the last quarter of the eighteenth century the British population had been increasing with extraordinary speed. Dynamic growth in manufacturing, backed by more sophisticated financial institutions, rapid technological advances, and improvements in transport, accelerated the urbanization of that population. By 1850 the emergence of industrial capitalism as the dominant mode of production had effected permanent structural changes in British society. Here, in a favourite phrase of the time, was The Age of Great Cities—Britain as the first modern urban and industrial nation. Mightiest of the cities, of course, was London, its population grown from less than 900,000 in 1801 to nearly 2,500,000 by 1851, and set to pass 5,000,000 by 1911. London had become the metropolis, a world-city, the capital of capital itself, and the hub of empire. Fanning out from this centre, imperial enterprise sought new markets, new sources of raw material, new opportunities for investment and speculation, and new lands to absorb those people who were surplus to the requirements of the domestic economy.

Frequently, such objectives could only be attained by violence. Military force was used to open Chinese ports to British trade, to round up Aborigines in Tasmania and New South Wales, to support settlers as they grabbed land from the Maoris in New Zealand, to secure the expansion of Cape Colony against Boers and black Africans alike. Leading the imperialist charge was the campaign of annexation conducted across the north of the Indian subcontinent: Assam in 1826, Sind in 1842, the Punjab in 1846, Oudh in 1856. In response to all this, a number of early Victorian poets were eager to wave the flag. Smug and simple-minded, Eliza Cook's popular ballad 'The Englishman' (c.1845) sees Britain's 'vast domain' as the proper reward for national superiority 'In Arms, in Arts, or Song'. This seems almost innocent when set against the coarse triumphalism with which the balladeers of *Bentley's Miscellany* greeted victories in India: Sheehan's 'The Campaign of the Sutlej' (1846), included in this anthology, is characteristic. At the other emotional pole are the sombre elegiacs of Richard Chevenix Trench occasioned by the disastrous Afghanistan campaign in the winter of 1841–2 —though Trench's reflections serve only to reaffirm Britain as 'The justicer of righteous Heaven'. Alongside such reactions to campaigns of military conquest, successful and otherwise, Charles Mackay's sequence of poems 'The Emigrants' (1856) depicts the colonial settlement of Canada as a great civilian adventure, conquering the unpeopled wilderness to create 'a new and happy land'.

'Something more than shop':
Rebellion in India and the New Shape of Empire

'The Emigrants' is buoyant with hope, confident that Anglo-Saxon pluck and enterprise can build an imperial future which will have 'Fair elbow-room for men to breathe'. Despite the social distress and class struggles of the 1830s and 1840s, Britain had been largely untouched by the revolutionary movements that had shaken Europe in 1848, and the 1851 Great Exhibition seemed to mark the beginning of a new era of prosperity. Although the concert of nations had been shattered by the Crimean War (1854–6), the defeat of Russia was seen to safeguard British strategic interests, despite the organizational incompetence that had made a shambles out of the whole campaign. Although Dickens's *Little Dorrit* (1856–7) execrated 'this right little, tight little island', to the eyes of most·people in the mid-1850s Britain and its Empire stood secure. Then, in May 1857, native Indian troops in Meerut mutinied, killing their British officers. The rebellion became a wider struggle for independence and spread across Hindostan with extraordinary speed; British compounds, caught wholly unprepared, were overwhelmed; Delhi was taken and the end of colonial rule in India was proclaimed. The British response was savage; mass executions in the name of order prompted Indian reprisals, most notoriously at Cawnpore; military action to contain the rising became a racist vendetta, and the rising was suppressed in what was at times a frenzy of blood-letting.

The Indian Mutiny, as the British called it, came as a profound shock to public opinion, but it also served to engage the public imagination with the issue of empire as never before. Something of this is evident in the diverse ways in which poets tried to grapple with what had happened. Gerald Massey essayed the grand manner in the blood and thunder narrative of *Havelock's March* (1860); at the other end of the scale, though possibly even more melodramatic, is the domestic focus of Christina Rossetti's 'In the Round Tower at Jhansi' (1857). Very different from either are the poems of Alfred Lyall, who was an eyewitness to events and who subsequently became a distinguished Indian administrator: included here, from his collection *Verses Written in India* (1889), are the sympathetic 'Rajpoot Rebels', written at the time of the rising, and the wryly retrospective 'Badminton' (1876). As important as any of these reactions was that of *Punch*. Founded in 1841 and quickly established as a vehicle for liberal middle-class opinion, *Punch* had shown little interest in the Empire before the Mutiny. Afterwards, for half a century, its pages are full of items on imperial issues, only a handful of which it has been possible to include in this anthology. The three Mutiny poems reprinted here

encapsulate what would become central concerns of the period-
ical in its response to the Empire: the efficiency, or otherwise, of
the imperial government in 'What Gammon!' (1857); the finan-
cial costs and obligations of imperialism, in 'The Pagoda Tree'
(1859); and the higher mission of empire, in 'Our Army of
Martyrs' (1858). These different points of focus are telling,
particularly the last. They reflect an important shift in attitude
towards Britain's imperial role, a shift brought about by a major
development in the structure of the Empire consequent upon
the Mutiny.

In 1858 the East India Company, widely blamed for allowing
the Mutiny to happen, was abolished, and India was brought
directly under the Crown for the first time. The period of the
British Raj—a Hindi word that simply means 'rule'—now
properly began. India became the key component—economic,
strategic, and ideological—of what has since been called the
formal empire: those territories acquired by Britain and ruled
directly, albeit through a labyrinth of local administrations.
Distinct from these were the colonies of white settlement—at
this date, Canada, Australia, and New Zealand—which had a
considerable measure of legislative autonomy. Outside both the
formal empire and the white colonies was the shifting shape of
the informal empire, made up of client states and territories
where British interests were effectively hegemonic. Here was the
context in which British imperialism came to full consciousness:
direct rule over millions of subject people; indirect rule over
millions more; the settlement of vast, supposedly empty tracts of
the earth's surface. What did such unparalleled dominion mean?
What was it for? Surely not just 'That wealth, with unabated
flood/To England's shore might flow?'. *Punch*, answering its
own question, was positive: 'Our heroes were designed to bleed/
For something more than Shop'. Quite what that 'something
more' was, would come to occupy a large part of British
consciousness in the rest of the nineteenth century.

'Mightiest of all peoples under heaven': Tennyson and the Mythology of Empire

Building on the tradition of Thomson and Garrick, of Cowper
and Campbell, of Hemans and Cook, a mythology of empire
emerged as a central project in British, particularly English

culture from the 1860s. The mythical components were histor-
ical, scientific, racial, moral, religious; they embraced the ethics
of duty, national destiny, the Pax Britannica, and the progress of
civilization. The myth-makers were idealistic men and women,
politicians on the make, and downright crooks. The mythology
they engendered, married—usually surreptitiously—to the im-
peratives of capitalist free enterprise, was sent out into the world
to justify not only the existing Empire, but also its expansion
into south east Asia, through the islands of the Pacific, and,
most of all, across the great reaches of the African continent.
The full mythology of Britain's Empire took time to construct,
and, like imperial themes generally, attracted little attention
from the major poets writing during the period of its emergence.
Robert Browning and Matthew Arnold seem not to have written
about the Empire at all; Swinburne's political interests were
focused on Europe, at least until his old age; William Morris
was imaginatively focused on other realms altogether; Elizabeth
Barrett Browning's widely publicized poem 'The Runaway Slave
at Pilgrim's Point' (1850) tackled the question of race, but only
with reference to the continuation of slavery in America. For
others, imperialism and the Empire provided matter for odd
poems: Rossetti's 'In the Round Tower at Jhansi' has already
been mentioned; Clough wrote the quirkily angled 'Columbus'
(1852), and Kingsley the touching domestic drama of 'The
Mango Tree' (1870)—though he made a major contribution to
the mythologizing of imperial history with his novel *Westward
Ho!* (1855).

Even Alfred Tennyson, in the first two decades of the Laure-
ateship that began in 1850, approached the subject less often
than might have been expected. He did write (and publish
anonymously) a group of xenophobic poems during the invasion
scare that followed Louis Napoleon's *coup d'état* in December
1851. Among them was 'For the Penny Wise' (1852), included
here, in which he seems unconscious of the irony of being indig-
nant because British troops in 'uncivilised' Africa were confront-
ing enemies better equipped than themselves. His 'Boadicea' of
1859 rewrites Cowper's poem in a far more energetic, but also
far more confusing manner: it is hard to tell whether the warrior
queen, 'Mad and maddening all that heed her', is to be admired
or deplored. In 1872, during an Anglo-American squabble about
compensation claims arising from the *Trent* affair, he recycled

a poem written forty years earlier that demonstrated how thoroughly English the old American colonies had been in demanding their independence.

Clearly, these somewhat desultory performances were not engaging the Laureate's full attention: that was committed for much of the 1850s and 1860s to completing *Idylls of the King*. V.G. Kiernan has argued for the importance of the imperial strain throughout the *Idylls*, and this seems right: but it is in the 'Epilogue to the Queen', first added to the *Idylls* in 1872, that Tennyson engages the Empire directly. Grounding the poem's rhetorical elevation is a firm understanding of the Empire's political constitution. Surveying the imperial realm, Tennyson sees two great estates. The one comprises the colonies of white settlement, secured by naval power, with a capacity for extension, and for accommodating British emigrants, that he imagines as limitless: this is the 'ocean-empire with her boundless homes/ For ever-broadening England'. The other is the formal empire enthroned in India, the centre of 'our vast Orient'. The morality of imperial sway is not at issue: it is the historical consequence of those military triumphs, epitomized by 'the roar of Hougoumont', that made the British 'mightiest of all peoples under heaven'; and it is backed by 'the faith/That made us rulers'. But faith in what? Not, it appears, in God, but in ourselves: the British may rule 'under heaven', but Tennyson stops short of claiming that they do so under Heaven. Effectively, it is a secular faith in an imperial destiny. But it comes at a price, and Tennyson argues that faith is being undermined by carping about paying the bill—specifically, by contemporary disputes about expenditure in Canada. The proposal, on economic grounds, to separate Canada from Britain is a betrayal of 'the tone of empire', but it focuses for Tennyson an absence in imperial self-awareness: Britain 'knows not her own greatness', and if, coming to that knowledge, she 'dreads' its consequences, then 'we are fallen'. Loyalty to the Queen, to whom Tennyson offers the *Idylls*, affords the symbolic link between the nation at home and the nation overseas, between Britain and its Empire. And the *Idylls* themselves are intended to link the present with the past, to recover the legendary matter of Arthur and British origins, and thus to help bring Britain to a knowledge of 'her own greatness'. What the 'Epilogue to the Queen' does, of course, is to define the late Victorian cultural project that we described above—the construction of a mythology of empire. And the project is urgent, for to fail is to risk Britain's becoming 'Some third-rate isle half lost among her seas'. The possibility is acknowledged even as it is dismissed: as so often in Tennyson, the apparently positive is counterpointed by a strain of melancholy, the 'signs of storm' that forebode 'The darkness of the battle in the West' where Arthur's kingdom died away. To invoke empire, it would seem, is also to invoke the spectre of a final futility.

Mythology and the Advent of Imperialism

Despite its subversive melancholy, the 'Epilogue to the Queen' signalled Tennyson's engagement with the mythology of empire, and in 1878 he published two narrative poems that contributed to its formation: 'The Revenge' and 'The Defence of Lucknow'. The all-action excitement of the first, and the breathless immediacy of the second, give both much in common with the prose stories for boys discussed by Martin Green in *Dreams of Adventure, Deeds of Empire*. Like many of these tales, both of Tennyson's poems reconstruct episodes from British history as exemplary moments in an implicit imperial saga. Despite inevitable defeat, the Elizabethan sea-dogs of 'The Revenge' show the qualities that laid the foundations of British naval supremacy. Despite overwhelming odds, the defenders of Lucknow show the same qualities in keeping the Empire in existence. Both poems also identify such qualities with a quintessential Britishness or, more narrowly, Englishness: at Lucknow 'the banner of England' is interchangeable with 'the banner of Britain'. And both poems effectively deploy the potent image identified by Victor Kiernan as 'England ... on the defensive, a small nation surviving by quality and courage' ('Tennyson, King Arthur, and Imperialism', in Samuel and Jones (eds), *Culture, Ideology and Politics. Essays for Eric Hobsbawm*, 1982). In 'The Defence of Lucknow' this trope disguises the overall political situation by isolating the individual event from the history to which it belongs (that of enforced British rule over India) and relocating it within a different history (that of heroic England embattled by alien hordes). In political discourse about a more recent imperialist war, American films have employed very similar images about Vietnam.

[23]

It is not, of course, accidental that Tennyson should have seen the need for an imperialist mythology, and helped provide one, when he did. Eric Hobsbawm gives his book on the period from 1875 to 1914 the title *The Age of Empire* (1987), and he emphasizes its significance in the formation of the modern world.

> Between 1880 and 1914 ... most of the world outside Europe and the Americas was formally partitioned into territories under the formal rule or informal domination of one of a handful of states ... Two major regions ... were, for practical purposes, entirely divided up: Africa and the Pacific. (pp. 57–8)

The rapid economic development of Western Europe and the United States redrew the globe, establishing a sharp division between the 'successful' Western nations and the rest. Hobsbawm points out that the very term 'imperialism' dates from these years.

> The word first enters politics in Britain in the 1870s, and was still regarded as a neologism at the end of that decade. It exploded into general use in the 1890s. By 1900, when the intellectuals began to write books about it, it was, to quote one of the first of them, the British Liberal J.A. Hobson, 'on everybody's lips, and used to denote the most powerful movement in the current problems of the western world'. (p. 60; quoting J.A. Hobson, *Imperialism*, 1902, Preface)

If imperialism presented itself as a 'problem' to the nations of the West, one can only wonder what it felt like to those millions of people who were on the receiving end.

Grabbing the Lion's Share: the Imperial Scramble in Africa and the East

The main prize for the rival colonial powers in the last quarter of the nineteenth century was Africa. The speed and rapacity with which they divided up the continent in what became known as 'the scramble for Africa' are alike extraordinary. There were two phases to the scramble. The first, between the late 1870s and mid-1880s, was largely concerned to secure trading interests, particularly around the coasts, and to impose a measure of control on the supply of raw materials needed by the advanced capitalist economies of Europe. Implementation was frequently left to private companies, like the British Niger in West Africa and the company launched by the Belgian King, Leopold, to exploit the resources of the Congo. The second, more intensive phase occupied the 1890s. With the colourable excuse of extinguishing the internal African slave trade, the imperialist powers broke up surviving native economies in the attempt to create a free labour pool on classic capitalist lines. This process involved far more direct colonial intervention: the sequence of territorial annexations that followed had effected the complete partition of Africa by the early years of the twentieth century.

In the 1870s, as the scramble began, British interests were concentrated on the Cape, on West Africa, and on the East African coast trading with India. The bankruptcy of the Egyptian government in 1876—brought about largely by attempts to 'modernize'—gave the British Prime Minister, Benjamin Disraeli, the chance to buy the Khedive's 44 per cent interest in the newly opened Suez Canal. This established Anglo-French dominance in Egypt, and secured Britain's control over the Canal, the 'quick route' to India and the Pacific. In 1882 the crushing of Arabi Pasha's nationalist revolt gave Britain colonial ascendancy and converted the Egyptian administration into a client government. In southern Africa, Cape Colony was extended northward and eastward, though far from smoothly: a whole regiment was annihilated at Isandhlwana before British troops eventually overcame the warriors of Cetewayo in the Zulu War of 1878–9, and the Afrikaner victory at Majuba Hill in the Anglo-Boer War of 1881 checked the attempt to swallow the Dutch settler republics of Transvaal and Orange Free State. British East Africa was established, exploration and settlement pushing inland from the coast over the area that eventually became Kenya. In West Africa, Anglo-French control over the Niger was formalized at the Berlin Conference of 1885, one of a package of deals that brought the first phase of the scramble to an end.

In the same year as the Conference, however, the great gold-field of Witwatersrand in the Transvaal was discovered, and became the spur that drove on Britain's South African ambitions

in the scramble's second phase. The vast territory of Bechuana-
land was annexed and subsequently attached to Cape Colony.
Under the direction of Cecil Rhodes, premier of the Cape and
head of the British South Africa Company, settlers penetrated
beyond Bechuanaland to claim the lands that they named
Rhodesia after their patron. The intransigent Afrikaner states
were effectively surrounded, and in 1899 provoked into war.
Immensely costly in both lives and money, the Boer War
(1899–1902) ultimately brought the whole of southern Africa,
with its immense natural resources, under British imperial rule.
In the reconstruction policy that followed the war, Boer loyalty
to the Crown was purchased at the expense of black African
rights: no black representatives were present at the 1910 confer-
ence which created the Union of South Africa, and with it the
framework of the system that in time would become apartheid.
Meanwhile, north of the area being settled as Rhodesia, British
colonies were being carved out of Uganda and Nyasaland. The
consolidation of British power in West Africa led to the founda-
tion of Nigeria. And from Egypt, in 1898–9, forces commanded
by Kitchener drove deep to the south to conquer the Arab feder-
ation that had been formed by the Mahdi, thus bringing the
whole of the western Sudan under Anglo-Egyptian rule and
establishing British control over the headwaters of the Nile.

As the British Lion was swallowing what he could of Africa,
the Raj entered upon its meridian with the creation of Victoria
as Empress of India in 1876. Imperial expansion based upon
India led to the establishment of a protectorate over Malaya in
the 1870s, the acquisition of much of Baluchistan in the 1880s,
and the annexation of Burma in 1885–6, as well as periodic
forays against Afghanistan and an invasion of China as part of
combined European operations during the Boxer Rising of
1899–1901. And in the Pacific—where Australian politicians
were particularly strident in urging a policy of colonial annexa-
tion—Fiji, North Borneo and Sarawak, southern New Guinea,
the Solomons, the Gilbert and Ellice group, Tonga, and a
miscellaneous scattering of other islands, were all swept into the
imperial bag in the final quarter of the nineteenth century.
Satiety was reached in 1901 when the Union Jack was raised
over Ocean Island: it is aptly described by the authors of the
Atlas of the British Empire (1989) as 'a particularly large pile of
guano' (p. 169).

'A trust of Heaven':
Mythology, Culture, and Mission at the Height of Empire

In the climate of the last twenty-five years of Victoria's reign the mythology of empire attained full bloom, nourished by imperial expansion and providing ideological sustenance for it in return. The impact upon British culture was both wide and deep. In fiction, the battle honours of the fleet and the promotion of naval power across the globe fed thousands of tales of nautical derring-do. Captain Marryat's sea stories, popular since their first appearance in the 1830s, were joined on the briny by the novels of W. Clark Russell, W.H.G. Kingston, and Gordon Stables, the founding editor of *Boy's Own Paper*. Garnering thrills from the wilder margins of empire, R.M. Ballantyne offered his eager audience novels like *The Young Fur Traders. Or, Snowflakes and Sunbeams from the Far North* (1856), *The Gorilla Hunters. A Tale of the Wilds of Africa* (1861), and, best known of all, *The Coral Island: A Tale of the Pacific Ocean* (1858). The vast unknown of the African interior proved as imaginatively compelling as it was economically tempting: somewhere beyond the real-life fast-nesses that called Livingstone and other explorers were the fantasy realms of lost tribes and treasure hoards that gave Rider Haggard a string of successes, most notably in *King Solomon's Mines* (1885) and *She* (1887). As the Empire extended geographically, so also it stretched chronologically: the imperial past was as fabled a site as the imperial present. No author ransacked the history of Britain and its Empire more thoroughly than that tireless writer of boys' adventures, George Alfred Henty. His novels, of which the following are just a few, stand like mile-stones along the route of the imperial progress: *The Dragon and the Raven. Or, The Days of King Alfred* (1880), *St George for England. A Tale of Cressy and Poitiers* (1885), *Under Drake's Flag. A Tale of the Spanish Main* (1883), *With Clive in India. Or, The Beginnings of an Empire* (1884), *With Wolfe in Canada. Or, The Winning of a Continent* (1887), *One of the 28th. A Tale of Waterloo* (1890), *Through the Sikh War. A Tale of the Conquest of the Punjaub* (1894). Alongside such fictional versions of the mythology of empire there are many varieties of visual repres-entation: from the Academy art of John Everett Millais's *The Boyhood of Raleigh* (1870), to the battle-pieces that folded out from the pages of *The Illustrated London News*; from the cabinet photographs of Our Empire in India, to the brightly coloured cuts of Victoria's colonial generals. And enveloping books and pictures alike was the material and commercial culture: the Empire Theatre in Leicester Square, the Imperial Theatre in Westminster, the Imperial Hotel in Russell Square; the Imperial Tobacco Company, the Pacific and Orient line, Home and Colonial Stores; suburban streets named after now-forgotten leaders of the Empire, bungalows in the home counties, Board School atlases with all that red on the map.

Poetry was only one element, though an important one, in late Victorian imperialism's complex of representation and self-representation. Poems often centred on the individual heroes of empire, the people whose lives—and, more often, deaths—could be layered into the cumulative stuff of imperial mythology. From many that could have been chosen we have included *Punch*'s elegy on David Livingstone (1874), Alfred Austin's lines on the diplomat Sir Bartle Frere (1884), Andrew Lang's commemoration of the dashing Colonel Burnaby (1885), and a number of poems on the demise of that eminent Victorian, General Charles Gordon—of whom more subsequently. But heroes did not have to be well-known figures: the mythology of empire could promote—partly it functioned in order to promote—the otherwise anonymous into exemplary types. This is what Francis Hastings Doyle does in 'The Private of the Buffs' (1866), and what Douglas Sladen tries to do in 'Mrs Watson. A Queensland Hero' (1883) with unfortunately ludicrous results. Personal at one end of the scale, the mythology of empire was panoramic at the other, and Victoria's Golden Jubilee of 1887 encouraged the grand sweep.

Among the many efforts called forth by the Jubilee celebrations, Lewis Morris's 'A Song of Empire' (1887) is both one of the most ambitious and one of the most instructive. Developing a theme found in Tennyson's 'Epilogue to the Queen', Morris identifies loyalty to the throne not only as a binding force of empire, but also as an implicit acknowledgement of Victoria's identity with England and Englishness: 'Thy life is England's', 'Therefore it is that we/Take thee for head and symbol of our name'. Her imperial realm is a wondrous birth, part nature, part destiny, 'a great tree' whose 'vital seeds' have blown across the earth, but which also appears to 'issue' 'from the shaping hand of fate'. As imperial matriarch, Victoria is also imperial superhero who has taken the life of Empire into herself, but—some-how—given birth to that life as well. With so personal a sense of the imperial family there are clear dangers of a kind of meta-phorical miscegenation: how *could* our own dear Queen have conceived all those black people and brown people? As the imperial children troop to the Jubilee, Morris gives firm priority to the colonies of white settlement: Australia is the 'Greater England of the Southern Sea', New Zealand 'our Southern Britain that shall be', and Canada the 'nurse of stalwart British hearts and strong'. India and the West Indies are also there, but the former as 'the ancient land' with 'unnumbered subject millions', and the latter as a gorgeous landscape where 'Our fathers' dusky freedmen toil'. Africa, 'the unhappy Continent', is only gradually emerging from 'the long history of blood and pain', though white settlement to come is foreshadowed in the 'scanty band of strong self-governed men' who make their way to the foot of the imperial throne. The dearest offspring of all, of course, are 'Thy people of these little Northern Isles', though their relationship to their mother—Victoria, or England, or Empire, or all three—is further confused by comparing them to the 'perfumed heart' of 'thy Rose', which keeps safe 'the seed of the miraculous flower'. An odd companion to Morris's 'A Song of Empire' is Oscar Wilde's Jubilee poem, 'Ave Imperatrix' (1887). Odd, firstly, because Wilde's stance as aesthetic anarch-ist makes him such an unlikely celebrant of the Empire. Secondly, because the particular mythology he develops con-structs imperialism as a self-sacrificial mission, the ultimate purpose of which is transfiguring and redemptive: 'with thorn-crowned head,/Up the steep road must England go'. There is no indication that Wilde is being ironic or parodic, and though he is far more concerned than is Morris with the human cost of empire, that cost is registered only in terms of English lives; colonized peoples figure merely as exotic extras. The reality of imperialism is blurred into moral uplift by Wilde's lush religiosity just as surely as it is by Morris's fuddled metaphors of fecundity.

Few poems before Wilde's christianize the imperial enterprise quite so explicitly, though the missionary poems discussed earlier see the Empire as a conduit for evangelism. More usual is the secular (though often religiose) belief that identified expan-sion with the diffusion of British ideals of liberty—a concept that can be traced back at least as far as James Thomson. It is there in Morris's 'A Song of Empire', and recurs as a central element in his ode 'The Imperial Institute' (1893), where Britain wields 'the sole sceptre of the Free'. It was easier to see liberty at work in the colonies of white settlement, which could be construed for ideological purposes as unpeopled—or, at least, populated only by 'savages' who could be discounted. *Punch* was particularly pleased with Australia, congratulating the state of Victoria on its progress in 1875, and New South Wales on achieving a civilized centenary in 1888: 'All England cries, through *Punch*'s pen,/ "Advance, Australia!"' It is also white settlement that William Watson has in mind in his 1890 poem 'England and Her Colonies', where he deploys Morris's image of the Empire as a mighty tree, 'a thousand-wintered', with 'New nations fostered in her shade/And linking land with land'. The formal empire, more obviously the product of conquest and annexation, was less amenable to myths of natural growth. Nature needed to be replaced conceptually by prescriptive culture, and imperialism presented in the form of paternalist tuition. This was a key formulation in later Victorian consciousness: Britain ruled the subject peoples of the Empire for their own good, and though, like children, they might chafe under discipline, it was wholesome and they would find it beneficial in the end. In 1876, irritated by the Disraelian *coup de théâtre* that turned Victoria into Empress of India, *Punch* took the opportunity to remind everybody that the Raj held India's 'swarming millions', 'but as a trust of Heaven,/ To civilise and educate to her best teaching given'.

This kind of mission statement was wholly in accord with the imperial role envisaged by Morris, Wilde, and the scores of other poets who hymned the 1887 Jubilee. It also went admirably with the ethos of duty promoted incessantly by the English public schools that trained the imperial captains of the future: the masters of the Empire—so the argument ran—were in reality its self-denying servants. Henry Newbolt, lifelong pupil of Clifton School, turned this ethos into the core of his literary career, most famously in 'Vitaï Lampada' (1898).

> The river of death has brimmed his banks,
> And England's far, and Honour a name,
> But the voice of a schoolboy rallies the ranks:
> 'Play up! play up! and play the game!'

Playing the game, Newbolt knew, was not always so agreeably martial, nor did the schoolboy always get to rally the ranks. The anonymous death on some obscure frontier could also be a thing of duty, as it is in 'He Fell Among Thieves' (1898), an imaginary variant of the exemplary lives commemorated in so much of the elegiac poetry of imperialism. Set against such sacrificial high-mindedness, the simple relish of William McGonagall's patriotism comes as something of a relief. As innocent of intellectual complexity as of the rules of scansion, his *Poetic Gems* of 1890 includes three thumping celebrations of British victories over Arab forces, 'The Battle of Tel-el-Kebir', 'The Battle of El-Teb', and 'The Battle of Abu Klea', the first of which is reprinted here. Even so, McGonagall's no-nonsense attitude seems as far from the realities of battle as does Newbolt's patrician stoicism: 'it must have been a glorious sight', he opines of Tel-el-Kebir, 'To see Sir Garnet Wolseley in the thickest of the fight!'.

'Vain the Dream!': Imperial Misgivings

For all its confidence and conviction, the late Victorian mythology of empire covered a deep and ironic unease. This is well put by the authors of the *Atlas of the British Empire* in their discussion of the establishment of British imperial rule in Africa.

> Never had such large areas of the map been coloured red so rapidly, nor with so little apparent effort. But never were the Briish forced to move so hurriedly to cover up their weaknesses. Throughout the nineteenth century, the continent of Africa had been regarded by Britain as its own reserve, protected, if largely unexploited. In the last two decades of the century, however, Africa was broken into by a number of European powers ... The last great spectacle of British imperial expansion, which so excited the Victorians, was in reality a grim rearguard action by a country whose statesmen half knew that it was already past the peak of its power. (p. 143)

After the 1860s growth in the domestic economy began to slow, Britain's lead in key areas of industrial production was overhauled by younger capitalist economies, particularly those of Germany and the United States, and competition for overseas markets intensified. In the face of cheap grain imports, agriculture went into sharp decline; the forces of Labour, organized by the new unionism, renewed their struggle against Capital on a larger scale than ever before; experts seeking a way out of the protracted economic slump of the 1880s complained limply of a worsening in the terms of trade; doubts even began to be entertained about free trade itself, the gospel on which British enterprise had built its success. In this context the mythology of empire may be seen to have functioned not only to justify, but also to reassure—even to console. One result is a detectable uncertainty, a kind of queasiness, in some late Victorian poetry on imperial themes.

We have already noticed the pessimism that suffuses Tennyson's 'Epilogue to the Queen'. His sentiments are less clouded in 1880s poems like 'Hands All Round', written to celebrate the Queen's birthday in 1883, and 'Politics' (1885), ringingly simplistic in its claim that 'The fleet of Britain is her all-in-all'. Also apparently untroubled is the imperial unity that rounds off 'Opening of the Indian and Colonial Exhibition by the Queen' of May 1886: 'One life, one flag, one fleet, one Throne'. Yet this is more of a wish than an assertion, an appeal made necessary because the danger of disunity is all too apparent. And, as the poem progresses, confidence leeches from the affirmative chorus 'Britons, hold your own'—increasingly unconvincing as it becomes increasingly vague. *Punch*'s unease is evident in the scepticism with which 'Ba! Ba! Black Sheep!' (1873) addresses the Ashanti War, and in the 1877 poem 'Kaiser-I-Hind', already quoted. But the most dramatic focus for imperialist anxieties came in the following decade with the death of General Gordon. Dispatched to Khartoum in 1884 with orders to withdraw Anglo-Egyptian forces from what Gladstone's government judged to be an unnecessary conflict with the Mahdi, Gordon defended the city instead. When news of his lonely—though self-inflicted—plight reached London, he was turned into a hero, and, when the relief column arrived just too late, a martyr. Mythologies need martyrs, and Gordon became a symbol of imperialist rectitude to set against the shifts and compromises of politicians. In 'Mirage!', written as early as April 1884 and perhaps the first poetic contribution to the affair, *Punch* recognized the opportunism of the attacks on Gladstone, but over the months that followed became increasingly transfixed by the heroic figure in the desert. Austin's elegy to Frere, who died at the time, is uncompromising: 1884 is 'a year conceived in shame'. The apprehensions that Tennyson's 'Epilogue to the Queen' had expressed about England's sense of greatness, have come to pass: 'The very fear of Empire strikes us numb,/Fumbling with pens, who brandished once the blade'. Once it was all over the elegies came out in a rush. The two we have included strike very different notes. George MacDonald finds consolation in the thought of Gordon as one of Christ's own Imperial General Staff. For Andrew Lang, in 'The White Pacha' (1885), there is no comfort. The old tales of heroic return, the legends of Charlemagne and Arthur, are hollow: like them, Gordon will 'never come again'. Lang's pessimism, eerily close to Tennyson's own, resounds beyond its immediate occasion and finds echo in the very fabric of empire: 'though fair the vision seem ... Whate'er sick Hope may whisper, vain the dream!'

'The Jingo-Englishman': Myths of Nation and Race

The obverse of such doubt was stridency. In particular, it was the militant nationalism, the blustering advocacy of imperialist expansion, that was given the name 'jingoism'. The word was coined in 1878 to label support for Disraeli's foreign policy, the aggressiveness of which was most often a matter of rhetoric cynically designed for domestic consumption. *Punch* hated jingoism, and was goaded to some of its most effective poetry as a result: the villanelle '"In Wain!"', and the Eliza Cook parody 'The Jingo-Englishman', both of 1878, are examples. Jingoism at its crudest was more concerned with sloganizing than versifying: of the poems included here, Owen Seaman's 'The Spacious Times' (1896) is probably most explicit in its attitudes, though they are tempered by a measure of self-mockery. Seaman was no fool, however, and his poem is revealing about what it was in jingoism that liberal imperialists found especially offensive. In foregrounding British self-interest, jingoism not only affronted imperialism's higher moral claims, it suggested, uncomfortably, that they were little more than the camouflage produced by squeamishness: dress imperialism up however you liked, the reality was a global enterprise run so that Britain could profit. Jingoism ensured that, ideologically, the Empire lost its clothes. It demythologized empire.

Too dangerous not to accommodate or sublimate, jingoism's strains (in more than one sense) are apparent in much of the imperialist poetry of the late nineteenth and early twentieth centuries, and may well account for an intensification of rhetoric evident from the end of the 1880s. One element of this—and one to which jingoism certainly contributed—has been observed by John Lucas in *England and Englishness* (1991). He argues that Victorian poetry constructed 'a myth of Englishness which became increasingly troubling as the century progressed because it was increasingly xenophobic and eventually racist' (p. 173). The mythopoeic process and its products were more diverse than this suggests, but the development Lucas identifies is clear enough. British responses to the Indian Mutiny were shot through with racial fears, and the paternalist discourses of the Raj are partly premised on the racial otherness of the subcontinent's 'swarming millions'. Doyle's 'Private of the Buffs' is dramatized as a model of English stubborness—always thought of as a good thing—by means of derogatory racial contrast: 'Let dusky Indians whine and kneel:/An English lad must die'. The argument of William Rossetti's sonnet 'Emigration' (*c*.1881) is based upon the pseudo-biological category of 'Imperial races', rather than that of 'imperialist states', and thus collapses history and culture into nature—the primary function of bourgeois mythology according to Barthes. Rossetti can then validate the historical moment of white colonization as the outcome of natural law, inevitable and therefore guiltless. A similar strategy lingers in the metaphor of natural growth employed in Morris's 'A Song of Empire' (1887), where it reinforces the overt promotion of the colonies of white settlement, and in Watson's 'England and Her Colonies' (1890). Racial destiny can also be read as a component of the English imperial martyrdom that is Wilde's subject in 'Ave Imperatrix', and it is race and religiosity again that merge in the self-sacrificial fervour of W.E. Henley's 'England, my England' (1892). But it is the latter's Boer War elegy, 'Last Post' (1900), that is most explicit.

> Blow, you bugles of England, blow!
> That her Name as a sun among stars might glow,
> Till the dusk of Time, with honour and worth:
> That, stung by the lust and the pain of battle
> The One Race ever might starkly spread
> And the One Flag eagle it overhead!

Febrile, more than a little hysterical, Henley's sexual fantasies—
the Swinburnean longing to be 'stung' into consummation by
'lust' and 'pain'—are sublimated in the single fantasy of racial
dominance, and legitimized as part of the mythology of empire
itself. Henley's case may be extreme, but it is far from unique.
Francis Thompson's elegy 'Cecil Rhodes' (1902) is concerned,
in part at least, with admiring the racist ambitions of its sub-
ject—'He saw the Teuton and the Saxon grip/Hands round the
warded world'—and a cognate megalomania lurks behind the
august rhetoric of 'Land of Hope and Glory' (1901): 'Wider still
and wider shall thy bounds be set;/God, who made thee mighty,
make thee mightier yet'.

'Lyra Heroica':
Poetry and Empire in the 1890s

'England, my England', under its more orotund title 'Pro Rege
Nostro', and 'Last Post' were both included in later editions of
the anthology *Lyra Heroica*, which Henley himself first edited in
1891. Tellingly, it carries the subtitle *A Book of Verse for Boys*.
In *Dreams of Adventure, Deeds of Empire*, Martin Green argues
for a dichotomy between the novels of nineteenth-century high
culture, concerned primarily with personal relationships and set
in a domestic sphere, and stories of action set in a public sphere
which is predominantly male. Though subject to many qualifica-
tions, not least in its definitions of 'high' and 'popular' cultures,
Green's distinction usefully draws attention to the masculinist
values that imaginatively constructed the world of action. In the
mythology of empire the world of action could coextend with the
world of actuality. Where better to live the imagination than in
an empire which circled the globe itself? And how better to
deliver it from defamation, from the charge of mere commercial
self-interest, than by lives of heroic action?

In the preface to *Lyra Heroica*, Henley spells out his project.

> My purpose has been to choose and sheave a certain
> number of those achievements in verse which, as express-
> ing the simpler sentiments and more elemental emotions,
> might fitly be addressed to such boys—and men, for that
> matter—as are privileged to use our noble English tongue.

Verse 'addressed to ... boys—and men, for that matter'; certainly not to girls—or women, for that matter. Henley goes on to outline the anthology's defining 'sentiments' and 'emotions', the matrix of values that for him and his intended audience are peculiarly male.

> To set forth, as only art can, the beauty and joy of living, the beauty and blessedness of death, the glory of battle and adventure, the nobility of devotion—to a cause, an ideal, a passion even—the dignity of resistance, the sacred quality of patriotism, that is my ambition here.

The values of adventure mesh with the mythological construction of imperialism: the melodies played on Henley's heroic lyre are orchestrated to the Empire's tunes of glory. His anthology presents the poems in chronological order, beginning with Shakespeare's *Henry V* and ending with some contemporary pieces. His progress, significantly for Green's argument, takes in both popular verse (a sizeable selection of border ballads) and verse that belongs in the 'high' bracket (Milton, Wordsworth, and the apostle of culture himself, Matthew Arnold). The choice of contemporary poems shows Henley's preferences very clearly: the American Bret Harte's 'What the Bullet Sang'; Austin Dobson's 'A Ballad of the Armada'; Lang's 'The White Pacha', included, one presumes, without any sense of its final, despairing irony; Robert Louis Stevenson's 'Mother and Son', in which the mother happily stays at home while her son roams the world 'like a sword ... On nobler missions sent'; and 'Prayers' by another American, Henry Charles Beeching, with its pledge to God of 'the strength of a man'. There are also two poems by Rudyard Kipling, 'A Ballad of East and West' and 'The Flag of England'. Later editions of *Lyra Heroica* do not seem to have increased this number, although Kipling was recognized both at the time and since as the definitive poet of the late Victorian and Edwardian Empire.

Kipling and the Diversity of Empire

Kipling's relatively limited representation in *Lyra Heroica* does not seem accidental: indeed, it follows from the extent of his engagement with the matter of empire. The Empire was far too involved a historical phenomenon, far too multifaceted, too complex in its ideas, its myths and discourses, to allow of its being contained in the simple ethos of Henley's heroics. Kipling wrote out of this diversity more fully than any other British poet. And not only as a poet, but also as a journalist, a writer of short stories, and a novelist: it was not for nothing that he was awarded the Nobel Prize for Literature in 1907. Kipling's range is wide, and the selection we have made can only hope to indicate this. Though what he writes is projected from a consciousness of Britain's position as an imperialist power, Kipling's Empire is very much a political, cultural, and—above all—a historical reality: it is not the monolithic object of patriotic worship as it is so often for the likes of Henley. His poetry certainly deals with heroism, and with a set of values that he persistently identifies as masculine. But heroics and values alike tend to be rendered as functions of experience, and are qualified or ironized in the process. They belong to the people who kept the Empire in being: to the petty officials of the Indian Civil Service, to the soldiers on garrison duty or footslogging through yet another colonial campaign, to the engineers building bridges and railways up-country, to the ships' crews plying the long passage between home and the distant East. Spoken from within the specifics of experience, their poems resist conversion into the abstract terms of imperialist rhetoric. Individual speakers may generalize about the Empire, but the generalizations remain theirs, anchored in the particulars of time and place.

Such qualities are especially clear in the early collections, *Departmental Ditties* (1886) and *Barrack Room Ballads* (1892). From the first we have included 'The Story of Uriah', an acid tale of hill-station adultery, and 'Arithmetic on the Frontier', which reduces the solitary death in the service of empire— mythologized by Newbolt in 'He Fell Among Thieves' (1898)— to the random outcome of an ironic calculus.

> A scrimmage in a Border Station—
> A canter down some dark defile—
> Two thousand pounds of education
> Drops to a ten-rupee *jezail*.

'Shillin' a Day' and the famous 'Mandalay', both from *Barrack Room Ballads*, are concerned with what colonial soldiering meant to the working-class men who made up the army's 'other ranks'—and the later poem, in particular, is a long way from the hard masculine values idealized by public school imperialists. Indeed, 'The Widow at Windsor', from the same collection, makes a particularly telling comparison with 'England, my England', published in the same year. While Henley, safe at home, can fantasize over how he might answer the imperial bugle, Kipling's soldiers know that they are 'poor beggars in red' who cannot 'get away from the tune that they play/To the bloomin' old rag over'ead'.

In much of his poetry of the later 1890s, however, Kipling changes perspective: rather than reading the Empire through the eyes of this man or that, he assumes the role of imperial spokesman. He does this most elaborately in 'A Song of the English' (1896), and, for all its verve and local intensity, the imperial testament turns out to be an amalgam of standard elements from the late Victorian mythology of empire. The English must keep 'the Faith our Fathers sealèd us', and 'the Law' that they must obey is one of service: 'Clear the land of evil, drive the road and bridge the ford'. Imagined by colonially minded visionaries who 'yearned beyond the sky-line where the strange roads go down', the Empire was purchased by England's dead: 'We have strawed our best to the weed's unrest/To the shark and the sheering gull'. It will be sustained by a continuity of effort, and by the ties of race: 'Truly', England answers her offspring, 'ye come of The Blood'. Powerful as much of the poetry is, this is the Kipling of imperialist incantation, conjuring a vision of empire from a highly dubious mix of race, religion, and romance. Even so, 'A Song of the English' does manage to ground itself in the material and quotidian: the 'Song of the Cities' is a roll-call of real places, of great ports and naval bases; they speak to one another through the deep sea cables, not through the medium of some imperial ether; and their life-blood flows in the sea lanes of international trade, not in the mystical nonsense of race.

Nevertheless, it is racial myth that determines Kipling's most notorious poem, 'The White Man's Burden' (1898). Addressed principally to the United States, where expansion had already taken white colonization across continental America to the Pacific seaboard, the poem converts paternalist mission into a racial crusade. The complicating ironies typical of earlier poems here become those ironies of sacrifice and ingratitude which serve only to reinforce a conviction of racial superiority: we whites are not merely better, we are also misunderstood. One of the few things that can be said for the poem is that it buys into the mythology of race less militaristically and less hysterically than does Henley's 'Last Post': or perhaps it is merely more dangerous as a result. And yet, in the preceding year, 'Recessional' had eschewed the flag-waving and self-congratulation of Victoria's Diamond Jubilee for a warning about hubris and the fragility of empire. In 'The Islanders' (1902) Kipling attacked the insular complacency of the British, and, in particular, the cult of games—'the flannelled fools at the wicket or the muddied oafs at the goals'—that the public school ethos believed was the moral backbone of Empire. And with the 'Service Poems' of 1903, Kipling could return, in a metrical *tour de force* like 'Boots', to the experience of the ordinary British soldier, who marched endlessly and, sometimes, died anonymously, to keep the Empire in place. Kipling's range, as we said before, is wide, and it embraces a large measure of contradiction: here, rather than in any allegiance to an imperialist mythology, lies Kipling's claim to being the Empire's definitive poet.

Voices against Empire: Blunt, Belloc, Buchanan

Kipling's poetry was premised on an acceptance of the Empire as a fact: for all his diversity of approach it was not imaginatively possible for him to accommodate a radical rejection of the enterprise itself. Deeply engaged in all that concerned the imperial fabric, Kipling could probe its dark corners, reprimand its owners, even query the soundness of its foundations: what he could not do was ask whether it should have been built at all. Others could. As more of the world map was painted red, as imperialism assumed a definite ideological shape and its attendant mythological discourse grew more dominant, the thesis of empire generated its antithesis. From the last decades of the nineteenth century an increasing number of people began to dissent from the whole business, and a few of them did so in verse.

The maverick Tory Wilfrid Scawen Blunt was the most remarkable of these. His early sonnet 'Gibraltar' (1880) expresses the kind of sentiment to be expected of a Victorian traveller on his way home, excited by the sound of the regimental 'fifes upon the breeze' and the sight of the 'red coats marching from the hill'. But in December 1881 Blunt met the Egyptian nationalist leader Ahmad Arabi, and became a strong supporter. He tried unsuccessfully to act as a mediator between Arabi and the British government, and when Arabi's forces were defeated at the battle of Tel-el-Kebir—as celebrated by McGonagall—it was Blunt who arranged for Arabi's legal defence and for his exile to Ceylon. From 1882 onwards Blunt opposed imperialism in all its forms. His poem 'The Wind and the Whirlwind' (1883) is an account of the recent events in Egypt from this critical point of view. Next, in March 1885, Blunt joined the Irish Land League, working for the independence of Ireland from Britain. Visiting Ireland in the following year, he met Dr Duggan, the Roman Catholic Bishop of Clonfert, who told him how the English landlords continued to destroy the lives of their Irish tenants, and said that if he were not a priest he would be 'going about in your dockyards and ports, blowing up your ironclads with dynamite' (Blunt, *Land War in Ireland*, 1912, pp. 65–6). It is Duggan's voice behind that of the Irish priest who speaks Blunt's dramatic monologue, 'The Canon of Aughrim' (1888). Blunt himself defied the new Crimes Act in Ireland by holding a public meeting to protest against the eviction of Irish farmers, and was arrested and sentenced to two months' imprisonment.

Undeterred by the experience of gaol, which he described in his 1889 sonnet sequence *In Vinculis*, Blunt continued to take a radical line. In 1899, the year after the outbreak of the Boer War, he published the extraordinary poem *Satan Absolved. A Victorian Mystery*. An entry in Blunt's diary for 17 October 1898 makes clear his adversarial intent: 'Swinburne has just published a ridiculous sonnet in favour of the war, and Kipling has also been in the "Times". My "Satan Absolved" must stand for poetry on the other side' (*My Diaries*, 1932, p. 333). So, rather eccentrically, it does. In the poem Satan explains to a somewhat unobservant God that things have gone badly wrong down on earth, though responsibility for the mayhem rests not with him but with man, the 'lewd bare-bottomed ape' to whom God has rashly given supreme power. Above all it is 'Anglo-Saxon man'—subject of so many panegyrics from the Empire's mythmakers—whose pursuit of profit has plundered continents and laid waste the earth, an accusation which strikingly anticipates the arguments of environmentalism. In the midst of the diatribe, Kipling's claim that white imperialism has loftier purposes is stripped of its pretensions: 'The White Man's Burden, Lord, is the burden of his cash'. There have been few more succinct deconstructions of the mythology of empire.

Blunt did not shift his position, and his later 'Quatrains of Life' (1914), a work of autobiographical retrospection, contains some of his most successful anti-imperialist poetry. The last section of 'Quatrains' takes the poet to the Orient, where his feelings of affinity with the Bedouin are outraged by the 'Saxon multitude' marching in to make war, and, most of all, by the rapacious arrogance of the British.

> Chief of the sons of Japhet he, with hand
> Hard on the nations of the sea and land,
> Intolerant of all, tongues, customs, creeds,
> Too dull to spare, too proud to understand.

In memory Blunt returns to his first realization of the evils of imperialism, to the eve of Tel-el-Kebir and the two armies encamped before battle. In the one, Islamic warriors called to prayer; in the other, men of 'the slums' spending what might be their last night on earth in 'Drink and debauchery', entertained by the 'strains of the music halls'. The contrast, and Blunt's class-based élitism, are alike revealing. His radicalism could carry him to a generous anger on behalf of those peoples subjugated by the Empire. It did not enable him to understand that the same economic interests that drove the Empire also systematically impoverished the British working class, and then exploited that poverty to recruit the soldiers and sailors needed to guarantee the security of the imperial investment.

Blunt's stance was highly individualistic, but his anti-imperialism was not unique. Parody and satire were favourite weapons of attack. George R. Sims's savagely funny 'Ode and Paid to Kahu' (1883) takes to task a South Seas chieftain for massacring a rival tribe in the name of Christianity: 'To slaughter men in Heaven's name/Is Christian England's private game'. *Punch*, steering between its broad support for the Empire and its dislike of jingoism, attacked imperialism's assumptions about the superiority of European civilization, as in the jaunty little poem 'Ask a White Man!' (1890), included here. Far more ambitious in scope than these occasional pieces is Hilaire Belloc's *The Modern Traveller* (1898). Belloc held what came to be known as

'Little England' views, sentiments that focused on the home country and, by implication, deplored the imperialist project that others saw as so triumphant a statement of Englishness. The modern traveller of the title is Mr Rooter, and through his narrative Belloc ridicules the cult of manly adventure, partly by suggesting its association with selling stories profitably to the popular press, in this case the *Daily Menace*. But the poem has a more serious target as well: the chartered companies who managed much of the scramble for Africa on behalf of the imperialist powers. Rooter is accompanied by the semi-allegorical figures of Commander Sin and Captain Blood, and their object is to spy out the land on which they can launch a wholly fraudulent speculative company. If necessary the company's enterprise can be backed by force, and at one point Blood memorably summarizes the technological superiority in firearms that helped make Western imperialism so successful:

> He stood upon a little mound,
> Cast his lethargic eyes around,
> And said beneath his breath:
> 'Whatever happens we have got
> The Maxim Gun, and they have not.'

The year after *The Modern Traveller* appeared, Robert Buchanan brought out *The New Rome: Ballads and Poems of our Empire*. Despite the success of his earlier literary career, by 1899 Buchanan was impoverished, largely forgotten, and nearing the end of his life; he died destitute in 1901. *The New Rome* is a remarkable performance, a vigorous, at times frantic, attack upon the Empire and the mythology that helped sustain it. The decadence of the Roman Empire is replayed in contemporary Britain. Commercial self-interest runs everything under the hypocritical cover of patriotism and Christianity: the 'Image in the Forum'—the title of one of the poems—is 'Not Baal, but Christus-Jingo'. Weaker nations are destroyed for the sanctified benefit of the European powers: ''Tis meet that the heathen tribes should starve, and the Christian dogs be fed'. Imperialists like Joseph Chamberlain—attacked in the poem 'Patriotism'—crucify the true Christ daily. And the national bard who leads the bragging and the celebration is Kipling, 'whose name and fame have spread/As far as the Flag of England waves, and the

Tory prints are read'. The cumulative power of *The New Rome* can only be felt when it is read in full: the three poems we have chosen—'A Song of Jubilee', 'Tommy Atkins', and 'The Charter'd Companie'—indicate something of Buchanan's range, and his rage.

The Boer War:
Imperial Mythology and the Crisis of Reality

It is doubtful whether the dissent of writers like Blunt, Belloc, and Buchanan did anything much to dent the confidence of the imperialists. Historical events, however, did just that. The mythology of empire faced the test of reality in the Boer War and, palpably, it failed. Britain's most extensive and most costly military campaign since the Crimean War was fought against a few thousand colonial farmers whose obstinate independence stood in the way of the thorough exploitation of South Africa's goldfields. There were, of course, occasions for heroism, self-sacrifice, the public school virtues generally; and the garrisons of Ladysmith and Mafeking put in cameo performances of British grit under siege. But the war also revealed alarming inadequacies in the British high command, and the protracted final stages of the Boer guerrilla campaign were only ended when Kitchener, no stranger to brutality, adopted a scorched earth policy and introduced mass internment: the compounds into which the Afrikaners were herded were called concentration camps. Cynically provoked by British economic interests, short on glory, finishing with women and children in barbed wire cages, there was little that was chivalrous or elevating about the Boer War. When it was all over, Kipling, in 'The Lesson' (1902), delivered a headmasterly reprimand.

> Not on a single issue, or in one direction or twain,
> But conclusively, comprehensively, and several times
>   and again,
> Were all our most holy illusions knocked higher than
>   Gilderoy's kite.
> We have had a jolly good lesson, and it serves us jolly
>   well right!

The lesson Kipling had in mind was primarily military; but in retrospect we can see it as ideological as well. The Boer War not only cost the mythology of empire much of its credibility, it also broke the relative harmony of the cultural establishment that had invested so heavily in that mythology.

More poems were written about the war than any previous British conflict, and their lack of unanimity reflects the extent to which the ethos of imperialism had been compromised. In this context, the case of William Watson is particularly revealing. Unlike Blunt, he was a cultural insider, tipped as a possible successor to Tennyson in the Laureateship. As we have seen, his 1890 poem 'England and Her Colonies' endorses the Empire in a wholly orthodox way. Soon after, however, his views began to change, and the failure of the European powers to prevent Turkish atrocities in the Balkans convinced him of the hollow-ness of much of the imperialist rhetoric. His 1897 collection, *The Year of Shame*—from which we include 'How Weary is Our Heart!'—was the result. Two years later he publicly opposed the war in South Africa and, denounced as pro-Boer, withdrew into literary silence for its duration. Watson's retrospective volume, *For England* (1904)—from which we have taken a number of poems—seems more an expression of sorrow than of anger: but it also reveals the extent to which he finds the old mythology of empire no longer tenable.

Among the imperialists, Henley contributed *For England's Sake* (1900), in which appeared 'Last Post', discussed earlier. Swinburne, his earlier radicalism (such as it was) long forgotten, produced several exercises in armchair bellicosity, including 'Transvaal' (1899)—the 'ridiculous sonnet' of Blunt's diary entry quoted above—and the triumphalist 'First of June' (1902). More dignified was Newbolt. 'April on Waggon Hill' (1900) and 'The Only Son' (*c*.1900) both try, in different ways, to grapple with the personal costs of dying for the Empire, costs that are regis-tered far less abstractly than in any of his pre-war poems. Perhaps rather surprisingly, Newbolt admired Thomas Hardy's poetry and dedicated his 1907 *Collected Poems* to him. Hardy's own 'War Poems', written 1899–1900, strike a note different from that of either the imperialists or their opponents. Almost all have a domestic focus, principally on the wives and families left behind, and the war itself is consistently presented as alien, estranging—nowhere more so than in the famous 'Drummer Hodge'. A wider perspective is established by evoking a histor-ical context that suggests the futility of any attempt to build civilization upon conquest. Hardy's own stance is withdrawn, wry, that of a bystander unable to influence events that are governed by forces beyond his control. There is wryness of a different sort in A.E. Housman's Boer War elegy, 'Astronomy', and in the deftly managed lyric 'Lancer', its bisexual innuendoes subversively reinterpreting the martial glamour that was so important an element in the mythology—and masculinity—of empire.

Entering upon the Eclipse: the Empire in the early Twentieth Century

After the Boer War the mythology of imperialism never recovered the ascendancy it had achieved in middle- and upper-class culture over the last decades of Victoria's reign. Although the Edwardian period staged spectacular displays of imperial power, notably in the Indian Durbars of 1903 and 1912, the status of the Empire from the viewpoint of British domestic politics was changing. As Davis and Huttenback have shown in *Mammon and the Pursuit of Empire* (1988), the cost of imperial defence, borne almost wholly by the British taxpayer, became ever more burdensome to the national economy. Successive British administrations had been unable to pressure the colonies of white settlement into providing for their own defence: although the extension of legislative independence in Australia (federated in 1901), New Zealand (granted dominion status in 1907), and South Africa (formed into a federal union in 1910) brought some alleviation to the home country, it also meant a further slackening of the Crown's already attenuated authority. In India, attempts to balance the budget were continually frustrated by the need to reconcile the Raj to indigenous socio-economic interests. The Empire was not only expensive, it was proving increasingly difficult to manage in Britain's interests. At home, the idea of the Empire's importance was also affected by the progressive extension of the franchise, which gradually introduced working-class representation into the formal political process. To the great mass of the British proletariat—something above 70 per cent of the population—the Empire was simply there, the backdrop to a consciousness that was far more concerned with the immediate problems of wages and living conditions. Similarly, British socialism, closely tied into the trade union movement, concentrated upon the intensifying domestic struggle with the forces of Capital. When socialists spoke about the Empire—as Keir Hardie, for one, sometimes did—they condemned it as one of the more pernicious products of international capitalism.

The most substantial contribution to the poetry of empire during this period was Alfred Noyes's *Drake* (1906–8). An epic reworking of the origins of British sea power, it marks the end point of a process of mythologization that can be tracked in Kingsley's *Westward Ho!*, Tennyson's 'The Revenge', and Newbolt's 'Drake's Drum', and that had its origins way back in the eighteenth century. The quasi-mystical patriotism impelling *Drake* has a more contemporary counterpart in 'The Empire Builders' (1907), where Noyes—moved perhaps by the stirrings of democracy—distributively assigns the credit for empire to the self-sacrificial devotion of the ordinary people of Britain: 'For all are Empire-builders here,/Whose hearts are true to heaven and home'. There is no evidence that ordinary people were much moved by such pieties. For popular culture, the Empire was far more imaginatively engaging as a setting for exotic yarns, as in Jacky Hayes's exuberantly melodramatic monologue 'The Green Eye of the Little Yellow God' (1911).

Even if only as part of the background texture of a night out at the music-hall, patriotism and its associated assumptions about the rightness of the British Empire remained the norm in the years leading up to the outbreak of the First World War in August 1914. But the core values of the mythology of empire, those listed by Henley in his preface to *Lyra Heroica*, could not survive the reality of mechanized warfare: together they constituted what Wilfrid Owen called 'the old lie'. Soldiers, probably, had always known the truth; now it was patent not just to a professional army but to a whole nation of conscripts. For many who fought, the entire ideological construction of the Empire and its history fell at Loos, on the Somme, at Passchendaele. Here indeed was 'that battle in the West' that Tennyson had dreaded, and the Arthur whose legend he had summoned from the mist to the imperial cause fell too. In 'Hospital Barge at Cérisy' Owen comes to understand 'How unto Avalon, in agony,/Kings passed in the dark barge, which Merlin dreamed'. Kipling, who well knew of his own complicity in the imperial narrative, and whose son was killed, wrote of the dead's 'Common Form': 'If any question why we died,/Tell them, because our fathers lied'. The armed forces of the Empire died alongside those from Britain: poetry written by members of those forces is beyond the scope of this anthology. The only British poems that take the Empire as a theme seem to be those produced for the consumption of the Home Front, celebrating imperial solidarity and the colonial contribution to the war effort: by way of example we include the music-hall monologue 'The Answer of the Anzacs' (1916).

Between the Wars: Occasional Songs

As a geopolitical entity the Empire, of course, survived the First World War: ironically, indeed, it achieved its greatest territorial extent with the acquisition of former German colonies under the terms of the Treaty of Versailles. But after the war the Empire virtually disappeared as a subject for poetry. These were the years that saw the liberal questioning of British imperialism in E.M. Forster's *A Passage to India* (1923), and the more radical critique of George Orwell in his autobiographical *Burmese Days* (1934). We have found no equivalents to these works in the poetry of the time. Eliot's *Waste Land* (1922) may set London, the 'Unreal City', among the other capitals of fallen empires, but its main enterprise is to suggest a general human condition. Yeats's poetry certainly attacks British policies in Ireland, but it is written from the point of view of the colonized rather than the colonizer, and so falls outside our scope. Even the left-wing poets of the 1930s who might have been expected to attack imperialism seem more typically to have focused their attention on internal British politics, and in particular on the economic crisis of the decade.

One area in which the Empire did survive as matter for verse, however, was in variety theatre, both at the popular level in the music-hall, and, at the level of the smart set, in revue. From the first we have included Billy Bennett's anarchic 'Mandalay' (1929) and Alan Sanders's cockney monologue 'Tommy out East' (1932): both, in their different ways, take the Kipling of *Barrack Room Ballads* as their starting point. From the second we have included two lyrics by Noël Coward, the famous 'Mad Dogs and Englishmen' (1934), and a song he wrote while in India during the Second World War, 'I Wonder What Happened to Him' (1944). Both, tellingly enough, mock the social habits of an empowered class, the satire bright but careful not to penetrate below the mannered surface. They have neither the chaotic subversiveness of Bennett's piece, nor the sense of alienation that lurks in Sanders's poem. After all, fashionably cynical though Coward's audience might have been, it still belonged to the same class as the managers of empire. A solitary poem from the period represents the continuation of an attitude to the Empire uncomplicated by irony, John Masefield's 'Australia' (1936). It is a personal record of a visit to Australia, so apolitical and direct in the warmth of its feelings as to be disarming. Extraordinarily, Masefield's enthusiasm takes us back—who knows how consciously—to the naïve optimism of the very dawn of colonialism, to the creation of 'Earth's newest race of men, whose bodies' beauty/Surpasses all the peoples of the world'.

After Empire

Neither the impact of the Second World War upon imperialism, nor the ending of the British Empire as, one by one, its former colonies gained their independence, seem to have provoked much direct poetic response—although further research may prove this remark to be too sweeping. Auden's 'Partition' (1948) reflects with sardonic detachment on the winding-up of the Raj; some twenty years later, with most of the Empire dismantled, Philip Larkin's 'Homage to a Government' (1968) sneers at the cost-cutting which he imputes to the final stages of Britain's colonial withdrawal. Both writers, from very different perspectives, see the end of empire as an expedient act, rather than a positive political achievement. Although their direct approach to the theme seems relatively unusual, Britain's imperial eclipse may have had a more indirect, but also more pervasive, poetic influence. In *Minotaur. Poetry and the Nation State* (1992), Tom Paulin finds its effect underlying the nostalgic or melancholy mood of much English postwar poetry, particularly that of Larkin. The former British Empire has certainly not disappeared altogether from the subject matter of more recent British poetry, but neither has it been given a prominent role. Geoffrey Hill's meditations on the British in India place the subject in the context of a general questioning of Victorian culture and its values in 'An Apology for the Revival of Christian Architecture in England' (1978). Jon Stallworthy's 'An Ode for Trafalgar Day' (1965) vividly contrasts the confident outward-looking gaze of Victorian Englishmen with the constrained inwardness attributed to the modern Englishman, and attempts a balanced evaluation of the whole enterprise—though maybe still allowing 'energy' and 'courage' to excuse the violence on which the Empire was founded.

However the story is not yet over. The contention behind this anthology is that the past informs the present in many, often unrecognized ways which we need to understand. If the end of empire left some English poets feeling culturally deprived, it gave opportunities for many voices from the former Empire to make themselves heard: the Australian Les Murray and the West Indian Derek Walcott being perhaps the most distinguished so far. Hence our earlier direction of the reader to anthologies of poetry from all the formerly colonized areas of the world. There is also the question of the effects of imperialism on the present population of Great Britain. As Salman Rushdie has argued, it is the fact of empire that has led to the mixed population that now inhabits these islands: Defoe's True-Born Englishman was never more various, and of course he is now often a woman. The fact that this anthology contains few poems by women reflects the gendering of the idea of empire in its heyday. Whether contemporary British culture can bring together our new multi-racial society in a harmonious way only time can tell. Rushdie is doubtful. Hulse, Kennedy, and Morley, the editors of *The New Poetry* (1993), are more optimistic: writers of the 1980s and early 1990s, they claim, 'have discovered a new pluralism and are starting to define a believable role for poetry' (p. 25). The black contribution to English poetry is only just beginning to be recognized: among recent works that deal directly with the issues of empire is David Dabydeen's *Turner* (1994), its title referring to the Turner painting *Slave Ship*, mentioned earlier in this Introduction. For British black poetry generally, there is an excellent discussion by Fred D'Aguiar in Robert Hampson and Peter Barry's *New British Poetries: The Scope of the Possible* (1994). What is undoubtedly true is that, in the words of Edward Said:

> No one today is purely *one* thing. Labels like Indian, or woman, or Muslim, or American are no more than starting points, which if followed into actual experience for only

a few moments are quickly left behind. Imperialism consolidated the mixture of cultures and identities on a global scale. But its worst and most paradoxical gift was to allow people to believe that they were only, mainly, exclusively, white, or black, or Western, or Oriental. (pp. 407–8)

If this anthology helps to question that legacy by allowing us to look carefully at its construction, it will have served its purpose.

TEXTUAL NOTE

Wherever possible the texts of the poems in this anthology have been taken from standard or first editions, or from first printings. We have retained original spellings and, to a large extent, original typographical conventions. Obvious errors in spelling and punctuation have been silently corrected.

GEORGE CHAPMAN

'DE GUIANA, CARMEN EPICUM', 1596

Poet, classical scholar, and a leading Jacobean dramatist, Chapman (1559–1634) produced the first complete translation of the works of Homer, one of the central literary achievements of the English Renaissance. 'De Guiana, Carmen Epicum' ('Of Guiana, an Epic Song') was written as a poetic preface to Lawrence Kemys's *A Relation of the Second Voyage to Guiana*. It is addressed to Kemys's master, the adventurer and explorer Sir Walter Raleigh, and urges him to take possession of Guiana, on the South American coast, for Elizabeth and England. It is one of the first English poems to engage the idea of an overseas empire: significantly, even at this early stage, Chapman thought the theme an appropriate one for the epic voice.

> WHAT worke of honour and eternall name,
> For all the worlde t'enuie and vs t'atchieue,
> Filles me with furie, and giues armed handes
> To my heartes peace, that els would gladlie turne
> My limmes and euery sence into my thoughtes
> Rapt with the thirsted action of my mind?
> O *Clio, Honors Muse*, sing in my voyce,
> Tell the attempt, and prophecie th'exploit
> Of his *Eliza*-consecrated sworde,
> That in this peacefull charme of *Englands* sleepe,
> Opens most tenderlie her aged throte,
> Offring to poure fresh youth through all her vaines,
> That flesh of brasse, and ribs of steele retaines.
>
> *Riches*, and *Conquest*, and *Renowme* I sing,
> *Riches* with honour, *Conquest* without bloud,
> Enough to seat the Monarchie of earth,
> Like to *Ioues* Eagle, on *Elizas* hand.
> *Guiana*, whose rich feet are mines of golde,
> Whose forehead knockes against the roofe of Starres,
> Stands on her tip-toes at faire *England* looking,
> Kissing her hand, bowing her mightie breast,
> And euery signe of all submission making,
> To be her sister, and the daughter both
> Of our most sacred Maide: whose barrennesse

Is the true fruite of vertue, that may get,
Beare and bring foorth anew in all perfection,
What heretofore sauage corruption held
In barbarous *Chaos*; and in this affaire
Become her father, mother, and her heire.

Then most admired Soueraigne, let your breath
Goe foorth vpon the waters, and create
A golden worlde in this our yron age,
And be the prosperous forewind to a Fleet,
That seconding your last, may goe before it
In all successe of profite and renowme:
Doubt not but your election was diuine,
(As well by *Fate* as your high iudgement ordred)
To raise him with choise Bounties, that could adde
Height to his height; and like a liberall vine,
Not onelie beare his vertuous fruit aloft,
Free from the Presse of squint-eyd *Enuies* feet,
But decke his gracious Proppe with golden bunches,
And shroude it with broad leaues of *Rule* oregrowne
From all blacke tempestes of inuasion.

Those Conquests that like generall earthquakes shooke
The solid world, and made it fall before them,
Built all their braue attemptes on weaker groundes,
And lesse persuasiue likelihoods then this;
Nor was there euer princelie Fount so long
Powr'd foorth a sea of Rule with so free course,
And such ascending Maiestie as you:
Then be not like a rough and violent wind,
That in the morning rends the Forrestes downe,
Shoues vp the seas to heauen, makes earth to tremble,
And toombes his wastfull brauerie in the Euen:
But as a riuer from a mountaine running,
The further he extends, the greater growes,
And by his thriftie race strengthens his streame,
Euen to ioyne battale with th'imperious sea
Disdaining his repulse, and in despight
Of his proud furie, mixeth with his maine,
Taking on him his titles and commandes:
So let thy soueraigne Empire be encreast,
And with *Iberian Neptune* part the stake,
Whose *Trident* he the triple worlde would make.
You then that would be wise in Wisdomes spight,
Directing with discredite of direction,

And hunt for honour, hunting him to death,
With whome before you will inherite gold,
You will loose golde, for which you loose your soules;
You that choose nought for right, but certaintie,
And feare that value will get onlie blowes,
Placing your faith in *Incredulitie*;
Sit till you see a woonder, *Vertue* rich:
Till *Honour* hauing golde, rob golde of honour;
Till as men hate desert that getteth nought,
They loath all getting that deserues not ought,
And vse you gold-made men, as dregges of men;
And till your poysoned soules, like Spiders lurking
In sluttish chinckes, in mystes of Cobwebs hide
Your foggie bodies, and your dunghill pride.

O *Incredulitie*, the wit of Fooles,
That slouenlie will spit on all thinges faire,
The *Cowards castle*, and the *Sluggards cradle*,
How easie t'is to be an Infidell?

But you *Patrician* Spirites that refine
Your flesh to fire, and issue like a flame
On braue endeuours, knowing that in them
The tract of heauen in morne-like glorie opens,
That know you cannot be the Kinges of earth,
(Claiming the Rightes of your creation)
And let the Mynes of earth be Kinges of you;
That are so farre from doubting likelie driftes,
That in things hardest y'are most confident;
You that know death liues, where power liues vnusde,
Ioying to shine in waues that burie you,
And so make way for life euen through your graues;
That will not be content like horse to hold
A thread-bare beaten waie to home affaires:
But where the sea in enuie of your raigne,
Closeth her wombe, as fast as tis disclosde,
That she like *Auarice* might swallowe all,
And let none find right passage through her rage:
There your wise soules as swift as *Eurus* lead
Your Bodies through, to profit and renowne,
And skorne to let your bodies chooke your soules,
In the rude breath and prisoned life of beastes:
You that heerein renounce the course of earth,
And lift your eies for guidance to the starres,
That liue not for your selues, but to possesse

[53]

Your honour'd countrey of a generall store;
In pitie of the spoyle rude self-loue makes,
Of them whose liues and yours one aire doth feede,
One soile doeth nourish, and one strength combine;
You that are blest with sence of all things noble
In this attempt your compleat woorthes redouble.

But how is *Nature* at her heart corrupted,
(I meane euen in her most ennobled birth?)
How in excesse of Sence is Sence bereft her?
That her most lightening-like effectes of lust
Wound through her flesh, her soule, her flesh vnwounded;
And she must neede incitements to her good,
Euen from that part she hurtes. O how most like
Art thou (heroike Author of this Act)
To this wrong'd soule of *Nature*: that sustainst
Paine, charge, and perill for thy countreys good,
And she much like a bodie numb'd with surfets,
Feeles not thy gentle applications
For the health, vse, & honor of her powers.
Yet shall my verse through all her ease-lockt eares
Trumpet the Noblesse of thy high intent,
And if it cannot into act proceed,
The fault and bitter pennance of the fault
Make red some others eyes with penitence,
For thine are cleare; and what more nimble spirites
Apter to byte at such vnhooked baytes,
Gaine by our losse; that must we needs confesse
Thy princelie valure would haue purchast vs.
Which shall be fame eternall to thy name,
Though thy contentment in thy graue desires,
Of our aduancement, faile deseru'd effect,
O how I feare thy glorie which I loue,
Least it should dearelie growe by our decrease.
Natures that stick in golden-graueld springs,
In mucke-pits cannot scape their swallowings.

But we shall foorth I know; Golde is our Fate,
Which all our actes doeth fashion and create.

Then in the *Thespiads* bright Propheticke Fount,
Me thinkes I see our Liege rise from her throne,
Her eares and thoughts in steepe amaze erected,
At the most rare endeuour of her power.
And now she blesseth with her woonted Graces

Th'industrious Knight, the soule of this exploit,
Dismissing him to conuoy of his starres.
And now for loue and honour of his woorth,
Our twise-borne Nobles bring him Bridegroome-like,
That is espousde for vertue to his loue
With feastes and musicke, rauishing the aire,
To his *Argolian* Fleet, where round about
His bating Colours English valure swarmes
In haste, as if *Guianian Orenoque*
With his Fell waters fell vpon our shore.
And now a wind as forward as their spirits,
Sets their glad feet on smooth *Guianas* breast,
Where (as if ech man were an *Orpheus*)
A world of Sauadges fall tame before them,
Storing their theft-free treasuries with golde,
And there doth plentie crowne their wealthie fieldes,
There *Learning* eates no more his thriftlesse books,
Nor *Valure* Estridge-like his yron armes.
There *Beautie* is no strumpet for her wantes,
Nor *Gallique* humours putrifie her bloud:
But all our Youth take *Hymens* lightes in hand,
And fill each roofe with honor'd progenie.
There makes *Societie* Adamantine chaines,
And ioins their harts with wealth, whom wealth disioyn'd.
There healthfull Recreations strowe their meades,
And make their mansions daunce with neighborhood,
That here were drown'd in churlish *Auarice*.
And there do Pallaces and temples rise
Out of the earth, and kisse th'enamored skies,
Where new *Britania*, humblie kneeles to heauen,
The world to her, and both at her blest feete,
In whom the Circles of all Empire meet.

MICHAEL DRAYTON

'TO THE VIRGINIAN VOYAGE', 1606

Drayton (1563–1631) was a prolific poet who wrote mainly on patriotic and historical themes. The occasion of this poem was the voyage backed by London entrepreneurs that, in 1607, established the first permanent British settlement in the New World, at Jamestown in Virginia—the town named after James I, the colony after the Virgin Queen, Elizabeth. Drayton's last verse commends the works of Richard Hakluyt, chronicler of Elizabethan voyages of discovery, and founding father of the literature of English sea power.

YOU Brave Heroique Minds,
Worthy your Countries Name,
   That Honour still pursue,
   Goe, and subdue,
Whilst loyt'ring Hinds
Lurke here at home, with shame.

Britans, you stay too long,
Quickly aboord bestow you,
   And with a merry Gale
   Swell your stretch'd Sayle,
With Vowes as strong,
As the Winds that blow you.

Your Course securely steere,
West and by South forth keepe,
   Rocks, Lee-shores, nor Sholes,
   When EOLUS scowles,
You need not feare,
So absolute the Deepe.

And cheerefully at Sea,
Successe you still intice,
   To get the Pearle and Gold,
   And ours to hold,
VIRGINIA,
Earth's onely Paradise.

Where Nature hath in store
Fowle, Venison, and Fish,
   And the fruitfull'st Soyle,
   Without your Toyle,
Three Harvests more,
All greater then your Wish.

And the ambitious Vine
Crownes with his purple Masse,
   The Cedar reaching hie
   To kisse the Sky,
The Cypresse, Pine
And use-full Sassafras.

To whose, the golden Age
Still Natures lawes doth give,
   No other Cares that tend,
   But Them to defend
From Winters age,
That long there doth not live.

When as the Lushious smell
Of that delicious Land,
   Above the Seas that flowes,
   The cleere Wind throwes,
Your Hearts to swell
Approching the deare Strand.

In kenning of the Shore
(Thanks to God first given,)
   O you the happy'st men,
   Be Frolike then,
Let Cannons roare,
Frighting the wide Heaven.

And in Regions farre
Such *Heroes* bring yee foorth,
   And those from whom We came,
   And plant Our name,
Under that Starre
Not knowne unto our North.

[57]

And as there Plenty growes
Of Lawrell every where,
   APOLLO's Sacred tree,
   You it may see,
A Poets Browes
To crowne, that may sing there.

Thy Voyages attend,
Industrious HACKLUIT,
   Whose Reading shall inflame
   Men to seeke Fame,
And much commend
To after-Times thy Wit.

MICHAEL DRAYTON

From *POLY-OLBION*, 1622

Drayton's lengthy poem attempts to give a full topographical
account of England. Book XIX, from which this extract is taken,
describes and celebrates English seamen, including Frobisher,
Drake, and Raleigh.

    Then *Forbosher*, whose fame flew all the Ocean o'r,
Who to the Northwest sought, huge *China's* wealthy shore,
When nearer to the North, that wandring Sea-man set,
Where hee in our hotst Mon'ths of June and July met
With Snow, Frost, Haile, & Sleet, and found stern Winter
With mighty Iles of Ice, and Mountaines huge and long.
Where as it comes and goes, the great eternall Light,
Makes halfe the yeare still day, and halfe continuall night.
Then for those Bounds unknown, he bravely set againe,
As he a Sea-god were, familiar with the Maine.
    The Noble *Fenton* next, and *Jackman* we preferre,
Both Voyagers, that were with famous *Forbosher*.
    And *Davies*, three times forth that for the Northwest made;
Still striving by that course, t'inrich the English Trade:
And as he well deserv'd to his eternall fame.
There by a mightie Sea, Imortaliz'd his Name.
    With noble *Gilbert* next, comes *Hoard* who tooke in hand
To cleere the course scarse knowne into the *New-found* Land,
And view'd the plenteous Seas, and fishfull Havens, where
Our neighbouring Nations since have stor'd them every yeare.
    Then Globe-engirdling *Drake*, the Navall Palme that wonne,
Who strove in his long Course to emulate the Sunne:
Of whom the *Spaniard* us'd a Prophecie to tell,
That from the British Isles shoud rise a Dragon fell,
That with his armed wings, should strike th' *Iberian* Maine,
And bring in after time much horror upon *Spaine*.
This more then man (or what) this Demie-god at Sea,
Leaving behind his backe, the great *America*,
Upon the surging Maine his wel-stretch't Tacklings flewd,
To fortie three Degrees of North'ly Latitude;
Unto that Land before to th' Christian world unknowne,
Which in his Countries right he nam'd New *Albion*;
And in the Westerne *Inde*, spight of the power of *Spaine*,

He Saint *Iago* tooke, *Domingo*, *Cartagene*:
And leaving of his prowesse, a marke in every Bay,
Saint *Augustins* surpriz'd, in *Terra Florida*.

Then those that foorth for Sea, Industrious *Rawleigh* wrought,
And them with every thing, fit for discovery fraught;
That *Amadas*, (whose Name doth scarsely English sound)
With *Barlow*, who the first *Virginia* throughly found.
As *Greenvile*, whom he got to undertake that Sea,
Three sundry times from hence, who touch'd *Virginia*.
In his so rare a choyce, it well approov'd his wit;
That with so brave a Spirit, his turne so well could fit.
O *Greenvile*, thy great Name, for ever be renown'd,
And borne by *Neptune* still, about this mightie Round;
Whose Navall Conflict wanne thy Nation so much fame,
And in th' *Iberians* bred feare of the English name.

Andrew Marvell

'BERMUDAS', written c.1654

———

Very much a man of affairs as well as a man of letters, Marvell (1621–78) was the most urbane of the Metaphysical poets. Although a supporter of the Cromwellian Commonwealth, he was sufficiently deft politically to retain a position of influence after the Restoration. In this poem he mythologizes Bermuda, first settled by British colonists in 1609, as an earthly paradise complete with reformed religion, contrasting it with the troubled England of the Civil War period.

WHERE the remote *Bermudas* ride
In th' Oceans bosome unespy'd,
From a small Boat, that row'd along,
The listning Winds receiv'd this Song.
   What should we do but sing his Praise
That led us through the watry Maze,
Unto an Isle so long unknown,
And yet far kinder than our own?
Where he the huge Sea-Monsters wracks,
That lift the Deep upon their Backs.
He lands us on a grassy Stage;
Safe from the Storms, and Prelat's rage.
He gave us this eternal Spring,
Which here enamells every thing;
And sends the Fowl's to us in care,
On daily Visits through the Air.
He hangs in shades the Orange bright,
Like golden Lamps in a green Night.
And does in the Pomgranates close,
Jewels more rich than *Ormus* show's.
He makes the Figs our mouths to meet;
And throws the Melons at our feet.
But Apples plants of such a price,
No Tree could ever bear them twice.
With Cedars, chosen by his hand,
From *Lebanon*, he stores the Land.
And makes the hollow Seas, that roar,
Proclaime the Ambergris on shoar.
He cast (of which we rather boast)

The Gospels Pearl upon our Coast.
And in these Rocks for us did frame
A Temple, where to sound his Name.
Oh let our Voice his Praise exalt,
Till it arrive at Heavens Vault:
Which thence (perhaps) rebounding, may
Eccho beyond the *Mexique Bay*.
Thus sung they, in the *English* boat,
An holy and chearful Note,
And all the way, to guide their Chime,
With falling Oars they kept the time.

JOHN DRYDEN

From *ANNUS MIRABILIS*, 1667

As poet, playwright, and essayist, Dryden (1631–1700) was one of the most influential writers of the later decades of the seventeenth century. Charles II made him Poet Laureate in 1670 and much of his work was deployed in the interests of the court party, most notably the verse satires he produced during the protracted succession crisis of the 1680s. *Annus Mirabilis*—which chronicles the events of The Year of Wonders, 1666—is the most important of his earlier political poems. Its opening stanzas, given here, review the success of the British against the Dutch in the war of 1665–6 and assess the threat posed by France. The commercial basis of British expansion depended in large part on replacing Holland as the leading European economic power, and much British policy—which included war when expedient—was directed to this end, with eventual success. With a canny eye on both classical precedent and *realpolitik*, Dryden sees the Second Dutch War as a parallel to the Second Punic War in which the commercial ascendancy of Carthage was overthrown by the nascent imperial power of Rome.

In thriving Arts long time had *Holland* grown,
    Crouching at home, and cruel when abroad:
Scarce leaving us the means to claim our own.
    Our King they courted, & our Merchants aw'd.

Trade, which like bloud should circularly flow,
    Stop'd in their Channels, found its freedom lost:
Thither the wealth of all the world did go,
    And seem'd but shipwrack'd on so base a Coast.

For them alone the Heav'ns had kindly heat,
    In Eastern Quarries ripening precious Dew:
For them the *Idumæan* Balm did sweat,
    And in hot Ceilon Spicy Forrests grew.

The Sun but seem'd the Lab'rer of their Year;
  Each wexing Moon suppli'd her watry store,
To swell those Tides, which from the Line did bear
  Their brim-full Vessels to the *Belg'an* shore.

Thus mighty in her Ships stood *Carthage* long,
  And swept the riches of the world from far;
Yet stoop'd to *Rome*, less wealthy, but more strong:
  And this may prove our second Punick War.

What peace can be where both to one pretend?
  (But they more diligent, and we more strong)
Or if a peace, it soon must have an end
  For they would grow too pow'rful were it long.

Behold two Nations then, ingag'd so far,
  That each seav'n years the fit must shake each Land:
Where *France* will side to weaken us by War,
  Who onely can his vast designs withstand.

See how he feeds th' *Iberian* with delays,
  To render us his timely friendship vain;
And, while his secret Soul on *Flanders* preys,
  He rocks the Cradle of the Babe of *Spain*.

Such deep designs of Empire does he lay
  O're them whose cause he seems to take in hand:
And, prudently, would make them Lords at Sea,
To whom with ease he can give Laws by Land.

APHRA BEHN

From *OF PLANTS*, 1689

Behn (1640–89) was the first Englishwoman to make a living by writing, mostly for the stage. She probably spent some time in Surinam, then a British colony, and wrote the novel *Oroonoko, or the History of the Royal Slave* (1688), in which a noble African is trapped into slavery and is executed when he later leads a rebellion. She wrote a good deal of poetry, but none of it is so explicitly concerned with race. The present extract from Book VI (lines 719–42), translated from the Latin of Abraham Cowley, celebrates the British Empire through praise of the oak tree, the material foundation of the navy.

> Oh how has Nature blest the British Land,
> Who both the valued *Indies* can command!
> What tho thy Banks the Cedars do not grace
> Those lofty Beauties of fam'd *Libanus*.
> The Pine, or Palm of *Idumean* Plaines,
> *Arabs* rich Wood or its sweet smelling Greens,
> Or lovely Plantan whose large leafy boughs
> A pleasant and a noble shade allows.
> She has thy warlike Groves and Mountains blest
> With sturdy Oak's, ore all the World the best,
> And for the happy Islands sure Defence
> Has wall'd it with a Mote of Seas immense,
> While to declare her Safety and thy Pride,
> With Oaken Ships that Sea is fortifi'd.
>   Nor was that Adoration vainly made,
> Which to the Oak the Ancient *Druids* paid,
> Who reasonably believed a God within,
> Where such vast wonders were produc'd and seen.
> Nor was it the dull Piety alone,
> And superstition of our *Albion*,
> Nor ignorance of the future Age, that paid
> Honours Divine to thy surprising shade.
> But they foresaw the Empire of the Sea,
> Great *Charles*, should hold from the Triumphant Thee.

DANIEL DEFOE

From *REFORMATION OF MANNERS*, 1702

Among the most enigmatic of English authors, Defoe (1660–1731) conducted his literary career as pamphleteer and satirist at the heart of the faction-ridden politics of the early eighteenth century. He is now best known for his novels, of which the first and culturally most influential, *Robinson Crusoe* (1719), casts much light on the ideology of colonialism in the age of mercantilism. In the poem from which this extract is taken, Defoe looks sardonically at various aspects of the life of London, including its investment in the slave trade. Slaving—one leg of the lucrative triangular trade between Britain, West Africa and the Caribbean—expanded rapidly as part of the national economy from 1689 when the trade, until then monopolized by companies like the Royal African, was opened up to all comers.

> Some fit out ships, and double freights ensure,
> And burn the ships to make the voyage secure:
> Promiscuous plunders through the world commit,
> And with the money buy their safe retreat.
> Others seek out to Afric's torrid zone,
> And search the burning shores of Serralone;
> There in insufferable heats they fry,
> And run vast risks to see the gold, and die:
> The harmless natives basely they trepan,
> And barter baubles for the souls of men:
> The wretches they to Christian climes bring o'er,
> To serve worse heathens than they did before.
> The cruelties they suffer there are such,
> Amboyna's nothing, they've outdone the Dutch.
> Cortez, Pizarro, Guzman, Penaloe,
> Who drank the blood and gold of Mexico,
> Who thirteen millions of souls destroyed,
> And left one third of God's creation void;
> By birth for nature's butchery designed,
> Compared to these are merciful and kind.
> Death could their cruellest designs fulfil,
> Blood quenched their thirst, and it sufficed to kill:
> But these the tender *coup de grâce* deny,
> And make men beg in vain for leave to die;

To more than Spanish cruelty inclined,
Torment the body and debauch the mind:
The ling'ring life of slavery preserve,
And vilely teach them both to sin and serve.
In vain they talk to them of shades below:
They fear no hell, but where such Christians go.
Of Jesus Christ they very often hear,
Often as his blaspheming servants swear;
They hear and wonder what strange gods they be,
Can bear with patience such indignity.
They look for famines, plagues, disease and death,
Blasts from above and earthquakes from beneath:
But when they see regardless heaven looks on,
They curse our gods, or think that we have none.
Thus thousands to religion are brought o'er,
And made worse devils than they were before.

ALEXANDER POPE

From *WINDSOR-FOREST*, 1713

Pope (1688–1744) was the great satirical poet of the age, his later work in particular combining technical mastery with the *saevo indignatio* that he drew from classical exemplars like Juvenal. *Windsor-Forest* is quite different in mood, in part reflecting the optimism engendered by the 1713 Treaty of Utrecht which ended the long wars of the reign of Queen Anne. Among other provisions, the Treaty secured a substantial extension of British colonies and plantations in America. In this extract the River Thames welcomes peace and envisages a glittering future for British maritime trade in a world where slavery will be abolished and colonized people will once again be free: there is no indication in the poem that Pope saw anything contradictory in such a proposition.

> Hail Sacred *Peace*! hail long-expected Days,
> That *Thames*'s Glory to the Stars shall raise!
> Tho' *Tyber*'s Streams immortal *Rome* behold,
> Tho' foaming *Hermus* swells with Tydes of Gold,
> From Heav'n it self tho' sev'nfold *Nilus* flows,
> And Harvests on a hundred Realms bestows;
> These now no more shall be the Muse's Themes,
> Lost in my Fame, as in the Sea their Streams.
> Let *Volga*'s Banks with Iron Squadrons shine,
> And Groves of Lances glitter on the *Rhine*,
> Let barb'rous *Ganges* arm a servile Train;
> Be mine the Blessings of a peaceful Reign.
> No more my Sons shall dye with *British* Blood
> Red *Iber*'s Sands, or *Ister*'s foaming Flood;
> Safe on my Shore each unmolested Swain
> Shall tend the Flocks, or reap the bearded Grain;
> The shady Empire shall retain no Trace
> Of War or Blood, but in the Sylvan Chace,
> The Trumpets sleep, while chearful Horns are blown,
> And Arms employ'd on Birds and Beasts alone.
> Behold! th'ascending *Villa*'s on my Side
> Project long Shadows o'er the Chrystal Tyde.
> Behold! *Augusta*'s glitt'ring Spires increase,
> And Temples rise, the beauteous Works of Peace.

I see, I see where two fair Cities bend
Their ample Bow, a new *White-Hall* ascend!
There mighty Nations shall inquire their Doom,
The World's great Oracle in Times to come;
There Kings shall sue, and suppliant States be seen
Once more to bend before a *British* QUEEN.
    Thy Trees, fair *Windsor!* now shall leave their Woods,
And half thy Forests rush into my Floods,
Bear *Britain*'s Thunder, and her Cross display,
To the bright Regions of the rising Day;
Tempt Icy Seas, where scarce the Waters roll,
Where clearer Flames glow round the frozen Pole;
Or under Southern Skies exalt their Sails,
Led by new Stars, and born by spicy Gales!
For me the Balm shall bleed, and Amber flow,
The Coral redden, and the Ruby glow,
The Pearly Shell its lucid Globe infold,
And *Phœbus* warm the ripening Ore to Gold.
The Time shall come, when free as Seas or Wind
Unbounded *Thames* shall flow for all Mankind,
Whole Nations enter with each swelling Tyde,
And Seas but join the Regions they divide;
Earth's distant Ends our Glory shall behold,
And the new World launch forth to seek the Old.
Then Ships of uncouth Form shall stem the Tyde,
And Feather'd People crowd my wealthy Side,
And naked Youths and painted Chiefs admire
Our Speech, our Colour, and our strange Attire!
Oh stretch thy Reign, fair *Peace!* from Shore to Shore,
Till Conquest cease, and Slav'ry be no more:
Till the freed *Indians* in their native Groves
Reap their own Fruits, and woo their Sable Loves,
Peru once more a Race of Kings behold,
And other *Mexico*'s be roof'd with Gold.
Exil'd by Thee from Earth to deepest Hell,
In Brazen Bonds shall barb'rous *Discord* dwell:
Gigantick *Pride*, pale *Terror*, gloomy *Care*,
And mad *Ambition*, shall attend her there.
There purple *Vengeance* bath'd in Gore retires,
Her Weapons blunted, and extinct her Fires:
There hateful *Envy* her own Snakes shall feel,
And *Persecution* mourn her broken Wheel:
There *Faction* roar, *Rebellion* bite her Chain,
And gasping Furies thirst for Blood in vain.

GEORGE BERKELEY

'ON THE PROSPECT OF PLANTING ARTS
AND LEARNING IN AMERICA', written 1726

Berkeley (1685–1753) was a distinguished Idealist philosopher
whose *Treatise concerning Human Knowledge* was published in
1710. He was also a high-ranking ecclesiastic, and in the 1720s
promoted the idea of a college in the Bermudas for training
missionaries. Between 1728 and 1731 he lived in America,
returning to Britain only when it was clear that government
monies promised for the college would never be forthcoming.
This poem expresses his hopes for the future of learning in the
New World, which he also encouraged practically by estab-
lishing scholarships at Yale and donating books to both Yale
and Harvard.

THE Muse, disgusted at an age and clime
   Barren of every glorious theme,
In distant lands now waits a better time,
   Producing subjects worthy fame;

In happy climes, where from the genial sun
   And virgin earth such scenes ensue,
The force of art by nature seems outdone,
   And fancied beauties by the true;

In happy climes, the seat of innocence,
   Where nature guides and virtue rules,
Where men shall not impose, for truth and sense,
   The pedantry of courts and schools:

There shall be sung another golden age,
   The rise of empire and of arts,
The good and great inspiring epic rage,
   The wisest heads and noblest hearts.

Not such as Europe breeds in her decay;
   Such as she bred when fresh and young,
When heavenly flame did animate her clay,
   By future poets shall be sung.

Westward the course of empire takes its way;
  The first four acts already past,
A fifth shall close the drama with the day:
  Time's noblest offspring is the last.

Frances Seymour

COUNTESS OF HERTFORD

'THE STORY OF INKLE AND YARICO', *c.*1726

Frances Seymour (1699–1754) wrote her poems for circulation among her friends, and adapted this one from the story as told by Richard Steele in *The Spectator*, 13 March 1711.

A YOUTH there was possessed of every charm,
Which might the coldest heart with passion warm;
His blooming cheeks with ruddy beauty glowed,
His hair in waving ringlets graceful flowed;
Through all his person an attractive mien,
Just symmetry, and elegance were seen:
But niggard Fortune had her aid withheld,
And poverty th' unhappy boy compelled
To distant climes to sail in search of gain,
Which might in ease his latter days maintain.
By chance, or rather the decree of Heaven,
The vessel on a barbarous coast was driven;
He, with a few unhappy striplings more,
Ventured too far upon the fatal shore:
The cruel natives thirsted for their blood,
And issued furious from a neighbouring wood.
His friends all fell by brutal rage o'erpowered,
Their flesh the horrid cannibals devoured;
Whilst he alone escaped by speedy flight,
And in a thicket lay concealed from sight!
  Now he reflects on his companions' fate,
His threatening danger, and abandoned state.
Whilst thus in fruitless grief he spent the day,
A negro virgin chanced to pass that way;
He viewed her naked beauties with surprise,
Her well-proportioned limbs and sprightly eyes!
With his complexion and gay dress amazed,
The artless nymph upon the stranger gazed;
Charmed with his features and alluring grace,
His flowing locks and his enlivened face.
His safety now became her tend'rest care,
A vaulted rock she knew and hid him there;

The choicest fruits the isle produced she sought,
And kindly to allay his hunger brought;
And when his thirst required, in search of drink,
She led him to a chrystal fountain's brink.
  Mutually charmed, by various arts they strove
To inform each other of their mutual love;
A language soon they formed, which might express
Their pleasing care and growing tenderness.
With tigers' speckled skins she decked his bed,
O'er which the gayest plumes of birds were spread;
And every morning, with the nicest care,
Adorned her well-turned neck and shining hair,
With all the glittering shells and painted flowers
That serve to deck the Indian virgin's bowers.
And when the sun descended in the sky,
And lengthening shades foretold the evening nigh,
Beneath some spreading palm's delightful shade,
Together sat the youth and lovely maid;
Or where some bubbling river gently crept,
She in her arms secured him while he slept.
When the bright moon in midnight pomp was seen,
And starlight glittered o'er the dewy green,
In some close arbour, or some fragrant grove,
He whispered vows of everlasting love.
Then, as upon the verdant turf he lay,
He oft would to th' attentive virgin say:
'Oh, could I but, my Yarico, with thee
Once more my dear, my native country see!
In softest silks thy limbs should be arrayed,
Like that of which the clothes I wear are made;
What different ways my grateful soul would find
To indulge thy person and divert thy mind!';
While she on the enticing accents hung
That smoothly fell from his persuasive tongue.
  One evening, from a rock's impending side,
An European vessel she descried,
And made them signs to touch upon the shore,
Then to her lover the glad tidings bore;
Who with his mistress to the ship descends,
And found the crew were countrymen and friends.
Reflecting now upon the time he passed,
Deep melancholy all his thoughts o'ercast:
'Was it for this,' said he, 'I crossed the main,
Only a doting virgin's heart to gain?
I needed not for such a prize to roam,

[73]

There are a thousand doting maids at home.'
While thus his disappointed mind was tossed,
The ship arrived on the Barbadian coast;
Immediately the planters from the town,
Who trade for goods and negro slaves, came down;
And now his mind, by sordid interest swayed,
Resolved to sell his faithful Indian maid.
Soon at his feet for mercy she implored,
And thus in moving strains her fate deplored:
  'O whither can I turn to seek redress,
When thou'rt the cruel cause of my distress?
If the remembrance of our former love,
And all thy plighted vows, want force to move;
Yet, for the helpless infant's sake I bear,
Listen with pity to my just despair.
Oh let me not in slavery remain,
Doomed all my life to drag a servile chain!
It cannot surely be! thy generous breast
An act so vile, so sordid must detest:
But, if thou hate me, rather let me meet
A gentler fate, and stab me at they feet;
Then will I bless thee with my dying breath,
And sink contented in the shades of death.'
  Not all she said could his compassion move,
Forgetful of his vows and promised love;
The weeping damsel from his knees he spurned.
And with her price pleased to the ship returned.

JAMES THOMSON

From *BRITANNIA. A POEM*, 1727

Thomson (1700–48) was a Scot who settled in London and
became the chief poetic exponent of the Whig commercial
ideology of the early eighteenth century. In this extract, directed
against the threat posed by the French navy, he advocates an
aggressive, world-wide expansion of naval power as the means
of enforcing British interests and securing a maritime trading
empire.

> And what, my thoughtless Sons, should fire you more,
> Than when your well-earn'd Empire of the Deep
> The least beginning Injury receives?
> What better Cause can call your Lightning forth?
> Your Thunder Wake? Your dearest Life demand?
> What better Cause, then when your Country sees
> The sly Destruction at her Vitals aim'd?
> For oh it much imports you, 'tis your All,
> To keep your Trade intire, intire the Force,
> And Honour of your Fleets; o'er These to watch
> Even with a Hand severe, and jealous Eye.
> In Intercourse be gentle, generous, just,
> By Wisdom polish'd, and of Manners fair;
> But on the Sea be terrible, untam'd,
> Unconquerable still: let none escape,
> Who shall but aim to touch your Glory there.
> Is there the Man, into the Lion's Den
> Who dares intrude, to snatch his Young away?
> And is a *Briton* seiz'd? and seiz'd beneath
> The slumbring Terrors of a *British* Fleet?
> Then ardent rise! Oh great in Vengeance rise!
> O'erturn the Proud, teach Rapine to *restore*:
> And as you ride sublimely round the World,
> Make every Vessel stoop, make every State
> At once their Welfare and their Duty know.
> This is your Glory; this your Wisdom; this
> The native Power for which you were design'd
> By Fate, when Fate design'd the firmest State,
> That e'er was seated on the subject Sea;
> A State, alone, where *Liberty* should live,

In these late Times, this Evening of Mankind,
When *Athens*, *Rome*, and *Carthage* are no more,
The World almost in slavish Sloth dissolv'd.
For this, these Rocks around your Coast were thrown;
For this, your Oaks, peculiar harden'd, shoot
Strong into sturdy Growth; for this, your Hearts
Swell with a sullen Courage, growing still
As Danger grows; and Strength, and Toil for this
Are liberal pour'd o'er all the fervent Land.
Then cherish this, this unexpensive Power,
Undangerous to the Public, ever prompt,
By lavish Nature thrust into your Hand:
And, unencumber'd with the Bulk immense
Of Conquest, whence huge Empires rose and fell,
Self-crush'd, extend your Reign from Shore to Shore,
Where'er the Wind your high Behests can blow,
And fix it deep on this eternal Base.

JAMES THOMSON

From *LIBERTY. A POEM*, 1735–6

In this extract from Book IV of this long poem, the Genius of
the Deep addresses the Goddess of Liberty on the subject of
Britain's entitlement to naval power.

     —"By Fate commission'd, go,
"MY SISTER-GODDESS now, to yon *blest Isle*,
"Henceforth the Partner of my rough Domain.
"All my dread Walks to BRITONS open lie.
"Those that refulgent, or with rosy Morn,
"Or yellow Evening, flame; those that, profuse
"Drunk by Equator-Suns, severely shine;
"Or those that, to the Poles approaching, rise
"In Billows rolling into *Alps* of Ice.
"Even, yet untouch'd by daring Keel, be theirs
"The vast *Pacific*; that on other Worlds,
"Their future Conquest, rolls resounding Tides.
"Long I maintain'd inviolate my Reign;
"Nor *Alexanders* me, nor *Cæsars* brav'd.
"Still, in the Crook of Shore, the coward Sail
"'Till now low-crept; and peddling *Commerce* ply'd
"Between near-joining Lands. For BRITONS, chief,
"It was reserv'd, with star-directed Prow,
"To dare the middle Deep, and drive assur'd
"To distant Nations thro' the pathless Main.
"Chief, for their fearless Hearts the Glory waits,
"Long Months from Land, while the black stormy Night
"Around them rages, on the groaning Mast
"With unshook Knee to know their giddy Way;
"To sing, unquell'd, amid the lashing Wave;
"To laugh at Danger. Theirs the Triumph be,
"By deep *Invention*'s keen pervading Eye,
"The Heart of *Courage*, and the Hand of *Toil*,
"Each conquer'd Ocean staining with their Blood,
"Instead of Treasure robb'd by ruffian War,
"Round social Earth to circle fair Exchange,
"And bind the Nations in a golden Chain.
"To these I honour'd stoop. Rushing to Light
"A Race of Men behold! whose daring Deeds

"Will in Renown exalt my nameless Plains
"O'er those of fabling Earth, as her's to mine
"In Terror yield. Nay, could my savage Heart
"Such Glories check, their unsubmitting Soul
"Would all my Fury brave, my Tempest climb,
"And might in spite of me my Kingdom force."

JAMES THOMSON AND DAVID MALLETT

From *ALFRED. A MASQUE*, 1740

In the first half of the eighteenth century the mythology of the
Anglo-Saxon King Alfred became firmly established: he had
defeated foreign invaders and united the English for the first
time; his laws formed the basis on which English liberty was
built; he was, not least, the founder of the navy. All this is
embodied in the masque *Alfred* which Thomson co-wrote with
David Mallett (1705–65). At the end of the play a Bard appears
and celebrates Alfred's victory over the Danes: his song, set to
music by Thomas Arne, urges Britons to ensure national liberty
by taking control of the world's oceans. It subsequently became
one of the most famous nationalist and imperialist anthems.
Following the Bard in the masque a Hermit reinforces the polit-
ical imperative with his forecast of the global triumph of British
arms and commerce.

> When *Britain* first, at heaven's command,
>   Arose from out the azure main;
> *This* was the charter of the land,
>   And guardian angels sung *this* strain:
>   "Rule, *Britannia*, rule the waves;
>   *Britons* never will be slaves."
>
> The nations, not so blest as thee,
>   Must, in their turns, to tyrants fall:
> While thou shalt flourish great and free,
>   The dread and envy of them all.
>   "Rule, &c.
>
> Thee haughty tyrants ne'er shall tame:
>   All their attempts to bend thee down,
> Will but arrouse thy generous flame;
>   But work their woe, and thy renown.
>   "Rule, &c.

Still more majestic shalt thou rise,
　　More dreadful, from each foreign stroke:
As the loud blast that tears the skies,
　　Serves but to root thy native oak.
　　　　"Rule, &c.

To thee belongs the rural reign;
　　Thy cities shall with commerce shine:
All thine shall be the subject main,
　　And every shore it circles thine.
　　　　"Rule, &c.

The Muses, still with freedom found,
　　Shall to thy happy coast repair:
Blest isle! with matchless beauty crown'd,
　　And manly hearts to guard the fair.
　　　　"Rule, *Britannia*, rule the waves;
　　　　Britons never will be slaves."

HERMIT:

Alfred, go forth! lead on the radiant years,
To thee reveal'd in vision.——Lo! they rise!
Lo! patriots, heroes, sages, croud to birth:
And bards to sing them in immortal verse!
I see thy commerce, *Britain*, grasp the world:
All nations serve thee; every foreign flood,
Subjected, pays its tribute to the *Thames*.
Thither the golden South obedient pours
His sunny treasures: thither the soft East
Her spices, delicacies, gentle gifts:
And thither his rough trade the stormy North.
See, where beyond the vast *Atlantic* surge,
By boldest keels untouch'd, a dreadful space!
Shores, yet unfound, arise! in youthful prime,
With towering forests, mighty rivers crown'd!
These stoop to *Britain*'s thunder. This new world,
Shook to its centre, trembles at her name:
And there, her sons, with aim exalted, sow
The seeds of rising empire, arts, and arms.

　Britons, proceed, the subject Deep command
Awe with your navies every hostile land.
In vain their threats, their armies all in vain:
They rule the balanc'd world, who rule the main.

JAMES THOMSON

From *THE SEASONS*, 1730; expanded 1744

Thomson's long reflective and descriptive poem meanders through many aspects of life. In the first extract here, taken from 'Summer', he describes one of the many horrors incidental to the slave trade; in the second, from 'Autumn', Thomson expatiates on his favourite theme, the prosperity of British commerce.

From 'SUMMER'

INCREASING still the Terrors of these Storms,
His Jaws horrific arm'd with threefold Fate,
Here dwells the direful Shark. Lur'd by the Scent
Of steaming Crouds, of rank Disease, and Death,
Behold! he rushing cuts the briny Flood,
Swift as the Gale can bear the Ship along;
And, from the Partners of that cruel Trade,
Which spoils unhappy *Guinea* of her Sons,
Demands his share of Prey, demands themselves.
The stormy Fates descend: one Death involves
Tyrants and Slaves; when strait, their mangled Limbs
Crashing at once, he dyes the purple Seas
With Gore, and riots in the vengeful Meal.

From 'AUTUMN'

THEN gathering Men their natural Powers combin'd,
And form'd a *Public*; to the general Good
Submitting, aiming, and conducting All.
For This the *Patriot-Council* met, the full,
The free, and fairly represented *Whole*;
For This they plann'd the holy Guardian-Laws,
Distinguish'd Orders, animated Arts,
And with joint Force *Oppression* chaining, set
Imperial Justice at the Helm; yet still
To them accountable: nor slavish dream'd
That toiling Millions must resign their Weal,
And all the Honey of their Search, to such
As for themselves alone themselves have rais'd.

HENCE every Form of cultivated Life
In Order set, protected, and inspir'd,
Into Perfection wrought. Uniting All,
Society grew numerous, high, polite,
And happy. Nurse of Art! the City rear'd
In beauteous Pride her Tower-encircled Head;
And, stretching Street on Street, by Thousands drew,
From twining woody Haunts, or the tough Yew
To Bows strong-straining, her aspiring Sons.

THEN Commerce brought into the public Walk
The busy Merchant; the big Ware-house built;
Rais'd the strong Crane; choak'd up the loaded Street
With foreign Plenty; and thy Stream, O THAMES,
Large, gentle, deep, majestic, King of Floods!
Chose for his grand Resort. On either Hand,
Like a long wintry Forest, Groves of Masts
Shot up their Spires; the bellying Sheet between
Possess'd the breezy Void; the sooty Hulk
Steer'd sluggish on; the splendid Barge along
Row'd, regular, to Harmony; around,
The Boat, light-skimming, stretch'd its oary Wings;
While deep the various Voice of fervent Toil
From Bank to Bank increas'd; whence ribb'd with Oak,
To bear the BRITISH THUNDER, black, and bold,
The roaring Vessel rush'd into the Main.

JAMES THOMSON

From *THE CASTLE OF INDOLENCE*, 1748

In this allegorical poem a contrast is drawn between Indolence
and Industry, the latter particularly associated with Britain, the
centre of economic activity. In these stanzas from the second
section, the poem moves towards its resolution as Industry
settles happily in Britain's congenial commercial climate.

> To crown his Toils, SIR INDUSTRY then spred
> The swelling Sail, and made for BRITAIN's Coast.
> A Sylvan Life till then the Natives led,
> In the brown Shades and green-wood Forest lost,
> All careless rambling where it lik'd them most:
> Their Wealth the Wild-Deer bouncing through the Glade;
> They lodg'd at large, and liv'd at Nature's Cost;
> Save Spear, and Bow, withouten other Aid,
> Yet not the *Roman* Steel their naked Breast dismay'd.

> He lik'd the Soil, he lik'd the clement Skies,
> He lik'd the verdant Hills and flowery Plains.
> Be This my great, my chosen Isle (he cries)
> This, whilst my Labours LIBERTY sustains,
> This Queen of Ocean all Assault disdains.
> Nor lik'd he less the Genius of the Land,
> To Freedom apt and persevering Pains,
> Mild to obey, and generous to command,
> Temper'd by forming HEAVEN with kindest firmest Hand.

> Here, by Degrees, his Master-Work arose,
> Whatever Arts and Industry can frame:
> Whatever finish'd Agriculture knows,
> Fair Queen of Arts! from Heaven itself who came,
> When *Eden* flourish'd in unspotted Fame:
> And still with Her sweet Innocence we find,
> And tender Peace, and Joys without a Name,
> That, while they rapture, tranquillize the Mind;
> Nature and Art at once, Delight and Use combin'd.

Then Towns he quicken'd by mechanic Arts,
And bade the fervent City glow with Toil;
Bade social Commerce raise renowned Marts,
Join Land to Land, and marry Soil to Soil,
Unite the Poles, and without bloody Spoil
Bring home of either *Ind* the gorgeous Stores;
Or, should Despotic Rage the World embroil,
Bade Tyrants tremble on remotest Shores,
While o'er th' encircling Deep BRITANNIA's Thunder roars.

Anonymous

'BOLD GENERAL WOLFE', 1759

The entanglement of the great powers in continental Europe during the Seven Years' War (1756–63) was skilfully exploited by the policy of the Earl of Chatham, Pitt the Elder, greatly to enhance the colonial power of Britain. The victories of Robert Clive and Eyre Coote in India consolidated and extended the rule of the East India Company, giving the British decisive ascendancy over the French on the subcontinent. In Canada, direct French colonial involvement was ended with the taking of Quebec in 1759 by British forces under James Wolfe, who died in the moment of victory: his triumph and death are commemorated in this ballad.

> BOLD General Wolfe to his men did say,
> Come, come, my lads and follow me,
> To yonder mountains that are so high
> All for the honour, all for the honour,
> Of your king and country.
>
> The French they are on the mountains high,
> While we poor lads in the vallies laid,
> I see them falling like moths in the sun,
> Thro' smoke and fire, thro' smoke and fire
> All from our British guns.
>
> The very first volley they gave to us,
> Wounded our General in his left breast,
> Yet he sits for he cannot stand,
> Fight on so boldly, fight on so boldly,
> For whilst I've life I'll have command.
>
> Here is my treasure lies all in gold,
> Take it and part it, for my blood runs cold,
> Take it and part it, General Wolfe did say,
> You lads of honour, you lads of honour,
> Who made such gallant play.

DAVID GARRICK

'HEART OF OAK', 1759

Garrick (1717–79) was one of the most celebrated actors of the eighteenth century, and one of the great tragedians of the English stage, specializing in Shakespearean roles. A pupil and friend of Dr Johnson, he was an intimate of literary and artistic circles in London, and manager of the Drury Lane Theatre from 1747 to 1776. Garrick made one of the largest theatrical fortunes of all time, and was buried in Westminster Abbey. He wrote plays of his own, as well as numerous prologues and epilogues, but his best known composition is this song, which was written to celebrate British triumphs in the Seven Years' War and which became one of the most popular of patriotic anthems. The 'wonderful year' of the first stanza, 1759, saw Wolfe's victory at Quebec.

> COME cheer up my lads, 'tis to glory we steer,
> To add something more to this wonderful year.
> To honour we call you, not press you like slaves,
> For who are so free as we sons of the waves?

> *Chorus*
> Heart of oak are our ships, heart of oak are our men;
> We always are ready—steady, boys, steady—
> We'll fight and we'll conquer again and again.

> We ne'er see our foes but we wish 'em to stay.
> They never see us but they wish us away.
> If they run, why, we follow and run 'em ashore,
> For if they won't fight us, we cannot do more.

> Heart of oak etc.

> They swear they'll invade us, these terrible foes.
> They frighten our women, our children and beaux.
> But should their flat-bottoms in darkness get o'er,
> Still Britons they'll find to receive them on shore.

Heart of oak etc.

We'll still make 'em run and we'll still make 'em sweat,
In spite of the devil and *Brussels Gazette.*
Then cheer up my lads, with one heart let us sing
Our soldiers, our sailors, our statesmen and King.

Heart of oak etc.

THOMAS MORRIS

'SAPPHICS: AT THE MOHAWK-CASTLE, CANADA', 1761

Morris (1732–1806?) was a professional soldier who served in
Canada. The Sapphic was a Greek lyric metre, used by some
English poets in the adapted form of three long lines followed by
one short, giving a deliberately Classical effect to the handling
of the colonial subject matter. Written from Morris's lonely
colonial outpost, the poem is addressed to his friend back in
England, Richard 'Dicky' Montgomery.

EASE is the pray'r of him who, in a whaleboat
Crossing Lake Champlain, by a storm's o'ertaken;
Not struck his blanket, not a friendly island
      Near to receive him.

Ease is the wish too of the sly Canadian;
Ease the delight of bloody Caghnawagas;
Ease, Richard, ease, not to be bought with wampum,
      Nor paper money.

Not colonel's pay, nor yet a dapper sergeant,
Orderly waiting with recovered halberd,
Can chase the crowd of troubles still surrounding
      Laced regimentals.

That sub lives best who, with a sash in tatters
Worn by his grandsire at the fight of Blenheim,
To fear a stranger, and to wild ambition,
      Snores on a bearskin.

Why like fine-fellows are we ever scheming,
We short-lived mortals? Why so fond of climates
Warmed by new suns? O who, that runs from home, can
      Run from himself too?

Care climbs radeaux with four-and-twenty pounders,
Not quits our light troops, or our Indian warriors,
Swifter than moose-deer, or the fleeter east wind,
      Pushing the clouds on.

He, whose good humour can enjoy the present,
Scorns to look forward; with a smile of patience
Temp'ring the bitter. Bliss uninterrupted
        None can inherit.

Death instantaneous hurried off Achilles;
Age far-extended wore away Tithonus:
Who will live longer, thou or I, Montgom'ry?
        Dicky or Tommy?

Thee twenty messmates, full of noise and laughter,
Cheer with their sallies; thee the merry damsels
Please with their titt'ring; whilst thou sitt'st adorned with
        Boots, sash and gorget.

Me to Fort Hendrick, midst a savage nation,
Dull Connajohry, cruel fate has driven.
O think on Morris, in a lonely chamber,
        Dabbling in Sapphic.

JAMES GRAINGER

From *THE SUGAR CANE*, 1764

Grainger (1721–66) was a doctor who spent the last years of his life in the West Indies, and wrote this long poem about its main product. In this extract from the opening of Book IV he pleads the case of the slaves who worked the plantations.

YET, planter, let humanity prevail.—
Perhaps thy negro, in his native land,
Possessed large fertile plains, and slaves, and herds:
Perhaps, when'er he deigned to walk abroad,
The richest silks, from where the Indus rolls,
His limbs invested in their gorgeous pleats:
Perhaps he wails his wife, his children, left
To struggle with adversity: perhaps
Fortune, in battle for his country fought,
Gave him a captive to his deadliest foe:
Perhaps, incautious, in his native fields
(On pleasurable scenes his mind intent)
All as he wandered, from the neighbouring grove,
Fell ambush dragged him to the hated main.—
Were they even sold for crimes; ye polished say!
Ye to whom Learning opes her amplest page!
Ye, whom the knowledge of a living God
Should lead to virtue! are ye free from crimes?
Ah pity, then, these uninstructed swains;
And still let mercy soften the decrees
Of rigid justice, with her lenient hand.
    Oh, did the tender Muse possess the power,
Which monarchs have, and monarchs oft abuse:
'Twould be the fond ambition of her soul
To quell tyrannic sway; knock off the chains
Of heart-debasing slavery; give to man,
Of every colour and of every clime,
Freedom, which stamps him image of his God.
Then laws, Oppression's scourge, fair Virtue's prop,
Offspring of Wisdom! should impartial reign,
To knit the whole in well-accorded strife:
Servants, not slaves; of choice, and not compelled;
The blacks should cultivate the Cane-land isles.

ANNE PENNY

'ODES SUNG IN COMMEMORATION OF
THE MARINE SOCIETY', 1773

Penny (1731–84) was married to two naval officers in succession. This poem shows her support for the charity for training boys for the sea founded in 1756 by the philanthropist Jonas Hanway.

On the occasion of their Anniversary Dinner at the Crown and Anchor Tavern in the Strand, the 22d Day of February, 1773

(i)

*Sung by a Choir of Boys marching round the Room,
at the Head of the Society's Poor Boys*

SOCIAL Virtue's liberal plan
Cheers the helpless race of man:
O'er the poor's defenceless head,
See! her healing wings are spread!

Plants from Britain's earth behold
(Britain, parent of the bold),
Snatched from Vice's horrid train,
Chilling penury and pain!

Raised by Virtue's powerful arm,
See! their throbbing bosoms warm!
Certain pledge how well they'll prove
What they owe to Social Love.

Hail! thou blessing all divine!
Still, O still through Albion shine;
Whilst thy golden chain's unbroke,
Her foes shall bend beneath her yoke.

(ii)

Sung at Table by the same Choir

SEE these happy youths, now made
Bulwarks of our wealth and trade.
From this glorious source will flow
Vigorous strength, to quell each foe.

May such noble plans sustain
GEORGE's empire on the main!
May rich Commerce, England's pride,
Still adorn her swelling tide!

While ye guardians of our isle,
Favoured by his gracious smile,
Band of patriot-brothers, tie
The knot of social amity;

Virtue hails the great design,
She owns the impulse quite divine;
Bids her patriot King approve
The golden band of Social Love!

PHILLIS WHEATLEY

'ON BEING BROUGHT FROM AFRICA TO AMERICA', 1773

———

Taken to Boston as a slave when a child, Wheatley (1753?–84) was bought by a tailor, John Wheatley. Converted to Christianity, she visited England and published her *Poems on Various Subjects, Religious and Moral* in London in 1773. The idea, here succinctly expressed, that divine mercy had permitted her enslavement so that she could become convinced of her need for salvation, was one of the common teachings of Calvinist evangelicalism.

'TWAS mercy brought me from my pagan land,
Taught my benighted soul to understand
That there's a God, that there's a Saviour too:
Once I redemption neither sought nor knew.
Some view our sable race with scornful eye:
'Their colour is a diabolic dye.'
Remember, Christians, negroes black as Cain
May be refined and join th' angelic train.

ANONYMOUS

'BOSTON IN DISTRESS', 1776

Accumulated grievances in the American colonies about trade, taxation, and representation, came to a head in 1773 when Britain tried to impose taxes to help defray the costs of the Seven Years' War. The colonists issued a Declaration of Rights in 1774, and the first clash with British troops followed at Lexington in the next year. In 1776 came the Declaration of Independence, but the war to secure it dragged on until 1781, when the main British army surrendered at Yorktown. With the loss of the American colonies, the First British Empire came to an end: although Canada remained under the Crown, the focus of the imperial enterprise shifted to India and the Far East. This anonymous poem, written as fighting in New England intensified, expresses the anguish felt by many people in Britain about the conflict, which is here viewed as a civil war.

WHILE pleasure reigns unrivalled on this shore,
The streets of Boston stream with British gore;
While like fall'n Romans for new joys we sigh,
Our friends drop breathless, or for mercy cry.
Perhaps the soldier, lost to pity's charms,
Now stabs the infant in the mother's arms;
Perhaps the husband sees his better part
Welt'ring in gore and bleeding from the heart;
Perhaps the lover, plunged in bitter woe,
Is torn from her whom most he loves below,
And sees the life he values as his own
Yielded in pangs, or hears the dying groan;
Perhaps the son, O agony of pain!
Sees, fatal sight! his aged parent slain;
Perhaps whole families, together hurled,
Seek the dread confines of another world.
O! scene of slaughter fiends alone enjoy,
Fiends who love death and wait but to destroy.
Are widows' tears that never cease to roll,
Are mothers' pangs that penetrate the soul,

Are shrieks of infants sacrificed to rage,
The horrid trophies of the present age?
Eternal Father! in they mercy quell
The flames of faction that arise from hell;
Pour into British hearts the balm of peace,
And bid, O bid, this cruel carnage cease;
Like Isaac's sons let Britons meet again,
Nor be one brother by the other slain.

ANNA SEWARD

From 'ELEGY ON CAPTAIN COOK', 1780

Nicknamed 'The Swan of Lichfield', Seward (1747–1809) estab-
lished a considerable reputation as a poet of Sensibility, though
the range of her writings was wider than this implies. Well
known in literary society, she was a friend of Samuel Johnson
and, after her death, her *Poetical Works* were edited by Walter
Scott. Captain James Cook, the subject of Seward's elegy,
undertook three voyages to the Pacific, in 1768–71, 1772–5, and
1776–9; on the last of these he was killed by hostile islanders
on Hawaii. Cook's expeditions are among the most remarkable
exploits of seaborne exploration, opening up the South Seas to
European interest as never before—and in the process allowing
Britain to stake an imperial claim for what would become
Australia and New Zealand. Seward's elegy ignores such worldly
benefits and assigns Cook's motives to the force of Benevolence,
a disinterested love for his fellow creatures. In the later parts
of the poem she describes his exploration of Antarctica, his
encounter with the Maoris, and with antipodean flora and fauna,
before the fatal visit to Hawaii.

> Say first, what Power inspir'd his dauntless breast
> With scorn of danger and inglorious rest,
> To quit imperial London's gorgeous domes,
> Where, deck'd in thousand tints, young Pleasure roams;
> In cups of summer-ice her nectar pours,
> Or twines, 'mid wint'ry snows, her roseate bowers;
> Where the warm Orient loads Britannia's gales
> With all the incense of Sabæan vales;
> Where soft Italia's silken sons prolong
> The lavish cadence of the artful song;
> Where Beauty moves with fascinating grace,
> Calls the sweet blush to wanton o'er her face,
> On each fond youth her soft artillery tries,
> Aims the light smile, and rolls the frolic eyes:
> What Power inspir'd his dauntless breast to brave
> The scorch'd Equator, and th' Antarctic wave?
> Climes, where fierce Suns in cloudless ardors shine,
> And pour the dazzling deluge round the Line;
> The realms of frost, where icy mountains rise,

'Mid the pale summer of the polar skies?—
It was BENEVOLENCE!—on coasts unknown,
The shiv'ring natives of the frozen zone,
And the swart Indian, as he faintly strays
"Where Cancer reddens in the solar blaze,"
She bade him seek;—on each inclement shore
Plant the rich seeds of her exhaustless store;
Unite the savage hearts, and hostile hands,
In the firm compact of her gentle bands;
Strew her soft comforts o'er the barren plain,
Sing her sweet lays, and consecrate her fane. ...

Lovely BENEVOLENCE!—O Nymph divine!
I see thy light step print the burning Line!
Thy lucid eye the dubious pilot guides,
The faint oar struggling with the scalding tides.—
On as thou lead'st the bold, the glorious prow,
Mild, and more mild, the sloping sun-beams glow;
Now weak and pale the lessen'd lustres play,
As round th' horizon rolls the timid day;
Barb'd with the sleeted snow, the driving hail,
Rush the fierce arrows of the polar gale;
And through the dim, unvaried, ling'ring hours,
Wide o'er the waves incumbent Horror low'rs.

   From the rude summit of yon frozen steep,
Contrasting Glory gilds the dreary deep!
Lo!—deck'd with vermil youth and beamy grace,
Hope in her step, and gladness in her face,
Light on the icy rock, with outstretch'd hands,
The Goddess of the new Columbus stands.
Round her bright head the plumy peterels soar,
Blue as her robe, that sweeps the frozen shore;
Glows her soft cheek, as vernal mornings fair,
And warm as summer-suns her golden hair;
O'er the hoar waste her radiant glances stream,
And courage kindles in their magic beam.
She points the ship its mazy path, to thread
The floating fragments of the frozen bed.
While o'er the deep, in many a dreadful form,
The giant Danger howls along the storm,
Furling the iron sails with numbed hands,
Firm on the deck the great Adventurer stands;
Round glitt'ring mountains hears the billows rave,
And the vast ruin thunder on the wave.—
Appal'd he hears!—but checks the rising sigh,

And turns on his firm band a glist'ning eye.—
Not for himself the sighs unbidden break,
Amid the terrors of the icy wreck;
Not for himself starts the impassion'd tear,
Congealing as it falls;—nor pain, nor fear,
Nor Death's dread darts, impede the great design,
Till Nature draws the circumscribing line.
Huge rocks of ice th' arrested ship embay,
And bar the gallant Wanderer's dangerous way.—
His eye regretful marks the Goddess turn
The assiduous prow from its relentless bourn.

And now antarctic Zealand's drear domain
Frowns, and o'erhangs th' inhospitable main.
On its chill beach this dove of human-kind
For his long-wand'ring foot short rest shall find,
Bear to the coast the olive-branch in vain,
And quit on wearied wing the hostile plain.—
With jealous low'r the frowning natives view
The stately vessel, and adventurous crew;
Nor fear the brave, nor emulate the good,
But scowl with savage thirst of human blood!
And yet there were, who in this iron clime
Soar'd o'er the herd on Virtue's wing sublime;
Rever'd the stranger-guest, and smiling strove
To sooth his stay with hospitable love;
Fann'd in full confidence the friendly flame,
Join'd plighted hands, and name exchang'd for name.
To these the Hero leads his living store,
And pours new wonders on th' uncultur'd shore;
The silky fleece, fair fruit, and golden grain;
And future herds and harvests bless the plain.
O'er the green soil the kids exulting play,
And sounds his clarion loud the bird of day;
The downy goose her ruffled bosom laves,
Trims her white wing, and wantons in the waves;
Stern moves the bull along th' affrighted shores,
And countless nations tremble as he roars ...

Now the warm solstice o'er the shining bay,
Darts from the north its mild meridian ray;
Again the Chief invokes the rising gale,
And spreads again in desert seas the sail;
O'er dangerous shoals his steady steerage keeps,
O'er walls of coral, ambush'd in the deeps. ...

On a lone beach a rock-built temple stands,
Stupendous pile! unwrought by mortal hands;
Sublime the ponderous turrets rise in air,
And the wide roof basaltic columns bear;
Through the long aisles the murm'ring tempests blow,
And Ocean chides his dashing waves below.
From this fair fane, along the silver sands,
Two sister-virgins wave their snowy hands;
First gentle Flora—round her smiling brow
Leaves of new forms, and flow'rs uncultur'd glow;
Thin folds of vegetable silk, behind,
Shade her white neck, and wanton in the wind;
Strange sweets, where'er she turns, perfume the glades,
And fruits unnam'd adorn the bending shades.
—Next Fauna treads, in youthful beauty's pride,
A playful Kangroo bounding by her side;
Around the Nymph her beauteous Pois display
Their varied plumes, and trill the dulcet lay;
A Giant-bat, with leathern wings outspread,
Umbrella light, hangs quiv'ring o'er her head.
As o'er the cliff her graceful steps she bends,
On glitt'ring wing her insect train attends.
With diamond-eye her scaly tribes survey
Their Goddess-nymph, and gambol in the spray ...

Now leads BENEVOLENCE the destin'd way,
Where all the Loves in Otaheite stray.
To bid the Arts disclose their wond'rous pow'rs,
To bid the Virtues consecrate the bow'rs,
She gives her Hero to its blooming plain:—
Nor has he wander'd, has he bled in vain!
His lips persuasive charm th' uncultur'd youth,
Teach Wisdom's lore, and point the path of Truth.
See! chasten'd love in softer glances flows,
See! with new fires parental duty glows.
Thou smiling Eden of the southern wave,
Could not, alas! thy grateful wishes save
That angel-goodness, which had blest thy plain?—
Ah! vain thy gratitude, thy wishes vain!
On a far distant, and remorseless shore,
Where human fiends their dire libations pour;
Where treachery, hov'ring o'er the blasted heath,
Poises with ghastly smile the darts of death,
Pierc'd by their venom'd points, your favorite bleeds,
And on his limbs the lust of hunger feeds!

JAMES FREETH

'BUNKER'S HILL,
OR THE SOLDIER'S LAMENTATION', 1780

Freeth (1731–1808) was a Birmingham radical. In this poem, put into the mouth of a British infantryman serving in the American War of Independence, he dramatizes the distress felt by many soldiers at having to fight people whom they regarded as their fellow countrymen—a sentiment similar to that of 'Boston in Distress'. The Battle of Bunker's Hill, fought in 1775, was as bloody as it was indecisive.

I AM a jolly soldier,
　　Enlisted years ago,
To serve my king and country,
　　Against the common foe.
But when across th' Atlantic
　　My orders were to go,
I grieved to think that English hearts
　　Should draw their swords on those
Who fought and conquered by their side,
　　When Frenchmen were their foes.

In drubbing French and Spaniards
　　A soldier takes delight,
But troops cooped up in Boston,
　　Are in so sad a plight,
That many think their stomachs more
　　Inclined to eat than fight,
And like us would be loth to stir;
　　For ev'ry vet'ran knows,
We fought and conquered side by side,
　　When Frenchmen were our foes.

'Twas on the seventeenth of June,
　　I can't forget the day,
The flower of our army
　　For Charles-Town sailed away.
The town was soon in ashes laid,
　　When bombs began to play:

But oh! the cruel scene to paint,
   It makes my blood run chill;
Pray heaven grant I never more
   May climb up Bunker's Hill.

America to frighten
     The tools of power strove,
But ministers are cheated,
     Their schemes abortive prove.
The men they told us would not fight
     Are to the combat drove,
And to our gallant officers,
   It proved a bitter pill,
For numbers dropped before they reached
   The top of Bunker's Hill.

I should not be amazed to hear
     Wolfe's ghost had left the shades,
To check that shameful bloody work
     Which England's crown degrades.
The lads, who scorn to turn their backs
     On Gallia's best brigades,
Undaunted stood, but frankly own
   They better had lain still,
Than such a dear-bought victory gain,
   As that of Bunker's Hill.

Did they, who bloody measures crave,
     Our toil and danger share,
Not one to face the rifle-men
     A second time would dare.
Ye Britons who your country love,
     Be this your ardent pray'r:
To Britain and her colonies,
   May peace be soon restored,
And knaves of high and low degree
   Be *destined to the cord*.

ANNA SEWARD

'VERSES INVITING STELLA TO TEA ON THE PUBLIC FAST-DAY, FEBRUARY, 1781'

The occasion of this epistolary poem was one of the official fasts proclaimed during the war in America. The invitation to tea gives Seward the opportunity for some wry, but also sympathetic reflections on the so-called Boston Tea Party of 1773, when colonists threw taxed tea into Boston harbour—an act that was taken to mark the start of the break with Britain. The final couplet refers to a recent murder, apparently by poisoned laurel-water.

DEAR Stella, midst the pious sorrow
Our Monarch bids us feel tomorrow,
The ah's! and oh's! supremely trist,
The abstinence from beef and whist,
Wisely ordained to please the Lord,
And force him whet our edgeless sword,
Till, skipping o'er th' Atlantic rill,
We cut provincial throats at will;
Midst all the penitence we feel
For merry sins—midst all the zeal
For vengeance on the saucy foe,
Who lays our boasted legions low,
I wish, when sullen evening comes,
To gild for me its falling glooms,
You would, without cold pause, agree
Beneath these walls to sip your tea.
From the chaste, fragrant Indian weed
Our sins no pampering juices feed;
And though the Hours, with contrite faces,
May banish the ungodly aces,
And take of food a sparing bit,
They'll gluttonise on Stella's wit.

'*Tea*,' cries a Patriot, 'on *that* day!
'Twere good you flung the drug away!
Remembering 'twas the cruel source
Of sad distrust, and long divorce,
'Twixt nations which, combined, had hurled
Their conquering javelin round the world.

'O Indian shrub! thy fragrant flowers
To England's weal had deadly powers,
When Tyranny, with impious hand,
To venom turned its essence bland;
To venom subtle, fierce and fell,
As drenched the dart of Isdabel.

'Have we forgot that cursed libation,
That cost the lives of half the nation?
When Boston, with indignant thought,
Saw poison in the perfumed draught,
And caused her troubled Bay to be
But one vast bowl of bitter tea;
While Até, chiefly-bidden guest,
Came sternly to the fatal feast,
And mingled with th' envenomed flood
Brothers', parents, children's blood:
Dire as the banquet Atreus served,
When his own sons Thyestes carved,
And Phoebus, shrinking from the sight,
Drew o'er his orb the pall of night.

'Tomorrow then, at least, refrain,
Nor quaff thy gasping country's bane!
For, O! reflect, poetic daugher,
'Twas vanquished Britain's laurel-water!'

GEORGE DALLAS

From *THE INDIA GUIDE*, 1781

In 1776 Dallas (1758–1833) went out to India in the service of
the East India Company, where he became a Collector—a prin-
cipal regional administrative officer. In the 1790s he returned to
Britain, a baronetcy, and a political career, writing pamphlets on
both India and Ireland. Subtitled 'Journal of a Voyage to the
East Indies in 1780', the long narrative poem from which this
extract comes was first published in Calcutta; it gives a lively,
apolitical account of the journey to India and of first experiences
there. The speaker here is a young English lady, Miss Emily
Brittles, who opens the poem.

    O! HOW shall I picture, in *delicate* strain,
The scene which ensued when I first crossed the main;
Or, how shall my muse in *clean* numbers bewail,
My early hard lot, when, reclined o'er a pail,
I was racked by sea-sickness and pains in my head,
Which gave me such torture I wished myself dead!
Forgive the chaste nymph should she wish to conceal
All the risings and swimmings too often I feel;
For whenever it happens the weather's not mild,
I'm as sick and as squeamish as Jenny with child.
You have seen bales of goods and mercantile wares
Raised by pulleys to windows up two pair of stairs;
So stuck in a chair, made on purpose for this,
Sailors hoist upon deck every India-bound miss:
When poised in the air, I happened to show
Too much of my legs to the boat's crew below,
Who, laughing, occasioned the blush of distress.
Indeed, dear Mama, I am obliged to confess,
That indecency so much on ship-board prevailed,
I scarce heard aught else from the moment I sailed.
    The noise in the ship, from every quarter,
Almost split the brain of your poor little daughter:
Twice a week 'twas the custom the drums loud to rattle,
As a signal below to prepare for a battle.
The sailors on deck were for ever a-brawling,
The ladies below in piano were squalling;
The bulkheads of cabins were constantly creaking,

In concert with pigs, who as often were squeaking;
Such a clatter above from the chick to the goose,
I thought the livestock on the poop had broke loose;
Dogs, puppies and monkeys of ev'ry degree,
Howled peals of loud discord in harsh symphony,
Whilst near to my cabin a sad noisy brute
Most cruelly tortured a poor German flute.
Another, a sprightly amusement to find,
A broken bad fiddle with three strings would grind;
And to add to discordance, our third mate Tarpawl
Some vulgar low tune would be certain to bawl.
But to picture the whole I am really unable,
'Twas worse than the noise at the building of Babel;
I declare my poor ears were so sadly distressed
That for many a week I ne'er got any rest. ...
   It was often the case on a rough squally day,
At dinner our ship on her beam-ends would lay;
Then tables and chairs on the floor all would jumble,
Knives, dishes and bottles upon us would tumble:
As late, when a roll brought us all to the floor,
Whilst the ladies were screaming, the gentlemen swore,
Our Purser, as big as a bullock at least,
Lay on poor little me, like an over-fed beast.
Not many weeks since, I had only to scoop
From my lap the contents of a tureen of soup;
And when with clean clothes I again had sat down,
A vile leg of mutton fell right on my gown.
Sometimes I was soiled from my head to my toe
With nasty pork chops, or a greasy pilau.

William Cowper

'BOADICEA', 1782

A gentle and pious man, Cowper (1731–1800) suffered for much of his life from bouts of religious melancholia, a condition that was exacerbated by the gloomy Calvinist cast of his evangelical faith. In literature he found relief from the depression that afflicted him, and from the late 1770s, as far as he was able, he devoted himself to writing poetry. The popularity of his work grew in the last years of his life, and he was widely read by the Victorians. In this poem from his first collection, Cowper dramatizes an imagined incident from early British history, when Boadicea, Queen of the Iceni, led a revolt against the Roman occupation. Though defeated, she is granted a vision of a future British Empire far more extensive than the imperial rule against which she is fighting.

WHEN the British warrior Queen,
   Bleeding from the Roman rods,
Sought, with an indignant mien,
   Counsel of her country's gods,

Sage beneath a spreading oak
   Sat the Druid, hoary chief,
Every burning word he spoke
   Full of rage, and full of grief:

"Princess! if our aged eyes
   Weep upon thy matchless wrongs,
'Tis because resentment ties
   All the terrors of our tongues.

"Rome shall perish—write that word
   In the blood that she has spilt;
Perish, hopeless and abhorr'd,
   Deep in ruin as in guilt.

"Rome, for empire far renown'd,
   Tramples on a thousand states;
Soon her pride shall kiss the gound—
   Hark! the Gaul is at her gates!

"Other Romans shall arise,
    Heedless of a soldier's name;
Sounds, not arms, shall win the prize,
    Harmony the path to fame.

"Then the progeny that springs
    From the forests of our land,
Armed with thunder, clad with wings,
    Shall a wider world command.

"Regions Cæsar never knew
    Thy posterity shall sway;
Where his eagles never flew,
    None invincible as they."

Such the bard's prophetic words,   .
    Pregnant with celestial fire,
Bending as he swept the chords
    Of his sweet but awful lyre.

She, with all a monarch's pride,
    Felt them in her bosom glow;
Rush'd to battle, fought and died;
    Dying, hurl'd them at the foe.

Ruffians, pitiless as proud,
    Heaven awards the vengeance due;
Empire is on us bestowed,
    Shame and ruin wait for you!

WILLIAM COWPER

From *THE TASK*, 1785

Cowper undertook this long, blank verse poem as a therapeutic
exercise—the Task of the title—on the suggestion of a sympath-
etic neighbour. It dwells· reflectively on many aspects of con-
temporary life. This extract from Book I, 'The Sofa', refers to
Omani, a Tahitian prince who had acted as interpreter to
Captain Cook on his fatal third voyage to the Pacific (1776–9),
and was brought back to England, where he was presented at
Court and painted by Sir Joshua Reynolds.

These therefore I can pity, placed remote
From all that science traces, art invents,
Or inspiration teaches; and enclosed
In boundless oceans, never to be pass'd
By navigators uninform'd as they,
Or plough'd perhaps by British bark again,
But far beyond the rest, and with most cause,
Thee, gentle savage! whom no love of thee
Or thine, but curiosity perhaps,
Or else vain-glory, prompted us to draw
Forth from thy native bowers, to show thee here
With what superior skill we can abuse
The gifts of Providence, and squander life.
The dream is past; and thou hast found again
Thy cocoas and bananas, palms and yams,
And homestall thatch'd with leaves.   But has thou found
Their former charms?   And having seen our state,
Our palaces, our ladies, and our pomp
Of equipage, our gardens, and our sports,
And heard our music; are thy simple friends,
Thy simple fare, and all thy plain delights
As dear to thee as once?   And have thy joys
Lost nothing by comparison with ours?
Rude as thou art, (for we return'd thee rude
And ignorant, except of outward show,)
I cannot think thee yet so dull of heart
And spiritless, as never to regret
Sweets tasted here, and left as soon as known.
Methinks I see thee straying on the beach,

And asking of the surge that bathes thy foot
If ever it has wash'd our distant shore.
I see thee weep, and thine are honest tears,
A patriot's for his country: thou art sad
At thought of her forlorn and abject state,·
From which no power of thine can raise her up.
Thus fancy paints thee, and, though apt to err,
Perhaps errs little when she paints thee thus.
She tells me too, that duly every morn
Thou climb'st the mountain top, with eager eye
Exploring far and wide the watery waste
For sight of ship from England.   Every speck
Seen in the dim horizon, turns thee pale
With conflict of contending hopes and fears.
But comes at last the dull and dusky eve,
And sends thee to thy cabin, well prepared
To dream all night of what the day denied.
Alas! expect it not.   We found no bait
To tempt us in thy country.   Doing good,
Disinterested good, is not our trade.
We travel far, 'tis true, but not for nought;
And must be bribed to compass earth again
By other hopes and richer fruits than yours.

JAMES FREETH

'BOTANY BAY', 1786

As far as is known, Captain Cook was the first European to land on the eastern coast of Australia: this he did in 1770 at Botany Bay, near what is now Sydney. In 1786 it was chosen as the site of a penal settlement to which Britain could transport its convicted felons. Major Semple, mentioned in the poem, was a notorious high-life adventurer, sentenced to seven years' transportation in 1786 for fraud: 'White Boys' were Irish nationalists.

AWAY with all whimsical bubbles of air,
Which only excite a momentary stare;
Attention to plans of utility pay,
Weigh anchor and steer towards Botany Bay.

Let no one think much of a trifling expense,
Who knows what may happen a hundred years hence;
The loss of America what can repay?
New colonies seek for at Botany Bay.

O'er Neptune's domain how extensive the scope!
Of quickly returning how distant the hope!
The Cape must be doubled, and then bear away
Two thousand good leagues to reach Botany Bay.

Of those *precious* souls which for nobody care,
It seems a large cargo the kingdom can spare;
To ship a few hundreds off make no delay,
They cannot too soon go to Botany Bay.

They go of an island to take special charge,
Much warmer than Britain, and ten times as large;
No Custom-house duty, no freightage to pay,
And tax-free they'll live when at Botany Bay.

This garden of Eden, this new promised land,
The time to set sail for is almost at hand;
Ye worst of land-lubbers, make ready for sea,
There's room for you all about Botany Bay.

As scores of each sex to this place must proceed,
In twenty years time—only think of the breed;
Major Semple, should Fortune much kindess display,
May live to be king over Botany Bay.

For a general good, make a general sweep,
The beauty of life is good order to keep;
With night-prowling hateful disturbers away,
And send the whole tribe into Botany Bay.

Ye chiefs who go out on this naval exploit,
The work to accomplish, and set matters right;
To Ireland be kind, call at Cork on your way,
And take a few White Boys to Botany Bay.

Commercial arrangements give prospect of joy,
Fair and firm may be kept ev'ry national tie;
And mutual confidence those who betray,
Be sent to the bottom of Botany Bay.

WILLIAM COWPER
'THE NEGRO'S COMPLAINT', 1788

Opposition to slaving, growing steadily—like the trade itself—throughout the eighteenth century, assumed the form of an organized campaign in 1787 with the formation of the Committee, subsequently the Society, for the Abolition of the Slave Trade. The Society was led by Granville Sharp, its President; Thomas Clarkson, whose seminal *Essay on the Slavery and Commerce of the Human Species* had appeared in 1786; and the influential evangelical William Wilberforce. Both evangelicalism and humanitarianism drew Cowper to the campaign, and in 1788, as a committee of the Privy Council met to inquire into the slave trade, he wrote a group of poems, of which this is one, vigorously supporting the abolitionist cause.

FORCED from home and all its pleasures,
  Afric's coast I left forlorn;
To increase a stranger's treasures,
  O'er the raging billows borne.
Men from England bought and sold me,
  Paid my price in paltry gold;
But, though slave they have enroll'd me,
  Minds are never to be sold.

Still in thought as free as ever,
  What are England's rights, I ask,
Me from my delights to sever,
  Me to torture, me to task?
Fleecy locks and black complexion
  Cannot forfeit nature's claim;
Skins may differ, but affection
  Dwells in white and black the same.

Why did all-creating Nature
  Make the plant for which we toil?
Sighs must fan it, tears must water,
  Sweat of ours must dress the soil.
Think, ye masters, iron-hearted,
  Lolling at your jovial boards,
Think how many backs have smarted
  For the sweets your cane affords.

Is there, as ye sometimes tell us,
　Is there One who reigns on high?
Has He bid you buy and sell us,
　Speaking from His throne, the sky?
Ask Him, if your knotted scourges,
　Matches, blood-extorting screws,
Are the means that duty urges
　Agents of His will to use?

Hark! He answers!—wild tornadoes
　Strewing yonder sea with wrecks,
Wasting towns, plantations, meadows,
　Are the voice with which He speaks.
He, foreseeing what vexations
　Afric's sons should undergo,
Fix'd their tyrants' habitations
　Where His whirlwinds answer—No.

By our blood in Afric wasted,
　Ere our necks received the chain;
By the miseries that we tasted,
　Crossing in your barks the main;
By our sufferings, since ye brought us
　To the man-degrading mart,
All sustain'd by patience, taught us
　Only by a broken heart!

Deem our nation brutes no longer,
　Till some reason ye shall find
Worthier of regard and stronger
　Than the colour of our kind.
Slaves of gold, whose sordid dealings
　Tarnish all your boasted powers,
Prove that you have human feelings
　Ere you proudly question ours!

WILLIAM COWPER

'PITY FOR POOR AFRICANS', 1788

One of Cowper's group of anti-slavery poems, guying those seeming liberals who expressed sympathy for the plight of slaves but could always find reasons why the abolition of the trade would be inexpedient.

I OWN I am shock'd at the purchase of slaves,
And fear those who buy them and sell them are knaves;
What I hear of their hardships, their tortures, and groans,
Is almost enough to draw pity from stones.

I pity them greatly, but I must be mum,
For how could we do without sugar and rum?
Especially sugar, so needful we see;
What, give up our desserts, our coffee, and tea!

Besides if we do, the French, Dutch, and Danes
Will heartily thank us, no doubt, for our pains;
If we do not buy the poor creatures, they will;
And tortures and groans will be multiplied still.

If foreigners likewise would give up the trade,
Much more in behalf of your wish might be said;
But, while they get riches by purchasing blacks,
Pray tell me why we may not also go snacks?

Your scruples and arguments bring to my mind
A story so pat, you may think it is coin'd,
On purpose to answer you, out of my mint;
But I can assure you I saw it in print.

A youngster at school, more sedate that the rest,
Had once his integrity put to the test;
His comrades had plotted an orchard to rob,
And ask'd him to go and assist in the job.

He was shock'd, sir, like you, and answer'd, "Oh no!
What! rob our good neighbour? I pray you don't go!
Besides, the man's poor, his orchard's his bread:
Then think of his children, for they must be fed."

"You speak very fine, and you look very grave,
But apples we want, and apples we'll have;
If you will go with us, you shall have a share,
If not, you shall have neither apple nor pear."

They spoke, and Tom ponder'd—"I see they will go;
Poor man! what a pity to injure him so!
Poor man! I would save him his fruit if I could,
But staying behind will do him no good.

"If the matter depended alone upon me,
His apples might hang till they dropp'd from the tree;
But since they will take them, I think I'll go too;
He will lose none by me, though I get a few."

His scruples thus silenced, Tom felt more at ease,
And went with his comrades the apples to seize;
He blamed and protested, but join'd in the plan;
He shared in the plunder, but pitied the man.

William Cowper

'SWEET MEAT HAS SOUR SAUCE', 1788

Another of Cowper's abolitionist poems, subtitled 'The Slave-Trade in the Dumps', this takes the form of a popular song and savagely burlesques the point of view of a trader pessimistic about the continuing profitability of his bloody business.

> A TRADER I am to the African shore,
> But since that my trading is like to be o'er,
> I'll sing you a song that you ne'er heard before,
> > Which nobody can deny, deny,
> > Which nobody can deny.
>
> When I first heard the news it gave me a shock,
> Much like what they call an electrical knock,
> And now I am going to sell off my stock,
> > Which nobody, &c.
>
> 'Tis a curious assortment of dainty regales,
> To tickle the negroes with when the ship sails,
> Fine chains for the neck, and a cat with nine tails,
> > Which nobody, &c.
>
> Here's supple-jack plenty, and store of ratan,
> That will wind itself round the sides of a man,
> As close as a hoop round a bucket or can,
> > Which nobody, &c.
>
> Here's padlocks and bolts, and screws for the thumbs,
> That squeeze them so lovingly till the blood comes;
> They sweeten the temper like comfits or plums,
> > Which nobody, &c.
>
> When a negro his head from his victuals withdraws,
> And clenches his teeth and thrusts out his paws,
> Here's a notable engine to open his jaws,
> > Which nobody, &c.
>
> Thus going to market, we kindly prepare
> A pretty black cargo of African ware,
> For what they must meet with when they get there,
> > Which nobody, &c.

'Twould do your heart good to see 'em below
Lie flat on their backs all the way as we go,
Like sprats on a gridiron, scores in a row,
    Which nobody, &c.

But ah! if in vain I have studied an art
So gainful to me, all boasting apart,
I think it will break my compassioate heart,
    Which nobody, &c.

For oh! how it enters my soul like an awl;
This pity, which some people self-pity call,
Is sure the most heart-piercing pity of all,
    Which nobody, &c.

So this is my song, as I told you before;
Come, buy off my stock, for I must no more
Carry Cæsars and Pompeys to sugar-cane shore,
    Which nobody, &c.

Hannah More

From *SLAVERY, A POEM*, 1788

More (1745–1833) was an energetic evangelical who wrote widely on religious and social issues, and was particularly concerned with promoting Christian education for the labouring classes. She was an early advocate of Sunday Schools, and the popularly targeted treatises she wrote during the unrest of the French Revolutionary period led to the establishment of the Religious Tract Society in 1799. More actively supported the Society for the Abolition of the Slave Trade from its beginning; the poem from which the following extract is taken belongs to the same phase of the campaign as Cowper's.

> Whene'er to Afric's shores I turn my eyes,
> Horrors of deepest, deadliest guilt arise;
> I see, by more than Fancy's mirror shown,
> The burning village, and the blazing town:
> See the dire victim torn from social life,
> See the scared infant, hear the shrieking wife!
> She, wretch forlorn! is dragged by hostile hands,
> To distant tyrants sold, in distant lands:
> Transmitted miseries, and successive chains,
> The sole sad heritage her child obtains.
> E'en this last wretched boon their foes deny,
> To weep together, or together die.
> By felon hands, by one relentless stroke,
> See the fond vital links of Nature broke!
> The fibres twisting round a parent's heart,
> Torn from their grasp, and bleeding as they part.
>   Hold, murderers! hold! nor aggravate distress;
> Respect the passions you yourself possess:
> Ev'n you, of ruffian heart, and ruthless hand,
> Love your own offspring, love your native land;
> Ev'n you, with fond impatient feelings burn,
> Though free as air, though certain of return.
> Then, if to you, who voluntary roam,
> So dear the memory of your distant home,
> O think how absence the loved scene endears
> To him, whose food is groan, whose drink is tears;
> Think on the wretch whose aggravated pains

To exile misery adds, to misery chains.
If warm *your* heart, to British feelings true,
As dear his land to him as yours to you;
And Liberty, in you a hallowed flame,
Burns, unextinguished, in his breast the same.
Then leave him holy Freedom's cheering smile,
The heaven-taught fondness for the parent soil;
Revere affections mingled with our frame,
In every nature, every clime the same;
In all, these feelings equal sway maintain;
In all, the love of home and freedom reign:
And Tempe's vale, and parched Angola's sand,
One equal fondness of their sons command.
The unconquered savage laughs at pain and toil,
Basking in Freedom's beams which gild his native soil.
    Does thirst of empire, does desire of fame,
(For these are specious crimes) our rage inflame?
No: sordid lust of gold their fate controls,
The basest appetite of basest souls;
Gold, better gained by what their ripening sky,
Their fertile fields, their arts, and mines supply.
    What wrongs, what injuries does Oppression plead
To smooth the crime and sanctify the deed?
What strange offence, what aggravated sin?
They stand convicted—of a darker skin!
Barbarians, hold! the opprobrious commerce spare,
Respect His sacred image which they bear.
Though dark and savage, ignorant and blind,
They claim the privilege of *kind*;
Let Malice strip them of each other plea,
They still are men, and men should still be free.
Insulted Reason loathes the inverted trade—
Loathes, as she views the human purchase made;
The outraged Goddess, with abhorrent eyes,
Sees Man the traffic, souls the merchandise!
Man, whom fair Commerce taught with judging eye,
And liberal hand, to barter or to buy,
Indignant Nature blushes to behold,
Degraded Man himself, trucked, bartered, sold;
O every native privilege bereft,
Yet cursed with every wounded feeling left.

WILLIAM BLAKE

'THE LITTLE BLACK BOY', 1789

———

A thorough-going radical in religion, politics, and poetic prac-
tice, Blake (1757–1827) brought together many of the elements
that were subsequently to be identified as key components of
English Romanticism. In Blake's own time, however, the
limited circulation of his work meant that his influence was very
restricted. His first important collection of poems, *Songs of Inno-
cence*, appeared in 1789; here the voice of innocence is that of a
negro boy confronting the way in which he is perceived by
whites.

My mother bore me in the southern wild,
And I am black, but oh, my soul is white;
White as an angel is the English child,
But I am black as if bereaved of light.

My mother taught me underneath a tree,
And sitting down before the heat of day
She took me on her lap and kissed me,
And pointing to the east began to say:

'Look on the rising sun: there God does live
And gives his light, and gives his heat away;
And flowers and trees and beasts and men receive
Comfort in morning joy in the noon day.

'And we are put on earth a little space,
That we may learn to bear the beams of love,
And these black bodies and this sun-burnt face
Is but a cloud, and like a shady grove.

'For when our souls have learned the heat to bear
The cloud will vanish, we shall hear his voice,
Saying: "Come out from the grove, my love and care,
And round my golden tent like lambs rejoice."'

Thus did my mother say, and kissed me;
And thus I say to little English boy:
When I from black and he from white cloud free
And round the tent of God like lambs we joy,

I'll shade him from the heat till he can bear
To lean in joy upon our Father's knee;
And then I'll stand and stroke his silver hair,
And be like him and he will then love me.

Erasmus Darwin

'VISIT OF HOPE TO SYDNEY COVE, NEAR BOTANY-BAY', 1789

Darwin (1731–1802) was a scientifically inclined poet, whose ideas in *The Botanic Garden* (1791) foreshadowed the theory of evolution to be developed by his grandson Charles. Here he expresses an optimistic view of the future of Britain's distant colony.

Where Sydney Cove her lucid bosom swells,
Courts her young navies, and the storm repels,
High on a rock amid the troubled air
Hope stood sublime, and waved her golden hair;
Calmed with her rosy smile the tossing deep,
And with sweet accents charmed the winds to sleep;
To each wild plain she stretched her snowy hand,
High-waving wood and sea-encircled strand.
  'Hear me,' she cried, 'ye rising realms! record
Time's opening scenes, and Truth's unerring word.
There shall broad streets their stately walls extend,
The circus widen, and the crescent bend;
There, rayed from cities o'er the cultured land,
Shall bright canals and solid roads expand;
There the proud arch colossus-like bestride
Yon glitt'ring streams, and bound the chasing tide;
Embellished villas crown the landscape scene,
Farms wave with gold, and orchards blush between:—
There shall tall spires and dome-capped towers ascend,
And piers and quays their massy structures blend;
While with each breeze approaching vessels glide,
And northern treasures dance on every tide!'
  Then ceased the nymph—tumultuous echoes roar,
And Joy's loud voice was heard from shore to shore—
Her graceful steps descending pressed the plain,
And Peace, and Art, and Labour joined her train.

WILLIAM COWPER

'SONNET TO WILLIAM WILBERFORCE, ESQ.', 1792

In 1792 Wilberforce, leading the anti-slavery crusade in Parliament, secured a majority vote in the Commons in favour of the phased abolition of the slave trade. Here Cowper congratulates him on the success of the campaign so far, and looks forward to complete victory in the near future. He was premature: vested interests managed to delay abolition for a further fifteen years.

THY country, Wilberforce, with just disdain,
    Hears thee by cruel men and impious call'd
    Fanatic, for thy zeal to loose the inthrall'd
From exile, public sale, and slavery's chain.
    Friend of the poor, the wrong'd, the fetter-gall'd,
Fear not lest labour such as thine be vain.

    Thou hast achieved a part; hast gain'd the ear
Of Britain's senate to thy glorious cause;
Hope smiles, joy springs, and, though cold caution pause
    And weave delay, the better hour is near
    That shall remunerate thy toils severe
By peace for Afric, fenced with British laws.

Enjoy what thou hast won, esteem and love
From all the just on earth, and all the blest above.

ROBERT SOUTHEY

'TO THE GENIUS OF AFRICA', 1795

A reviewer, essayist and scholar, as well as a prolific poet, Southey (1774–1843) was one of the early nineteenth century's most influential men of letters. Settling in Keswick in 1803, he came to be one of the group known as the Lake Poets, along with Coleridge, to whom he was related by marriage, and Wordsworth, with whom he maintained a long friendship. Southey's early poetry was politically radical though he became increasingly conservative as he grew older—as did his fellow Lake Poets. In 1813 he was sufficiently safe politically to be created Poet Laureate. As a young man he wrote a number of 'Poems concerning the Slave Trade', of which this is the most dramatic; it was written in Bristol, a centre of the trade.

O THOU, who from the mountain's height
Rollest thy clouds with all their weight
Of waters to old Nile's majestic tide;
Or o'er the dark sepulchral plain
Recallest Carthage in her ancient pride,
The mistress of the Main;
Hear, Genius, hear thy children's cry!
Not always should'st thou love to brood
Stern o'er the desert solitude
Where seas of sand heave their hot surges high;
Nor, Genius, should the midnight song
Detain thee in some milder mood
The palmy plains among,
Where Gambia to the torches' light
Flows radiant through the awaken'd night.

Ah, linger not to hear the song!
Genius, avenge thy children's wrong!
The demon Avarice on your shore
Brings all the horrors of his train,
And hark! where from the field of gore
Howls the hyena o'er the slain!
Lo! where the flaming village fires the skies
Avenging Power, awake! arise!

Arise, thy children's wrongs redress!
Heed the mother's wretchedness,
When in the hot infectious air
O'er her sick babe she bows opprest, ..
Hear her when the Traders tear
The suffering infant from her breast!
Sunk in the ocean he shall rest!
Hear thou the wretched mother's cries,
Avenging Power! awake! arise!

By the rank infected air
That taints those cabins of despair;
By the scourges blacken'd o'er,
And stiff and hard with human gore;
By every groan of deep distress,
By every curse of wretchedness;
The vices and the crimes that flow
From the hopelessness of woe;
By every drop of blood bespilt,
By Afric's wrongs and Europe's guilt,
Awake! arise! avenge!

And thou hast heard! and o'er their blood-fed plains
Sent thine avenging hurricanes
And bade thy storms with whirlwind roar
Dash their proud navies on the shore;
And where their armies claim'd the fight
Wither'd the warrior's might;
And o'er the unholy host with baneful breath,
There, Genius, thou hast breathed the gales of Death.

WILLIAM SHEPHERD

'ODE ON LORD MACARTNEY'S EMBASSY TO CHINA', 1797

Shepherd (1768–1847) was a Unitarian minister who was actively involved in the radical politics of the last years of the eighteenth century. In this strikingly outspoken poem he attacks the ruthlessness of British imperialism, evidenced by the military expansion of the East India Company in the 1790s, and by the continuing West African slave trade. The occasion of the poem was the diplomatic mission to Peking undertaken by Earl Macartney in 1792–4, rightly seen by Shepherd as an early move in the attempt to force the opening of China to British commerce.

SWIFT shot the curlew 'thwart the rising blast,
  As eve's dun shades enwrapped the billowy main;
Hoarse broke the waves against the sandy waste,
  And dim and cheerless swept the drizzling rain:
      When bending o'er the briny spray
      Stood thy genius, old Cathay,
      Her vestments floating on the gale;
      With angry glare her eyeballs roll,
      Horror shakes her inmost soul,
As thus along the strand swells her portentous wail:

      'Athirst for prey, what ruffian band
      Dares approach this happy land?
      Glimmering through the glooms of eve,
      What canvas flutters o'er the wave?
      Plunging through the swelling tide,
      What prows the whit'ning brine divide?
'Tis Albion's bloody cross that flouts the air,
  'Tis Albion's sons that skirt this peaceful shore;
Her cross, oppression's badge, the sign of war;
  Her sons that range the world, and peace is seen no more.

[126]

'Insatiate spoilers! that, with treach'rous smiles,
  In wreaths of olive hide the murderous sword:
Ill fare the tribes, unconscious of your wiles,
  Whose honest candour trusts your plighted word.
        Hence! ye harbingers of woe—
        Too well your deeds of blood I know:
        For mid the thickening gloom of night
        Oft, as I speed my watchful flight,
        A monitory voice I hear—
Keen Sorrow's thrilling cry awakes my list'ning ear.

        'A cry resounds from Ganges' flood;
        There Oppression's giant brood
        Wide the scythe of ruin sweep,
        And desolated districts weep.
        Terror waves the scourge on high,
        Patient Misery heaves the sigh;
Lo! meagre Famine drains the vital springs,
  And points from far where yawns the darksome grave;
Her gifts in vain profusive Plenty flings;
  Stern Avarice guards the store, nor owns the wish to save.

'From Niger's banks resounds the shriek of woe.
  There, inly pining, mourns the hapless slave;
Fraud proudly braves the light with shameless brow,
  And floating charnels plough the restless wave.
        Behold, in desolate array,
        The captives wind their silent way:
        Amid the ranks does Pity find
        A pair by fond affection joined?
        Fell Rapine, reckless of their pain,
        Blasts Misery's final hope—denies a common chain.
        'Hear, O my sons, the warning cry,
        And while you breathe the pitying sigh,
        Deep on Memory's tablet trace
        These triumphs of Britannia's race.
        From age to age, from sire to son,
        Let the eternal record run;
And when, with hollow hearts and honeyed tongues,
  These slaves of gold advance their blood-stained hand,
Shrink from the touch—Remember India's wrongs—
  Remember Afric's woes—and save your destined land.'

THOMAS CAMPBELL

'YE MARINERS OF ENGLAND. A NAVAL ODE',
1801; revised 1805

The son of an Edinburgh merchant whose colonial business was ruined by the American War of Independence, Campbell made a successful literary career for himself following the instant success of his first major poem *The Pleasures of Hope*, published in 1799. He wrote a number of patriotic and martial poems during the Napoleonic War, the most celebrated of which was 'Ye Mariners of England', based on the popular ballad 'Ye Gentlemen of England'. With 'Rule Britannia', it became a standard anthem in the ideology of British naval power as the means both of national security and of imperial expansion. The reference to Nelson in the second verse was included after the Battle of Trafalgar.

YE Mariners of England
That guard our native seas,
Whose flag has braved, a thousand years,
The battle and the breeze—
Your glorious standard launch again
To match another foe!
And sweep through the deep,
While the stormy winds do blow,—
While the battle rages loud and long,
And the stormy winds do blow.

The spirits of your fathers
Shall start from every wave!
For the deck it was their field of fame,
And Ocean was their grave.
Where Blake and mighty Nelson fell
Your manly hearts shall glow,
As ye sweep through the deep,
While the stormy winds do blow,—
While the battle rages loud and long,
And the stormy winds do blow.

Britannia needs no bulwarks,
No towers along the steep;
Her march is o'er the mountain waves,
Her home is on the deep.
With thunders from her native oak
She quells the floods below,
As they roar on the shore
When the stormy winds do blow,—
When the battle rages loud and long
And the stormy winds do blow.

The meteor flag of England
Shall yet terrific burn,
Till danger's troubled night depart
And the star of peace return.
Then, then, ye ocean warriors!
Our song and feast shall flow
To the fame of your name,
When the storm has ceased to blow,—
When the fiery fight is heard no more,
And the storm has ceased to blow.

WILLIAM WORDSWORTH

'TO TOUSSAINT L'OUVERTURE', written 1802

Lyrical Ballads, co-written by Wordsworth (1770–1850) and his friend Samuel Taylor Coleridge, attracted some critical acclaim when it first appeared in 1798, and this grew with the publication of the enlarged second edition of 1800. In the twenty years that followed, Wordsworth established his reputation as the leading poet of his generation and a central figure in what became known as the English Romantic Movement. He consciously developed a public voice in his poetry, particularly in his sonnets, many of which address historical themes and issues of state. Among these, collected later under the title 'Poems Dedicated to National Independence and Liberty', is this relatively early sonnet. Pierre Dominique Toussaint L'Ouverture was born a slave in the French colony of San Domingo, led the insurrection against the white planters that began in 1791, and subsequently became Governor of the whole island of Haiti. Napoleon's policy towards the French colonies resulted in Toussaint's betrayal and defeat, and he was imprisoned in France, where he died. Wordsworth's poem needs to be read in the double context of the Napoleonic War and the anti-slavery campaign in Britain.

TOUSSAINT, the most unhappy man of men!
Whether the whistling Rustic tend his plough
Within thy hearing, or thy head be now
Pillowed in some deep dungeon's earless den;—
O miserable Chieftain! where and when
Wilt thou find patience? Yet die not; do thou
Wear rather in thy bonds a cheerful brow:
Though fallen thyself, never to rise again,
Live, and take comfort. Thou hast left behind
Powers that will work for thee; air, earth, and skies;
There's not a breathing of the common wind
That will forget thee; thou hast great allies;
Thy friends are exultations, agonies,
And love, and man's unconquerable mind.

WILLIAM WORDSWORTH

'SEPTEMBER 1, 1802'

Composed shortly after the sonnet 'To Toussaint L'Ouverture'
and effectively a companion-piece to it, this recounts an experi-
ence of Wordsworth's returning from a visit to France during
the brief lull in the Napoleonic War that followed the Peace of
Amiens. The sonnet was introduced with the following explana-
tion: 'Among the capricious acts of tyranny that disgraced those
times, was the chasing of all Negroes from France by a decree of
the government: we had a Fellow-passenger who was one of the
expelled.'

WE had a female Passenger who came
From Calais with us, spotless in array,—
A white-robed Negro, like a lady gay,
Yet downcast as a woman fearing blame;
Meek, destitute, as seemed, of hope or aim
She sate, from notice turning not away,
But on all proffered intercourse did lay
A weight of languid speech, or to the same
No sign of answer made by word or face:
Yet still her eyes retained their tropic fire,
That, burning independent of the mind,
Joined with the lustre of her rich attire
To mock the Outcast—O ye Heavens, be kind!
And feel, thou Earth, for this afflicted Race!

WILLIAM BLAKE

From *VALA, OR THE FOUR ZOAS*, 1804

In his later years, Blake developed a complex mythology through which to express his radical vision of the world. Here, in an extract from Book IX, he alludes to the slave trade, prophesying a future of freedom for all mankind.

'Let the slave grinding at the mill run out into the field;
Let him look up into the heavens & laugh in the bright air;
Let the enchained soul, shut up in darkness & in sighing,
Whose face has never seen a smile in thirty weary years,
Rise & look out—his chains are loose, his dungeon doors are open.
And let his wife & children return from the oppressor's scourge.

'They look behind at every step & believe it is a dream:
Are these the slaves that groaned along the streets of Mystery?
Where are your bonds & taskmasters? Are these the prisoners?
Where are your chains, where are your tears? Why do you look
	around?
If you are thirsty, there is the river: go bathe your parched limbs.
The good of all the land is before you; for Mystery is no more!'

Then all the slaves from every earth in the wide universe
Sing a new song, drowning confusion in its happy notes
(While the flail of Urizen sounded loud, & the winnowing wind
	of Tharmas)
So loud, so clear in the wide heavens; & the song that they sung
	was this,
Composed by an African black, from the little earth of Sotha:

'Aha! Aha! How came I here so soon in my sweet native land?
How came I here? Methinks I am as I was in my youth,
When in my father's house I sat & heard his cheering voice;
Methinks I see his flocks & herds & feel my limbs renewed;
And lo, my brethren in their tents & their little ones around them!'

The song arose to the golden feast, the Eternal Man rejoiced:
Then the Eternal Man said: 'Luvah, the vintage is ripe: arise!
The sons of Urizen shall gather the vintage with sharp hooks,
And all thy sons, O Luvah, bear away the families of earth.

I hear the flail of Urizen; his barns are full, no room
Remains, & in the vineyards stand the abounding sheaves beneath
The falling grapes, that odorous burst upon the winds. Arise!
My flocks & herds trample the corn, my cattle browse upon
The ripe clusters; the shepherds shout for Luvah, prince of love!
Let the bulls of Luvah tread the corn, & draw the loaded waggon
Into the barn, while children glean the ears arcund the door.
Then shall they lift their innocent hands & stroke his furious nose,
And he shall lick the little girl's white neck, & on her head
Scatter the perfume of his breath, while from his mountains high
The lion of terror shall come down, & bending his bright mane
And couching at their side, shall eat from the curled boy's white lap
His golden food, and in the evening sleep before the door.'

WILLIAM WORDSWORTH
'TO THOMAS CLARKSON', 1807

The full title of this sonnet explains its occasion: 'On the Final Passing of the Bill for the Abolition of the Slave Trade'. After years of parliamentary obstruction, the 1806–7 ministry of Lord Grenville and Charles Fox finally abolished slaving throughout the British dominions. Wordsworth's sonnet salutes Clarkson's leadership throughout the long campaign; after 1807 Clarkson continued to work for the cause until abolition of slavery itself in British colonies was achieved in 1833.

CLARKSON! it was an obstinate hill to climb:
How toilsome—nay, how dire—it was, by thee
Is known; by none, perhaps, so feelingly:
But thou, who, starting in thy fervent prime,
Didst first lead forth that enterprise sublime,
Hast heard the constant Voice its charge repeat,
Which, out of thy young heart's oracular seat,
First roused thee.—O true yoke-fellow of Time,
Duty's intrepid liegeman, see, the palm
Is won, and by all Nations shall be worn!
The blood-stained Writing is for ever torn;
And thou henceforth wilt have a good man's calm,
A great man's happiness; thy zeal shall find
Repose at length, firm friend of human kind!

JAMES MONTGOMERY

From *THE WEST INDIES*, 1809

The son of a nonconformist missionary who died in the West
Indies, Montgomery (1771–1854) settled in the 1790s in Shef-
field, where he was twice imprisoned for involvement with
radical publications. He enjoyed some considerable success as a
poet in the first twenty years of the nineteenth century and in
later life was a warm supporter of philanthropic causes in Shef-
field. Montgomery identified strongly with the campaign against
slavery, and wrote the long historical and descriptive poem *The
West Indies*, from which the following extracts are taken, to
mark the British abolition of the slave trade in 1807.

After the arrival of Columbus and the Spanish in the 1490s
silver is discovered and the native Carib peoples, forced to work
the mines, are wiped out; from Part I.

> Where first his drooping sails Columbus furl'd,
> And sweetly rested in another world,
> Amidst the heaven-reflecting ocean, smiles
> A constellation of elysian isles;
> Fair as Orion when he mounts on high,
> Sparkling with midnight splendour from the sky:
> They bask beneath the sun's meridian rays,
> When not a shadow breaks the boundless blaze;
> The breath of ocean wanders through their vales
> In morning breezes and in evening gales:
> Earth from her lap perennial verdure pours,
> Ambrosial fruits, and amaranthine flowers;
> O'er the wild mountains and luxuriant plains,
> Nature in all the pomp of beauty reigns,
> In all the pride of freedom.—NATURE FREE
> Proclaims that MAN was born for liberty.
> She flourishes wher'er the sunbeams play
> O'er living fountains, sallying into day;
> She withers where the waters cease to roll,
> And night and winter stagnate round the pole:
> Man too, where freedom's beams and fountains rise,
> Springs from the dust, and blossoms to the skies;

Dead to the joys of light and life, the slave
Clings to the clod; his root is in the grave:
Bondage is winter, darkness, death, despair;
Freedom the sun, the sea, the mountains, and the air!

   In placid indolence supinely blest,
A feeble race these beauteous isles possess'd;
Untamed, untaught, in arts and arms unskill'd,
Their patrimonial soil they rudely till'd,
Chased the free rovers of the savage wood,
Insnared the wild-bird, swept the scaly flood;
Shelter'd in lowly huts their fragile forms
From burning suns and desolating storms;
Or when the halcyon sported on the breeze,
In light canoes they skimm'd the rippling seas;
Their lives in dreams of soothing languor flew,
No parted joys, no future pains, they knew,
The passing moment all their bliss or care;
Such as their sires had been the children were,
From age to age; as waves upon the tide
Of stormless time, they calmly lived and died.

   Dreadful as hurricanes, athwart the main
Rush'd the fell legions of invading Spain;
With fraud and force, with false and fatal breath,
(Submission bondage, and resistance death,)
They swept the isles.   In vain the simple race
Kneel'd to the iron sceptre of their grace,
Or with weak arms their fiery vengeance braved;
They came, they saw, they conquer'd, they enslaved,
And they destroy'd;—the generous heart they broke,
They crush'd the timid neck beneath the yoke;
Where'er to battle march'd their fell array,
The sword of conquest plough'd resistless way;
Where'er from cruel toil they sought repose,
Around the fires of devastation rose.
The Indian, as he turn'd his head in flight,
Beheld his cottage flaming through the night,
And, midst the shrieks of murder on the wind,
Heard the mute bloodhound's death-step close behind.

   The conflict o'er, the valiant in their graves,
The wretched remnant dwindled into slaves;
Condemn'd in pestilential cells to pine,
Delving for gold amidst the gloomy mine.

The sufferer, sick of life-protracting breath,
Inhaled with joy the fire-damp blast of death:
—Condemn'd to fell the mountain palm on high,
That cast its shadow from the evening sky,
Ere the tree trembled to his feeble stroke,
The woodman languish'd, and his heart-strings broke;
—Condemn'd in torrid noon, with palsied hand,
To urge the slow plough o'er the obdurate land,
The labourer, smitten by the sun's quick ray,
A corpse along the unfinish'd furrow lay.
O'erwhelm'd at length with ignominious toil,
Mingling their barren ashes with the soil,
Down to the dust the Charib people pass'd,
Like autumn foliage withering in the blast:
The whole race sunk beneath the oppressor's rod,
And left a blank among the works of GOD. .

To find labour for the cultivation of sugar cane on the islands,
Spain begins slaving from West Africa and the trade is taken up
by other European nations; from Part II.

AMONG the bowers of paradise, that graced
Those islands of the world-dividing waste,
Where towering cocoas waved their graceful locks,
And vines luxuriant cluster'd round the rocks;
Where orange-groves perfum'd the circling air,
With verdure, flowers, and fruit for every fair;
Gay myrtle-foliage track'd the winding rills,
And cedar forests slumber'd on the hills;
—An eastern plant, ingrafted on the soil,
Was till'd for ages with consuming toil;
No tree of knowledge with forbidden fruit,
Death in the taste, and ruin at the root;
Yet in its growth were good and evil found,—
It bless'd the planter, but it cursed the ground:
While with vain wealth it gorged the master's hoard,
And spread with manna his luxurious board,
Its culture was perdition to the slave,—
It sapp'd his life, and flourish'd on his grave.

When the fierce spoiler from remorseless Spain
Tasted the balmy spirit of the cane,
(Already had his rival in the west
From the rich reed ambrosial sweetness press'd,)

Dark through his thoughts the miser purpose roll'd
To turn its hidden treasures into gold.
But at his breath, by pestilent decay,
The Indian tribes were swiftly swept away;
Silence and horror o'er the isles were spread,
The living seem'd the spectres of the dead.
The Spaniard saw; no sigh of pity stole,
No pang of conscience touch'd his sullen soul:
The tiger weeps not o'er the kid;—he turns
His flashing eyes abroad, and madly burns
For nobler victims, and for warmer blood:
Thus on the Charib shore the tyrant stood,
Thus cast his eyes with fury o'er the tide,
And far beyond the gloomy gulph descried
Devoted Africa: he burst away,
And with a yell of transport grasp'd his prey. ...

Freighted with curses was the bark that bore
The spoilers of the west to Guinea's shore;
Heavy with groans of anguish blew the gales
That swell'd that fatal bark's returning sails;
Old Ocean shrunk as o'er his surface flew
The human cargo and the demon crew.
—Thenceforth, unnumber'd as the waves that roll
From sun to sun, or pass from pole to pole,
Outcasts and exiles, from their country torn,
In floating dungeons o'er the gulph were borne;
—The valiant, seized in peril-daring fight;
The weak, surprised in nakedness and night;
Subjects by mercenary despots sold;
Victims of justice prostitute for gold;
Brothers by brothers, friends by friends, betray'd;
Snared in her lover's arms the trusting maid;
The faithful wife by her false lord estranged,
For one wild cup of drunken bliss exchanged;
From the brute-mother's knee, the infant-boy,
Kidnapp'd in slumber, barter'd for a toy;
The father, resting at his father's tree,
Doom'd by the son to die beyond the sea:
—All bonds of kindred, law, alliance, broke;
All ranks, all nations, crouching to the yoke;
From fields of light, unshadow'd climes, that lie
Panting beneath the sun's meridian eye;
From hidden Ethiopia's utmost land;
From Zaara's fickle wilderness of sand;

From Congo's blazing plains and blooming woods;
From Whidah's hills, that gush with golden floods;
Captives of tyrant power and dastard wiles,
Dispeopled Africa, and gorged the isles.
Loud and perpetual o'er the Atlantic waves,
For guilty ages, roll'd the tide of slaves;
A tide that knew no fall, no turn, no rest,
Constant as day and night from east to west;
Still widening, deepening, swelling in its course,
With boundless ruin and resistless force.

Quickly by Spain's alluring fortune fired,
With hopes of fame and dreams of wealth inspired,
Europe's dread powers from ignominious ease
Started; their pennons stream'd on every breeze;
And still where'er the wide discoveries spread,
The cane was planted, and the native bled;
While, nursed by fiercer suns, of nobler race,
The Negro toil'd and perish'd in his place.

First, Lusitania,—she whose prows had borne
Her arms triumphant round the car of morn,
—Turn'd to the setting sun her bright array,
And hung her trophies o'er the couch of day.

Holland,—whose hardy sons roll'd back the sea,
To build the halcyon-nest of liberty,
Shameless abroad the enslaving flag unfurl'd,
And reign'd a despot in the younger world.

Denmark,—whose roving hordes, in barbarous times,
Fill'd the wide North with piracy and crimes,
Awed every shore, and taught their keels to sweep
O'er every sea, the Arabs of the deep,
—Embark'd, once more to western conquest led
By Rollo's spirit, risen from the dead.

Gallia,—who vainly aim'd, in depth of night,
To hurl old Rome from her Tarpeian height,
(But lately laid, with unprevented blow,
The thrones of kings, the hopes of freedom, low,)
—Rush'd o'er the theatre of splendid toils,
To brave the danger and divide the spoils.

Britannia,—she who scathed the crest of Spain,
And won the trident sceptre of the main,
When to the raging wind and ravening tide
She gave the huge Armada's scatter'd pride,
Smit by the thunder-wielding hand that hurl'd
Her vengeance round the wave-encircled world;
—Britannia shared the glory and the guilt,—
By her were Slavery's island-altars built,
And fed with human victims;—while the cries
Of blood demanding vengeance from the skies,
Assail'd her traders' grovelling hearts in vain,
—Hearts dead to sympathy, alive to gain,
Hard from impunity, with avarice cold,
Sordid as earth, insensible as gold.

   Thus through a night of ages, in whose shade
The sons of darkness plied the infernal trade,
Wild Africa beheld her tribes, at home,
In battle slain; abroad, condemn'd to roam
O'er the salt waves, in stranger isles to bear,
(Forlorn of hope, and sold into despair,)
Through life's slow journey, to its dolorous close,
Unseen, unwept, unutterable woes.

Inspired by the patriotic deaths of Nelson and Pitt, and by the
dying wish of Prime Minister Fox, Britain awakes to moral
responsibility and abolishes the slave trade; from Part IV.

   High on her rock in solitary state,
Sublimely musing, pale Britannia sate:
Her awful forehead on her spear reclined,
Her robe and tresses streaming with the wind;
Chill through her frame foreboding tremors crept!
The Mother thought upon her sons, and wept.
—She thought of Nelson in the battle slain,
And his last signal beaming o'er the main;
In Glory's circling arms the hero bled,
While victory bound the laurel on his head;
At once immortal, in both worlds, became
His soaring spirit and abiding name;
—She thought of Pitt, heart-broken on his bier;
And, "O my country!" echoed in her ear;
—She thought of Fox; she heard him faintly speak,

His parting breath grew cold upon her cheek,
His dying accents trembled into air;
"Spare injured Africa! the Negro spare!"

   She started from her trance!—and, round the shore,
Beheld her supplicating sons once more
Pleading the suit so long, so vainly tried,
Renew'd, resisted, promised, pledged, denied,—
The Negro's claim to all his Maker gave,
And all the tyrant ravish'd from the slave.
Her yielding heart confess'd the righteous claim,
Sorrow had soften'd it, and love o'ercame;
Shame flush'd her noble cheek, her bosom burn'd;
To helpless, hopeless Africa she turn'd;
She saw her sister in the mourner's face,
And rush'd with tears into her dark embrace:
"All hail!" exclaim'd the empress of the sea,—
"Thy chains are broken—Africa, be free!"

Mary Lamb

'CONQUEST OF PREJUDICE', 1809

After a fit of insanity in 1796 in which she killed her mother, Mary Lamb (1764–1847) spent most of her life under the care of her brother, the essayist and playwright Charles Lamb—himself subject to periodic mental breakdowns. She was a poet of the school of Sensibility, and collaborated with her brother in writing the famous *Lamb's Tales from Shakespeare* (1807). In this exemplary moral anecdote she promotes an enlightened approach to race relations.

UNTO a Yorkshire school was sent
  A Negro youth to learn to write,
And the first day young Juba went
  All gazed on him as a rare sight.

But soon with altered looks askance
  They view his sable face and form,
When they perceive the scorning glance
  Of the head boy, young Henry Orme.

He in the school was first in fame:
  Said he, 'It does to me appear
To be a great disgrace and shame
  A black should be admitted here.'

His words were quickly whispered round,
  And every boy now looks offended;
The master saw the change, and found
  That Orme a mutiny intended.

Said he to Orme, 'This African
  It seems is not by you approved;
I'll find a way, young Englishman,
  To have this prejudice removed.

'Nearer acquaintance possibly
  May make you tolerate his hue;
At least 'tis my intent to try
  What a short month may chance to do.'

Young Orme and Juba then he led
   Into a room, in which there were
For each of the two boys a bed,
   A table, and a wicker chair.

He locked them in, secured the key,
   That all access to them was stopt;
They from without can nothing see;
   Their food is through a sky-light dropt.

A month in this lone chamber Orme
   Is sentenced during all that time
To view no other face or form
   Than Juba's parched by Afric clime.

One word they neither of them spoke
   The first three days of the first week;
On the fourth day the ice was broke;
   Orme was the first that deigned to speak.

The dreary silence o'er, both glad
   To hear of human voice the sound,
The Negro and the English lad
   Comfort in mutual converse found.

Of ships and seas, and foreign coast,
   Juba can speak, for he has been
A voyager: and Orme can boast
   He London's famous town has seen.

In eager talk they pass the day,
   And borrow hours ev'n from the night;
So pleasantly time passed away,
   That they have lost their reckoning quite.

And when their master set them free,
   They thought a week was sure remitted,
And thanked him that their liberty
   Had been before the time permitted.

Now Orme and Juba are good friends;
   The school, by Orme's example won,
Contend who first shall make amends
   For former slights to Afric's son.

FELICIA HEMANS

'ENGLAND'S DEAD', 1813

Hemans's (1793–1835) prolific output included domestic and
sentimental lyrics, verse drama, historical narratives, and poems
on political and patriotic themes; as well as having a wide pop-
ular appeal, her work was admired by Wordsworth and Byron.
'England's Dead', written towards the end of the Napoleonic
War, reflects the expansion of British sea power and the global
nature of the trading and colonial interests that that power was
used to defend.

SON of the ocean isle!
Where sleep your mighty dead?
Show me what high and stately pile
Is reared o'er Glory's bed.

Go, stranger! track the deep,
Free, free, the white sail spread!
Wave may not foam, nor wild wind sweep,
Where rest not England's dead.

On Egypt's burning plains,
By the pyramid o'erswayed,
With fearful power the noonday reigns,
And the palm-trees yield no shade.

But let the angry sun
From heaven look fiercely red,
Unfelt by those whose task is done!—
There slumber England's dead.

The hurricane hath might
Along the Indian shore,
And far, by Ganges' banks at night,
Is heard the tiger's roar.

But let the sound roll on!
It hath no tone of dread
For those that from their toils are gone;—
There slumber England's dead!

Loud rush the torrent-floods
The western wilds among,
And free, in green Columbia's woods,
The hunter's bow is strung.

But let the floods rush on!
Let the arrow's flight be sped!
Why should *they* reck whose task is done?—
There slumber England's dead!

The mountain-storms rise high
In the snowy Pyrenees,
And toss the pine-boughs through the sky,
Like rose-leaves on the breeze.

But let the storm rage on!
Let the forest-wreaths be shed:
For the Roncesvalles' field is won,—
There slumber England's dead.

On the frozen deep's repose,
'Tis a dark and dreadful hour,
When round the ship the ice-fields close,
To chain her with their power.

But let the ice drift on!
Let the cold-blue desert spread!
Their course with mast and flag is done,
Even there sleep England's dead.

The warlike of the isles,
The men of field and wave!
Are not the rocks their funeral piles,
The seas and shores their grave?

Go, stranger! track the deep,
Free, free the white sail spread!
Wave may not foam, nor wild wind sweep,
Where rest not England's dead.

Reginald Heber

'FROM GREENLAND'S ICY MOUNTAINS', 1819

———

Heber (1783–1826) established an early reputation as a poet and hymnodist, and was an advocate of missionary expansion in the British colonies. He was appointed Bishop of Calcutta in 1822 and worked diligently in India before his early death a few years later. This hymn, his most famous, was written for a fund-raising service in support of the Society for the Propagation of the Gospel, one of the principal Anglican missionary organizations.

From Greenland's icy mountains,
   From India's coral strand,
Where Afric's sunny fountains
   Roll down their golden sand,
From many an ancient river,
   From many a palmy plain,
They call us to deliver
   Their land from error's chain.

What though the spicy breezes
   Blow soft o'er Ceylon's isle,
Though every prospect pleases
   And only man is vile,
In vain with lavish kindness
   The gifts of God are strown,
The heathen in his blindness
   Bows down to wood and stone.

Can we, whose souls are lighted
   With wisdom from on high,
Can we to men benighted
   The lamp of life deny?
Salvation! oh, salvation!
   The joyful sound proclaim,
Till each remotest nation
   Has learnt Messiah's name.

Waft, waft, ye winds, His story,
  And you, ye waters, roll,
Till, like a sea of glory,
  It spreads from pole to pole;
Till o'er our ransomed nature
  The LAMB for sinners slain,
Redeemer, King, Creator,
  In bliss returns to reign.

Thomas Campbell

'MEN OF ENGLAND', 1822

Victory in the Napoleonic War gave Britain naval supremacy and set the stage for the prodigious imperial expansion of the nineteenth century. In this poem Campbell's mythologizing of the tradition of English liberty, here particularly associated with the anti-monarchist leaders of the Civil War, is coupled with an implicit warning against militarism.

MEN of England! who inherit
　　Rights that cost your sires their blood!
Men whose undegenerate spirit
　　Has been proved on land and flood:—

By the foes ye've fought uncounted,
　　By the glorious deeds ye've done,
Trophies captured—breaches mounted,
　　Navies conquer'd—kingdoms won!

Yet, remember, England gathers
　　Hence but fruitless wreaths of fame,
If the patriotism of your fathers
　　Glow not in your hearts the same.

What are monuments of bravery,
　　Where no public virtues bloom?
What avail in lands of slavery,
　　Trophied temples, arch, and tomb?

Pageants!—Let the world revere us
　　For our people's rights and laws
And the breasts of civic heroes
　　Bared in Freedom's holy cause.

Yours are Hampden's, Russell's glory,
　　Sydney's matchless shade is yours,—
Martyrs in heroic story,
　　Worth a hundred Agincourts!

We're the sons of sires that baffled
　　Crowned and mitred tyranny:—
They defied the field and scaffold
　　For their birthrights—so will we!

James Montgomery

'INSCRIPTION UNDER THE PICTURE OF AN AGED NEGRO-WOMAN', 1826

———

After the 1807 abolition of the slave trade, Montgomery continued to support the campaign for complete emancipation. Here he appeals to the domestic sentiments of white middle-class humanitarianism.

ART thou a *woman?*—so am I; and all
That woman can be, I have been, or am;
A daughter, sister, consort, mother, widow.
Whiche'er of these *thou* art, O be the friend
Of one who is what thou canst never be!
Look on thyself, thy kindred, home and country,
Then fall upon thy knees, and cry "Thank GOD,
An English woman cannot be a SLAVE!"

Art thou a *man?*—Oh! I have known, have loved,
And lost, all that to woman man can be;
A father, brother, husband, son, who shared
My bliss in freedom, and my woe in bondage.
—A childless widow now, a friendless slave,
What shall I ask of thee, since I have nought
To lose but life's sad burthen; nought to gain
But heaven's repose?—these are beyond thy power;
Me thou canst neither wrong nor help;—what then?
Go to the bosom of thy family,
Gather thy little children round thy knees,
Gaze on their innocence; their clear, full eyes,
All fix'd on thine; and in their mother, mark
The loveliest look that woman's face can wear,
Her look of love, beholding them and thee:
Then, at the altar of your household joys,
Vow one by one, vow altogether, vow
With heart and voice, eternal enmity
Against oppression by your brethren's hands:
Till man nor woman under Britain's laws,
Nor son nor daughter born within her empire,
Shall buy, or sell, or hold, or be, a slave.

JAMES MONTGOMERY

From *THE PELICAN ISLAND*, 1827

The Pelican Island is Montgomery's most ambitious poem, an extraordinary attempt to reconcile the biblical creation myth with contemporary science in a visionary narrative about the evolution of a South Seas coral island. Ever since Cook's voyages, stories of man-eating Pacific islanders had multiplied and, in the final parts of the poem, Montgomery lingers luridly on cannibalism and depravity as decisive evidence of the unredeemed state of the native peoples. Such perceptions impelled the intensive missionary effort mounted by the colonial nations in the Pacific in the later nineteenth century, and gave religious justification to imperialist expansion. This extract is from Canto VI.

> I saw him sunk in loathsome degradation,
> A naked, fierce, ungovernable savage,
> Companion to the brutes, himself more brutal;
> Superior only in the craft that made
> The serpent subtlest beast of all the field,
> Whose guile unparadised the world, and brought
> A curse upon the earth which GOD had bless'd.
> That curse was here, without the mitigation
> Of healthful toil, that half redeems the ground
> Whence man was taken, whither he returns,
> And which repays him bread for patient labour,
> —Labour, the symbol of his punishment,
> —Labour, the secret of his happiness.
> The curse was here; for thorns and briars o'erran
> The tangled labyrinths,—yet briars bare roses,
> And thorns threw out their annual snow of blossoms:
> The curse was here; and yet the soil untill'd
> Pour'd forth spontaneous and abundant harvests,
> Pulse and small berries, maize in strong luxuriance,
> And slender rice that grew by many waters;
> The forests cast their fruits, in husk or rind,
> Yielding sweet kernels or delicious pulp,
> Smooth oil, cool milk, and unfermented wine,
> In rich and exquisite variety.
> On these the indolent inhabitants

Fed without care or forethought, like the swine
That grubb'd the turf, and taught them where to look
For dainty earth-nuts and nutritious roots;
Or the small monkeys, capering on the boughs,
And rioting on nectar and ambrosia,
The produce of that Paradise run wild:—
No,—these were merry, if they were not wise;
While man's untutor'd hordes were sour and sullen,
Like those abhorr'd baboons, whose gluttonous taste
They follow'd safely in their choice of food;
And whose brute semblance of humanity
Made them more hideous than their prototypes,
That bore the genuine image and inscription,
Defaced indeed, but yet indelible.
—From ravening beasts, and fowls that fish'd the ocean,
Men learn'd to prey on meaner animals,
But found a secret out which birds or beasts,
Most cruel, cunning, treacherous, never knew,
—The luxury of devouring one another.

    Such were my kindred in their lost estate,
From whose abominations while I turn'd,
As from a pestilence, I mourn'd and wept
With bitter lamentation o'er their ruin;
Sunk as they were in ignorance of all
That raises man above his origin,
And elevates to heaven the spirit within him,
To which the Almighty's breath gave understanding. . . .

They knew not shame nor honour, yet knew pride:
—The pride of strength, skill, speed, and subtilty;
The pride of tyranny and violence;—
Not o'er the mighty only, whom their arm
Had crush'd in battle, or had basely slain
By treacherous ambush, or more treacherous smiles,
Embracing while they stabb'd the heart that met
Their specious seeming with unguarded breast;
—The reckless savages display'd their pride
By vile oppression in its vilest forms,—
Oppression of the weak and innocent;
Infancy, womanhood, old age, disease,
The lame, the halt, the blind, were wrong'd, neglected,
Exposed to perish by wild beasts in woods,
Cast to the crocodiles in rivers; murder'd,

Even by their dearest kindred, in cold blood,
To rid themselves of Nature's gracious burdens,
In mercy laid on man to teach *him* mercy.

But their prime glory was insane debauch,
To inflict and bear excruciating tortures:
The unshrinking victim, while the flesh was rent
From his live limbs, and eaten in his presence,
Still in his death-pangs taunted his tormentors
With tales of cruelty more diabolic,
Wreak'd by himself upon the friends of those
Who now their impotence of vengeance wasted
On him, and drop by drop his life extorted
With thorns and briars of the wilderness,
Or the slow violence of untouching fire.

Vanity, too, pride's mannikin, here play'd
Satanic tricks to ape her master-fiend.
The leopard's beauteous spoils, the lion's mane,
Engirt the loins and waved upon the shoulders
Of those whose wiles or arms had won such trophies:
Rude-punctured figures of all loathsome things,
Toads, scorpions, asps, snakes' eyes and double tongue,
In flagrant colours on their tattoo'd limbs,
Gave proof of intellect, not dead, but sleeping,
And in its trance enacting strange vagaries.
Bracelets of human teeth, fangs of wild beasts,
The jaws of sharks, and beaks of ravenous birds,
Glitter'd and tinkled round their arms and ankles;
While skulls of slaughter'd enemies, in chains
Of natural elf-locks, dangled from the necks
Of those whose own bare skulls and cannibal teeth
Ere long must deck more puissant fiends than they.

Thomas Campbell

'LINES ON THE DEPARTURE OF EMIGRANTS FOR NEW SOUTH WALES', 1828

———

From the 1820s Australia was thought of increasingly as a colony of white settlement, rather than a mere dumping-ground for transported felons, and the British government began to encourage emigration as a remedy for poverty and unemployment in the United Kingdom. Campbell supported such a policy and this poem gives an extraordinary panoramic view—part epic adventure, part domestic idyll—of the life that emigrants may hope to have in their new country.

On England's shore I saw a pensive band,
With sails unfurled for earth's remotest strand,
Like children parting from a mother, shed
Tears for the home that could not yield them bread.
Grief marked each face receding from the view,
'Twas grief to nature honourably true.
And long, poor wanderers o'er the ecliptic deep,
The song that names but home shall bid you weep;
Oft shall ye fold your flocks by stars above
In that far world, and miss the stars ye love;
Oft, when its tuneless birds scream round forlorn
Regret the lark that gladdens England's morn,
And, giving England's names to distant scenes,
Lament that earth's extension intervenes.

But cloud not yet too long, industrious train,
Your solid good with sorrow nursed in vain:
For has the heart no interest yet as bland
As that which binds us to our native land?
The deep-drawn wish, when children crown our hearth,
To hear the cherub-chorus of their mirth,
Undamped by dread that want may e'er unhouse,
Or servile misery knit those smiling brows;
The pride to rear an independent shed,
And give the lips we love unborrowed bread;
To see a world, from shadowy forests won,
In youthful beauty wedded to the sun;

To skirt our home with harvests widely sown,
And call the blooming landscape all our own,
Our children's heritage, in prospect long—
These are the hopes, high-minded hopes and strong,
That beckon England's wanderers o'er the brine
To realms where foreign constellations shine,
Where streams from undiscovered fountains roll,
And winds shall fan them from th' Antarctic pole.
And what though doomed to shores so far apart
From England's home, that e'en the home-sick heart
Quails, thinking, ere that gulf can be recrossed,
How large a space of fleeting life is lost?
Yet there, by time, their bosoms shall be changed,
And strangers once shall cease to sigh estranged,
But jocund in the year's long sunshine roam
That yields their sickle twice its harvest-home.

There, marking o'er his farm's expanding ring
New fleeces whiten and new fruits upspring,
The grey-haired swain, his grandchild sporting round,
Shall walk at eve his little empire's bound,
Emblazed with ruby vintage, ripening corn,
And verdant rampart of acacian thorn,
While, mingling with the scent his pipe exhales,
The orange-grove's and fig-tree's breath prevails;
Survey with pride beyond a monarch's spoil,
His honest arm's own subjugated soil;
And, summing all the blessings God has given,
Put up his patriarchal prayer to Heaven
That, when his bones shall here repose in peace,
The scions of his love may still increase,
And o'er a land where life has ample room
In health and plenty innocently bloom.

Delightful land! in wildness even benign,
The glorious past is ours, the future thine.
As in a cradled Hercules, we trace
The lines of empire in thine infant face.
What nations in thy wide horizon's span
Shall teem on tracts untrodden yet by man!
What spacious cities with their spires shall gleam,
Where now the panther laps a lonely stream,
And all but brute or reptile life is dumb!
Land of the free! thy kingdom is to come—

Of states, with laws from Gothic bondage burst,
And creeds by chartered priesthoods unaccurst;
Of navies, hoisting their emblazoned flags
Where shipless seas now wash unbeaconed crags;
Of hosts, reviewed in dazzling files and squares,
Their pennoned trumpets breathing native airs,—
For minstrels thou shalt have of native fire,
And maids to sing the songs themselves inspire:
Our very speech, methinks, in after time,
Shall catch th' Ionian blandness of thy clime;
And, whilst the light and luxury of thy skies
Give brighter smiles to beauteous woman's eyes,
The arts, whose soul is love, shall all spontaneous rise.
Untracked in deserts lies the marble mine,
Undug the ore that 'midst thy roofs shall shine;
Unborn the hands—but born they are to be—
Fair Australasia, that shall give to thee
Proud temple-domes, with galleries winding high,
So vast in space, so just in symmetry,
They widen to the contemplating eye,
With colonnaded aisles in long array,
And windows that enrich the flood of day
O'er tesselated pavements, pictures fair,
And nichèd statues breathing golden air.
Nor there, whilst all that's seen bids fancy swell,
Shall music's voice refuse to seal the spell;
But choral hymns shall wake enchantment round,
And organs yield their tempests of sweet sound.

Meanwhile, ere arts triumphant reach their goal,
How blest the years of pastoral life shall roll!
Even should, some wayward hour, the settler's mind
Brood sad on scenes for ever left behind,
Yet not a pang that England's name imparts
Shall touch a fibre of his children's hearts;
Bound to that native land by nature's bond,
Full little shall their wishes rove beyond
Its mountains blue and melon-skirted streams,
Since childhood loved, and dreamt of in their dreams.

How many a name, to us uncouthly wild,
Shall thrill that region's patriotic child,
And bring as sweet thoughts o'er his bosom's chords
As aught that's named in song to us affords!

Dear shall that river's margin be to him
Where sportive first he bathed his boyish limb,
Or petted birds still brighter than their bowers,
Or twined his tame young kangaroo with flowers.
But more magnetic yet to memory
Shall be the sacred spot, still blooming nigh,
The bower of love where first his bosom burned
And smiling passion saw its smile returned.

Go forth and prosper, then, emprising band:
May He, who in the hollow of His hand
The ocean holds, and rules the whirlwind's sweep,
Assuage its wrath, and guide you on the deep!

THOMAS HOOD

'I'M GOING TO BOMBAY', 1832

A gifted and prolific comic writer in prose and verse, Hood (1799–1845) made his career in the vibrant but financially insecure world of early nineteenth-century literary journalism. Among many other ventures, he edited and largely wrote the *Comic Annual* from 1830 to 1839, and *Hood's Own* from 1838. As well as his extensive humorous output, Hood also wrote effective poems on contemporary social issues. His early death was largely brought about by overwork. This poem from the *Comic Annual* dramatizes the situation of a young lady about to leave for Bombay in search of a husband. Changing attitudes in the 1830s ended the common practice whereby British officials and merchants took Indian wives or mistresses: India thereafter became a marriage market for middle-class families with daughters who had failed to find a partner at home.

> My hair is brown, my eyes are blue,
> And reckon'd rather bright;
> I'm shapely, if they tell me true,
> And just the proper height;
> My skin has been admired in verse,
> And called as fair as day—
> If I *am* fair, so much the worse,
> I'm going to Bombay!
>
> At school I passed with some éclât;
> I learned my French in France;
> De Wint gave lessons how to to draw,
> And D'Egville how to dance;—
> Crevelli taught me how to sing,
> And Cramer how to play—
> It really is the strangest thing—
> I'm going to Bombay!

I've been to Bath and Cheltenham Wells,
But not their springs to sip—
To Ramsgate—not to pick up shells,—
To Brighton—not to dip.
I've tour'd the Lakes, and scour'd the coast
From Scarboro' to Torquay—
But tho' of time I've made the most,
I'm going to Bombay!

By Pa and Ma I'm daily told
To marry now's my time,
For though I'm very far from old,
I'm rather in my prime.
They say while we have any sun,
We ought to make our hay—
And India has so hot an one,
I'm going to Bombay!

My cousin writes from Hyderapot
My only chance to snatch,
And says the climate is so hot,
It's sure to light a match.—
She's married to a son of Mars,
With very handsome pay,
And swears I ought to thank my stars
I'm going to Bombay!

She says that I shall much delight
To taste their Indian treats,
But what she likes may turn me quite,
Their strange outlandish meats.—
If I can eat rupees, who knows?
Or dine, the Indian way,
On doolies and on bungalows—
I'm going to Bombay!

She says that I shall much enjoy,—
I don't know what she means,—
To take the air and buy some toy,
In my own palankeens,—
I like to drive my pony-chair,
Or ride our dapple gray—
But elephants are horses there—
I'm going to Bombay!

Farewell, farewell, my parents dear,
My friends, farewell to them!
And oh, what costs a sadder tear,
Good-buy to Mr. M!—
If I should find an Indian vault,
Or fall a tiger's prey,
Or steep in salt, it's all *his* fault,
I'm going to Bombay!

That fine new teak-built ship, the Fox
A, 1—Commander Bird,
Now lying in the London Docks,
Will sail on May the Third;
Apply for passage or for freight,
To Nichol, Scott, and Gray—
Pa has applied and seal'd my fate—
I'm going to Bombay!

My heart is full—my trunks as well;
My mind and caps made up,
My corsets shap'd by Mrs. Bell,
Are promised ere I sup;
With boots and shoes, Rivarta's best,
And dresses by Ducé,
And a special license in my chest—
I'm going to Bombay!

ALFRED TENNYSON

'O MOTHER BRITAIN LIFT THOU UP', 1833–4

As an undergraduate at Cambridge in the 1820s, Tennyson (1809–92) announced his intention of becoming the Great British Poet of the nineteenth century. It was an ambition he fulfilled triumphantly. Although the poetry he published in the early 1830s was adversely reviewed, the two-volume *Poems* of 1842 and *In Memoriam* of 1850 won wide public acclaim. In the latter year, on the death of Wordsworth, he accepted the Laureateship, a role for which he was uniquely equipped. Tennyson's poetry as Laureate, with its central national epic *Idylls of the King*, was written from the very heart of Victorian cultural, social, and religious concerns—among them, of course, the historical identity of Britain and the Empire. In 1884 he was created Baron Tennyson, the first man to be made a peer in recognition of services to the state that were wholly of a literary nature.

In this early poem, not published at the time, Tennyson celebrates the final success of the anti-slavery campaign in 1833, when the ministry of Earl Grey enacted the legislation that formally abolished slavery in all British possessions. The personification of Britain as imperial matriarch benignly granting freedom to her children is an important component in the ideology of the nineteenth-century Empire.

O mother Britain ·lift thou up,
　Lift up a joyful brow,
There lies not in the circled seas
　A land so great as thou.

O let the far-off shores be glad,
　The isles break out in song,
For thou didst buy them with a price
　To ransom them from wrong.

A time may come: this world of men
　Shall roll in broader light,
But never shall this world forget
　Who taught the peoples right.

O let the hills of canes rejoice,
　The palmy valleys ring!
What other people old or young
　Had done so just a thing?

A time may come. Forgotten Thames
　May curve his dreary rounds
By ruined hearths and heaps of brick
　And Babylonian mounds.

But thy good deed shall never die,
　It spreads from shore to shore,
And with the sun and moon renews
　Its light for evermore.

SAMUEL ROGERS

'WRITTEN IN 1834'

In the first half of the nineteenth century Rogers (1763–1855) was a leading figure in London literary circles. His considerable reputation as a poet rested upon a number of long contemplative and descriptive poems, of which *Italy* (1822) was the most acclaimed. Here, in a spirit of national self-congratulation, Rogers manages to celebrate the abolition of slavery as the consummation both of imperial expansion and of victory in the Napoleonic War.

WELL, when her day is over, be it said
That, though a speck on the terrestrial globe,
Found with long search and in a moment lost,
She made herself a name—a name to live
While science, eloquence, and song divine,
And wisdom, in self-government displayed,
And valour, such as only in the Free,
Shall among men be honoured.
       Every sea
Was covered with her sails; in every port
Her language spoken; and, where'er you went,
Exploring, to the east or to the west,
Even to the rising or the setting day,
Her arts and laws and institutes were there,
Moving with silent and majestic march,
Onward and onward, where no path-way was;
There her adventurous sons, like those of old,
Founding vast empires—empires in their turn
Destined to shine thro' many a distant age
With sun-like splendour.
      Wondrous was her wealth,
The world itself her willing tributary;
Yet, to accomplish what her soul desired,
All was as nothing; and the mightiest kings,
Each in his hour of strife exhausted, fallen,
Drew strength from Her, their coffers from her own
Filled to o'erflowing. When her fleets of war
Had swept the main—had swept it and were gone,
Gone from the eyes and from the minds of men,

Their dreadful errands so entirely done—
Up rose her armies; on the land they stood,
Fearless, erect; and in an instant smote
Him with his legions.
               Yet ere long 't was hers,
Great as her triumphs, to eclipse them all,
To do what none had done, none had conceived,
An act how glorious, making joy in Heaven;
When, such her prodigality, condemned
To toil and toil, alas, how hopelessly,
Herself in bonds, for ages unredeemed—
As with a god-like energy she sprung,
All else forgot, and, burdened as she was,
Ransomed the African.

GEORGE BEARD

From *THE HISTORY OF METHODISM* 1840

Beard was a Wesleyan minister whose naïvely written epic poem *The History of Methodism* was composed to celebrate the centenary of the movement. Beard had been a missionary in the West Indies and was directly involved in the evangelical campaign against slavery. In this passage from Book X he records the moment of the abolition of the last vestiges of formal slavery in the Empire on 1 August 1838 and, rather touchingly, recollects the scenes of his own missionary labours.

Oh, 'twas a day of jubilee indeed!
Of joy untold, to see our brethren freed;
The solemn hour of Slavery's funeral knell,
Hark to the sound,—for 'tis the sabbath bell:
The sable tribes, to Sion's courts repair,
The voice of joy, and gladness now is there:
To the Great Source of good, they raise the song,
"Salvation, strength, and pow'r, to God belong,
The glory give we him, with all his saints;
Who turns to shouts of joy, our long complaints:
Revives our souls, and makes us truly free,
Praise be to Him,—the Lord of liberty."

Thanks to the friends of freedom every where,
Who truly sought to pay, the long arrear;
Who faithful stood, and with a gen'rous heart,
Resolv'd the costly blessing to impart.
Thanks to the country, for the noble sum,
No stinted, mean, or paltry minimum.
The nation pours the tribute of her gold,
The sacred rights of freedom, to uphold;
And though impending gloom, her poor surrounds,
Her rich munificence prevails;—abounds. ...

Then lift your eyes, and gaze upon the scene,
The scatter'd churches, of the *Carribean*,
First of our Missions, planted by our COKE,
And now deliver'd from the galling yoke;

Your saved thousands,—glorious recompence,
Repays the ardor, and the love intense,
Of our apostles:—we their work pursue,
In the same spirit, with a zeal anew;
And our posterity, shall still proceed,
To carry on the philanthropic deed;
Unwearied in this all-converting toil,
While Heav'n shall cheer them, with its constant smile.

   Romantic isles! peace to your hills and dales,
Your flowing streamlets, and your fertile vales;
JAMAICA, where my babe's fair relics lie,
Where first I saw the bondman heave the sigh,
Where burning fever, sought to stop my breath,
But God "deliver'd from so great a death."
BAHAMAS too,—among your creeks and rocks,
Days of delight I've spent, with Salem's flocks;
With crowding Saints, on fair ST. VINCENT's isle,
Where hearts rejoice, and sabbaths wear a smile;
And TRINIDAD, where, for three circling years,
The pray'rs of hundreds oft allay'd my fears;
With green GRENADA last, a charming spot,
Where the frail Missionary is not forgot;
Peace to your sons and daughters, peace to you,
Amidst your homes, I found affection true;
Long will fond memory, cherish all the past,
And with retentive tenure hold it fast;
While hope shall point, unto that happy home,
Where pain, and grief, and parting never come;
Then peace within your sacred walls be found,
Prosperity encircle you around;
The richest dews of heaven *my brethren* bless,
Pour down ye skies, the show'r of righteousness;
And let these fields, unto the harvest white,
Regale our hearts with sanctified delight;
From century, to century still increase,
Brighten'd with light, and filled with love and peace;
While myriads rise, harmoniously to sing,
The hallelujah, to our heavenly king.

Richard Chevenix Trench

'Lines Written on the First Tidings of the Cabul Massacres', 1842

Trench (1807–86) was one of the most prolific of Victorian authors. As well as producing a substantial body of poetry, he wrote many works on theology and biblical exegesis, and was one of the outstanding philologists of his day. Remarkably, he combined this energetic authorship with a highly successful career in the Church, where he eventually rose to be Archbishop of Dublin. The subject of this poem is the disastrous British retreat from Kabul in the winter of 1841–2 during the First Afghan War; of nearly 16,000 soldiers and camp followers who set out, one man reached India alive.

> We sat our peaceful hearths beside,
> Within our temples hushed and wide
>   We worshipped without fear:
> With solemn rite, with festal blaze,
> We welcomed in the earliest days
>   Of this new-coming year.
>
> O ye that died, brave hearts and true,
> How in those days it fared with you
>   We did not then surmise;
> That bloody rout which still doth seem
> The fancy of a horrid dream,
>   Was hidden from our eyes:
>
> But haunts us now by day and night
> The vision of that ghastly flight,
>   Its shapes of haggard fear:
> While still from many a mourning home
> The wails of lamentation come,
>   And fill our saddened ear.
>
> O England, bleeding at thy heart
> For thy lost sons, a solemn part
>   Doth Heaven to thee assign.
> High wisdom hast thou need to ask,
> For vengeance is a fearful task,
>   And yet that task is thine.

Oh, then fulfil it, not in pride,
Nor aught to passionate hate allied;
   But know thyself to be
The justicer of righteous Heaven;
That unto thee a work is given,
   A burden laid on thee.

So thine own heart from guilty stains
First cleanse, and then, for what remains,
   That do with all thy might;
That with no faltering hand fulfil,
With no misgiving heart or will,
   As dubious of the right:

That do, not answering wrong for wrong,
But witnessing that truth is strong,
   And, outraged, bringeth woe.
'Tis this by lessons sad and stern,
To men who no way else would learn
   Which thou art set to show.

WILLIAM WORDSWORTH

'ASPECTS OF CHRISTIANITY IN AMERICA', 1842

In 1842 Wordsworth added this set of sonnets to the long series of *Ecclesiastical Sonnets* that he had published first in 1822. They offer a very particular, and partisan, view of the importance of the Anglican Church in the religious development of the United States. While paying due respects to the religious and political freedom of the former colonies, Wordsworth celebrates what he sees as the reliance of the American Episcopal Church upon its continuing communion with the Church of England. Bishop William White, apostrophized in the third sonnet, was particularly active in revitalizing Episcopalianism in the decades following the War of Independence.

I. THE PILGRIM FATHERS

WELL worthy to be magnified are they
Who, with sad hearts, of friends and country took
A last farewell, their loved abodes forsook,
And hallowed ground in which their fathers lay;
Then to the new-found World explored their way,
That so a Church, unforced, uncalled to brook
Ritual restraints, within some sheltering nook
Her Lord might worship and his word obey
In freedom.   Men they were who could not bend;
Blest Pilgrims, surely, as they took for guide
A will by sovereign Conscience sanctified;
Blest while their Spirits from the woods ascend
Along a Galaxy that knows no end,
But in His glory who for Sinners died.

II. CONTINUED

FROM Rite and Ordinance abused they fled
To Wilds where both were utterly unknown;
But not to them had Providence foreshown
What benefits are missed, what evils bred,
In worship neither raised nor limited
Save by Self-will. Lo! from that distant shore,
For Rite and Ordinance, Piety is led
Back to the Land those Pilgrims left of yore,
Led by her own free choice. So Truth and Love
By Conscience governed do their steps retrace.—
Fathers! your Virtues, such the power of grace,
Their spirit, in your Children thus approve.
Transcendent over time, unbound by place,
Concord and Charity in circles move.

III. CONCLUDED.—AMERICAN EPISCOPACY

PATRIOTS informed with Apostolic light
Were they, who, when their Country had been freed,
Bowing with reverence to the ancient creed,
Fixed on the frame of England's Church their sight,
And strove in filial love to reunite
What force had severed. Thence they fetched the seed
Of Christian unity, and won a meed
Of praise from Heaven. To Thee, O saintly WHITE,
Patriarch of a wide-spreading family,
Remotest lands and unborn times shall turn,
Whether they would restore or build—to Thee,
As one who rightly taught how zeal should burn,
As one who drew from our Faith's holiest urn
The purest stream of patient Energy.

ELIZA COOK

'THE ENGLISHMAN', *c.* 1845

———

Of working-class parents and the youngest of eleven children, Cook (1818–89) produced her first collection of poems in 1835. Her verse, homely, sentimental and patriotic, enjoyed considerable success and was widely published in magazines. Between 1849 and 1854 she edited her own periodical, *Eliza Cook's Journal*. 'The Englishman' was extremely popular, its unblushing celebration of national superiority providing an uncomplicated justification for imperial expansion.

THERE's a land that bears a world-known name,
   Though it is but a little spot;
I say 'tis first on the scroll of Fame,
   And who shall say it is not?
Of the deathless ones who shine and live
   In Arms, in Arts, or Song;
The brightest the whole wide world can give,
   To that little land belong.
   'Tis the star of earth, deny it who can;
The island home of an Englishman.

There's a flag that waves o'er every sea,
   No matter when or where;
And to treat that flag as aught but the free
   Is more than the strongest dare.
For the lion-spirits that tread the deck
   Have carried the palm of the brave;
And that flag *may* sink with a shot-torn wreck,
   But never float over a slave;
Its honour is stainless, deny it who can;
And this is the flag of an Englishman.

COOK (c.1845)

There's a heart that leaps with burning glow,
　The wronged and the weak to defend;
And strikes as soon for a trampled foe,
　As it does for a soul-bound friend.
It nurtures a deep and honest love;
　It glows with faith and pride;
And yearns with the fondness of a dove,
　To the light of its own fireside.
'Tis a rich, rough gem, deny it who can;
And this is the heart of an Englishman.

The Briton may traverse the pole or the zone,
　And boldly claim his right;
For he calls such a vast domain his own,
　That the sun never sets on his might.
Let the haughty stranger seek to know
　The place of his home and birth;
And a flush will pour from cheek to brow;
　While he tells his native earth.
For a glorious charter, deny it who can,
Is breathed in the words "I'm an Englishman."

JOHN SHEEHAN

'THE CAMPAIGN OF THE SUTLEJ', *c.*1846

A barrister by profession, Sheehan (1812–82) had a knockabout career in journalism both in Ireland, where he served a term of imprisonment for libel, and London. Under the pen-name 'The Irish Whiskey Drinker', he was one of a group of associated writers who contributed ballads to *Bentley's Miscellany* in the 1840s. Several of these ballads, like this one, celebrated the role of Irish troops in British colonial battles, and did so with brutal vigour wholly devoid of irony. In 1846 the valley of the Sutlej in north west India was the scene of decisive British victories at Aliwal and Sobraon in the First Sikh War, which terminated with the subsequent occupation of Lahore.

HAVE you not heard of the fighting in India, boys?
Sure 'twas at Moodkee a beautiful shindy, boys.
Better than hunting the fox from his cozy shaw
The hunt of the Sikhs from their camp at Ferozeshah.
At Alival, too, we complately astonish'd 'em,
Over the water we coax'd and admonish'd 'em,
Though bullets fly fast as bad eggs in the pillory,—
O we are the boys that can spike their artillery!

CHORUS

Come to the Sutlej, where loud the guns roar, my boys!
Come ere the fun and the fighting's all o'er, my boys!
Come where there's honour and plunder, galore, my boys!
O! who's for a shy at the siege of Lahore, my boys?

Hardinge's a hero; bowld Gough is another, boys,
Don't they call Napier "the divil's own brother," boys?
Ne'er in the East such a gallant commander was
Since on the Indus the great Alexander was.
Under Sir Harry Smith foes we could thump any:
Who'll serve the Queen and the East India Company?
Shew them our soldiers, the right sort of men are all;
Fight for the Crown and the Governor-General.

CHORUS

Come to the Sutlej, &c.

Rid the Ranee of her Punts and her Punches, boys!
Serve them a mouthful of lead for their lunches, boys!
Down at their river we will not stay long, my boys!
Smash into smith'reens their fine *tête-du-pong*, my boys.
If the powther is scarce, and the guns they won't play on it,
Try the cowld steel, and push on with the bayonet!
Once we're safe over, we'll then have a slap at all
Comes in our way, their cash, camels, and capital.

CHORUS

Then come to the Sutlej, where loud the guns roar, my boys!
Come ere the fun and the fighting's all o'er, my boys!
Come where there's honour and plunder, galore, my boys!
O! who's for a shy at the siege of Lahore, my boys?

ALFRED TENNYSON

'FOR THE PENNY-WISE', 1852

In 1851–2 British troops engaged in a war against native Africans in what was then known as Kaffraria—now part of South Africa—suffered a series of humiliating reverses: *The Times* reported that the Africans were equipped with better rifles. In this poem, published unsigned in *Fraser's Magazine* in February 1852, Tennyson waspishly accuses government economic retrenchment of jeopardizing imperial prestige and the lives of British soldiers.

We used to fight the French,
  And beat them, says the story;
But now the cry 're-trench'
  Has a little docked our glory.

We meant to beat the Kaffirs,
  We had the best intentions;
But the Kaffirs knocked us over,
  With the last inventions.

Poor little people, we,
  And in the world belated!
Our musket, as it seems,
  Is superannuated.

Friends! the soldier still
  Is worthy of his calling,
But who are they that want
  A little over-hauling?

ARTHUR HUGH CLOUGH

'COLUMBUS', written 1852

Reacting against the remorseless moral intensity of his education at Thomas Arnold's Rugby, Clough (1819–61) developed into a decidedly unusual Victorian poet—dubious about religion, ironic about many issues which his contemporaries approached with high seriousness. His relatively early death inspired the elegy 'Thyrsis' by his friend and fellow-poet, Matthew Arnold. Here, characteristically quizzical, Clough looks at one of the founding figures of Western imperial expansion, Christopher Columbus.

How in God's name did Columbus get over
   Is a pure wonder to me, I protest,
Cabot, and Raleigh too, that well-read rover,
   Frobisher, Dampier, Drake, and the rest.
      Bad enough all the same,
      For them that after came,
      But, in great Heaven's name,
      How *he* should ever think
      That on the other brink,
Of this wild waste terra firma should be,
Is a pure wonder, I must say, to me.

How a man ever should hope to get thither,
   E'en if he knew that there was another side;
But to suppose he should come any whither,
   Sailing straight on into chaos untried,
      In spite of the motion
      Across the whole ocean,
      To stick to the notion
      That in some nook or bend
      Of a sea without end
He should find North and South America,
Was a pure madness, indeed I must say, to me.

What if wise men had, as far back as Ptolemy,
  Judged that the earth like an orange was round,
None of them ever said, Come along, follow me,
  Sail to the West, and the East will be found.
      Many a day before
      Ever they'd come ashore,
      From the "San Salvador,"
      Sadder and wiser men
      They'd have turned back again;
And that *he* did not, but did cross the sea,
Is a pure wonder, I must say, to me.

CHARLES MACKAY

From 'THE EMIGRANTS', 1856

Few people were more central to the development of a literary mass market in the nineteenth century than was Mackay (1814–89): as well as being a highly successful journalist, he produced poems and songs, novels, popular history and topography, anthologies and miscellanies. Many of his songs—first collected in 1856—appeared between 1851 and 1855 with music by Sir Henry Bishop in supplements to the *Illustrated London News*, of which Mackay was editor. Among them was 'The Emigrants', a very popular set of twelve songs celebrating the new life promised by emigration to Canada: the songs follow a sketchy narrative sequence which begins with embarkation and ends with the settlers being joined by friends and relations from the old country.

'CHEER, BOYS! CHEER!'

CHEER, boys! cheer! no more of idle sorrow,
  Courage, true hearts, shall bear us on our way!
Hope points before, and shows the bright to-morrow,
  Let us forget the darkness of to-day!
So farewell, England! Much as we may love thee,
  We'll dry the tears that we have shed before;
Why should we weep to sail in search of fortune?
  So farewell, England! farewell evermore!
      Cheer, boys! cheer! for England, mother England!
        Cheer, boys! cheer! the willing strong right hand,
      Cheer, boys! cheer! there's work for honest labour—
        Cheer, boys! cheer!—in the new and happy land!

Cheer, boys! cheer! the steady breeze is blowing,
　To float us freely o'er the ocean's breast;
The world shall follow in the track we're going,
　The star of empire glitters in the west.
Here we had toil and little to reward it,
　But there shall plenty smile upon our pain,
And ours shall be the mountain and the forest,
　And boundless prairies ripe with golden grain.
　　　　Cheer, boys! cheer! for England, mother England!
　　　　Cheer, boys! cheer! united heart and hand!—
　　　　Cheer, boys! cheer! there's wealth for honest labour—
　　　　Cheer, boys! cheer!—in the new and happy land!

'FAR, FAR UPON THE SEA'

　　　Far, far upon the sea,
　　　The good ship speeding free,
Upon the deck we gather young and old;
　　　And view the flapping sail,
　　　Spreading out before the gale,
Full and round without a wrinkle or a fold:
　　　Or watch the waves that glide
　　　By the stately vessel's side,
And the wild sea-birds that follow through the air.
　　　Or we gather in a ring,
　　　And with cheerful voices sing,
'Oh! gaily goes the ship when the wind blows fair.'

　　　Far, far upon the sea,
　　　With the sunshine on our lee,
We talk of pleasant days when we were young,
　　　And remember, though we roam,
　　　The sweet melodies of home—
The songs of happy childhood which we sung.
　　　And though we quit her shore,
　　　To return to it no more,
Sound the glories that Britannia yet shall bear;
　　　That 'Britons rule the waves,'
　　　'And never shall be slaves.'
'Oh! gaily goes the ship when the wind blows fair.'

Far, far upon the sea,
Whate'er our country be,
The thought of it shall cheer us as we go.
And Scotland's sons shall join,
In the song of 'Auld lang Syne,'
With voice by memory soften'd, clear and low.
And the men of Erin's Isle,
Battling sorrow with a smile,
Shall sing 'St Patrick's Morning,' void of care;
And thus we pass the day,
As we journey on the way;—
'Oh! gaily goes the ship when the wind blows fair.'

'THE PIONEERS'

ROUSE! brothers, rouse! we've far to travel,
Free as the winds we love to roam,
Far through the prairie, far through the forest,
Over the mountains we'll find a home.
We cannot breathe in crowded cities,
We're strangers to the ways of trade;
We long to feel the grass beneath us,
And ply the hatchet and the spade.

Meadows and hills and ancient woodlands
Offer us pasture, fruit, and corn;
Needing our presence, courting our labour;—
Why should we linger like men forlorn?
We love to hear the ringing rifle,
The smiting axe, the falling tree;—
And though our life be rough and lonely,
If it be honest, what care we?

Fair elbow-room for men to thrive in!
Wide elbow-room for work or play!
If cities follow, tracing our footsteps,
Ever to westward shall point our way!
Rude though our life, it suits our spirit,
And new-born States in future years
Shall own us founders of a nation—
And bless the hardy Pioneers.

'UP THE STREAM! THROUGH THE WOOD!'

Up the stream! through the wood! Winter is past,
Hush'd is the cold angry voice of the blast;
Soft blow the breezes, and bright shines the day;
The fountains are gushing, the roses are blushing,
And rivers are rushing; away, lads, away!
Unruffled and blue, with the light on her breast,
Lake Erie lies calm, like an ocean at rest.
So gather, make ready, with rifle and bow,
And up the stream! through the woods! row, my lads, row!

Up the stream, through the wood, thousands of miles!
Breasting the rapids, and rounding the isles;
Ours is the wilderness, come when we may,
Teeming with treasure, and all for our pleasure,—
Our pleasure and profit; away, lads, away!
The nuggets we find are the squirrel and coon,
The beaver and white wolf that howls to the moon;
So gather, make ready, with rifle and bow,
And up the stream! through the woods! row, my lads, row!

Up the stream, through the wood, hardy and bold,—
'Twould curb our free souls to go digging for gold;
There's wealth in the forest—black, white, brown, and gray;
Our sport is to find it, and danger—who'd mind it?
'Tis danger gives pleasure—away, lads, away!
The full-bosom'd rivers flow merrily on;
The summer is short, 'tis our time to be gone;
So gather, make ready, with rifle and bow,
And up the stream! through the woods! row, my lads, row!

'LONG PARTED HAVE WE BEEN'

LONG parted have we been,
With an ocean wide between,
Since the weary day we left them on our good old English shore,
And we took a last farewell, to return to them no more.
  But they're coming, coming, coming,
    They are coming with the flowers,
  They are coming with the summer,
    To this new land of ours:
        And we'll all forget our sadness,
        And shake their hands with gladness,
And bid them joyous welcome to this new land of ours.

How often have we pray'd
They were here, both youth and maid,
The friends, the dear relations, and the lover fond and true,
To share our better fortune, and all the joys we knew.
  And they're coming, coming, coming,
    They are coming with the flowers,
  They are coming with the summer,
    To this new land of ours:
        And we'll give them cordial greeting,
        And have a merry meeting,
And a day of true rejoicing in this new land of ours.

In all our happiness
There seem'd a joy the less,
When we look'd around and miss'd them from the fireside's
    cheerful glow—
The old familiar comrades that we loved so long ago.
  But they're coming, coming, coming,
    They are coming with the flowers,
  They are coming with the summer,
    To this new land of ours:
        It needs but their embraces,
        And all their smiling faces,
To make us quite contented in this new land of ours.

PUNCH

First published in 1841 and running unbroken for nearly a century and a half, *Punch; or The London Charivari* was one of the most successful of all British periodicals. In format a weekly miscellany with topical commentary, humour and satire, in a mixture of prose, verse and cartoons, *Punch* rapidly became a cultural institution. Among its Victorian contributors were Mayhew, Thackeray, Jerrold and Grossmith, with Doyle, Leech, Tenniel, Du Maurier and Furniss among its many outstanding graphic artists. Under its four Victorian editors—Mark Lemon, Shirley Brooks, Tom Taylor and Francis Burnand—*Punch*'s political stance was broadly aligned with Gladstonian Liberalism and the values of bourgeois progress, though this shifted towards Conservatism in the last years of the century.

Punch's coverage of international affairs increased from the late 1840s, but it showed little interest in the Empire until the outbreak of the Indian Mutiny in 1857. Led by Sepoys—native troops in the employ of the East India Company—the speed with which the Mutiny spread, and the ease of its early successes, shook British public opinion. Injured self-esteem was replaced by something close to hysteria with the news of atrocities, the worst of which was the massacre of European women and children at Cawnpore. The suppression of the rebellion that followed had a viciousness unparalleled by any other episode in the Victorian Empire. Much of the blame for the Mutiny was subsequently placed upon official inaction and mismanagement by the East India Company. In this parody of Longfellow's 'Excelsior!', *Punch* attacks the government complacency that had ignored signs of the impending uprising.

THE price of funds was falling fast
When through the Commons' Lobby, past
A youth who grasped as firm as ice
This Ministerial device:
　　What Gammon!

His gills were stiff, his snowy hand,
Wore DENT's best kids we understand,
And like a penny-trumpet rung
The accents of that cheerful tongue:
    What Gammon!

In happy homes he'd seen the light
Of household mirth extinguished quite,
The storm-cloud gathered fast the while,
But still he muttered with a smile:
    What Gammon!

"Oh, stay!" one member said, "and think!
We stand upon an awful brink!"
He gently closed his left blue eye,
But still he answered with a sigh:
    What Gammon!

"Try not that dodge," another said,
"Dark lowers the tempest overhead;
The mutiny's spreading far and wide."
But still that cheerful voice replied:
    What Gammon!

Beware the Sepoy's pampered mood!
Beware our helpless womanhood!
This was the Opposition's cry,
A voice replied: "That's all my eye:
    And Gammon!"

Next day the wires electric bore
A horrid tale from red Cawnpore;
Still muttered by the Speaker's chair,
That youth with somewhat startled air:
    What Gammon!

True to his scent, as faithful hound,
That youth our own reporter found,
Still clenching in his grasp of ice,
That Ministerial device:
    What Gammon!

There, smoothing down his bran new hat,
Lifeless, but elegant he sat,
And 'mid the death-knell booming far,
A voice fell from that falling star:
    What Gammon!

CHRISTINA ROSSETTI

'IN THE ROUND TOWER AT JHANSI.
8 JUNE 1857'

For many years Rossetti (1830–94) was best known for her devotional poetry and verse for children, but the psychological depth, the particular inwardness, of her work is now increasingly recognized. Like other Victorian women poets she wrote very little on any matter connected with the Empire, and it is revealing that she was drawn to the particular incident from the Indian Mutiny that this poem dramatizes. The tragic couple involved were the British political agent at Jhansi, Captain Alexander Skene, and his wife.

A HUNDRED, a thousand to one; even so;
　　Not a hope in the world remained:
The swarming howling wretches below
　　Gained and gained and gained.

Skene looked at his pale young wife.
　　'Is the time come?'—'The time is come.'
Young, strong, and so full of life,
　　The agony struck them dumb.

Close his arm about her now,
　　Close her cheek to his,
Close the pistol to her brow—
　　God forgive them this!

'Will it hurt much?'—'No, mine own:
　　I wish I could bear the pang for both.'—
'I wish I could bear the pang alone:
　　Courage, dear, I am not loth.'

Kiss and kiss: 'It is not pain
　　Thus to kiss and die.
One kiss more.'—'And yet one again.'—
　　'Good-bye.'—'Good-bye.'

PUNCH

'OUR ARMY OF MARTYRS', 13 FEBRUARY 1858

Once the Mutiny had been put down and the East India Company abolished, the whole purpose of the British presence in India needed to be redefined. In a poem that anticipates something of the late Victorian rhetoric of imperial destiny, *Punch* claims that colonial rule is about far more than narrow economic interests—though quite what remains conveniently vague.

FOR what have all the martyrs died
    On India's crimson plains,
Now streaming with the generous tide,
    Outpoured from heroes' veins,
Where gallant NICHOLSON and NEILL
    Have found a soldier's grave,
And though unscathed by shot or steel,
    Fell HAVELOCK good and brave?

Were they whom hosts of orphans weep,
    Whom crowds of widows mourn,
In peace that we may eat and sleep
    From friends and kinsfolk torn?
Their toils, their pains, did they endure,
    And were their lives but sold,
That we might life enjoy secure,
    Whilst they in death are cold.

That we might safely count our gains,
    Increasing day by day,
Only for that, are their remains
    Now mouldering into clay?
That wealth, with unabated flood,
    To England's shores might flow,
Shed they alone their noble blood,
    And are they lying low?

Laid they their lives down but for this,
   That Commerce might pursue
Her thriving course, and rich men miss
   No doit of revenue?
Of pompous wealth, of mere purse-pride
   The champions, did they fall?
If so, they martyrs only died
   To Mammon after all.

Not so; those martyrs' blood, we trust,
   To better purpose sown,
Will not have sunk in Indian dust,
   To bear such fruit alone:
The blood of martyrs is a seed
   Whence springs another crop,
Our heroes were designed to bleed
   For something more than Shop.

Alfred Comyn Lyall

'RAJPOOT REBELS', written c.1858

For over thirty years Lyall (1835–1911) was a distinguished administrator in British India, and subsequently a member of the India Council in London. Many of the poems in his *Verses Written in India*—published in 1889 but composed over a number of years—reflect his personal knowledge of the Mutiny and its aftermath, and, as here, his sympathy with the native cultures that the Raj suppressed.

On the Sardah, 1858

WHERE the mighty cliffs are frowning
    Far o'er the torrents fall,
And the pine and the oak stand crowning
    The ridges of high Nepaul,

Sat twenty Rajpoot rebels,
    Haggard and pale and thin,
Lazily chucking the pebbles
    Into the foaming lynn.

Their eyes were sunken and weary,
    With a sort of listless woe
They looked from their desolate eyrie
    Over the plains below.

They turned from the mountain breezes
    And shivered with cold and damp,
They were faint with the fierce diseases
    Of the deadly jungle swamp.

Two had wounds from a sabre
    And one from an Enfield ball,
But no one cared for his neighbour,
    There was sickness or wounds on all.

The Rajpoot leader rose then
    Stiffly and slow from the ground,
He looked at the camp of his foes then,
    And he looked at his brethren round;

And he said: 'From my country driven
  'With the last of my hunted band,
'My home to another given,
  'On a foreign soil I stand.

'They have burnt every roof in the village,
  'They have slain the best of my kin,
'They have ruined and burnt and pillaged,
  'And yet we had done no sin;

'Our clans were heady and rude,
  'Our robbers many and tall,
'But our fighting never shed English blood,
  'Nor harried an English hall.

'The king took tithe if he might;
  'He was paid by a knave or a fool;
'For we held our lands on a firmer right
  'Than is given by parchment rule;

'Our fathers of old had cleared it
  'From the jungle with axe and sword,
'Our ancient rights had endeared it
  'To him who was chief and lord.

'Our father's curse with our father's land,
  'Like the wrath of a great god's blow
'May it fall on the head and the iron hand
  'And the heart of our English foe.

'As our fathers fought, we fight;
  'But a sword and a matchlock gun,
''Gainst the serried line of bayonets bright
  'A thousand moving like one!

'From the banks of Ganges holy,
  'From the towers of fair Lucknow,
'They have driven us surely and slowly,
  'They have crushed us blow on blow.

———

'When the army has slain its fill,
  'When they bid the hangman cease;
'They will beckon us down from the desert hill
  'To go to our homes in peace.

'To plough with a heavy heart,
  'And, of half our fields bereft,
''Gainst the usurer's oath, and the lawyer's art
  'To battle that some be left.

'At the sight of an English face
  'Loyally bow the head,
'And cringe like slaves to the surly race
  'For pay and a morsel of bread;

'Toil like an ox or a mule
  'To earn the stranger his fee—
'Our sons may brook the Feringhee's rule,
  'There is no more life for me!'

PUNCH

Indian revenues were exhausted after the Mutiny. Here *Punch* argues that centuries of commercial rapacity, not least by the British, should now give way to an enlightened policy of long-term investment and development. The poem's informing metaphor projects such future British rule as a type of benign imperial husbandry.

THE Land of Ind! the wondrous land—
　　The land of wealth from times of old:
Where pearls lay basking on the sand,
　　And golden waves Pactolus rolled;
Where in Golconda's darkling mines,
The diamond's buried sun-light shines.

India—a Queen of grace inert,
　　All golden-scarfed and jewel-crowned;
Her waist, with gem-like shawls engirt,
　　Her wrists and ancles silver-bound—
How rich and rare a prize was she,
Beneath the full Pagoda Tree!

Those long and lustrous eyes alone,
　　Those odorous streams of silken hair,
That waist which mocked the tiny zone,
　　Those hands and feet so small and fair,
All these were charms to tempt and please,
But wooers sought her not for these.

None came to woo—all came to win;
　　The stalwart Rajpoot calm and proud,
The polished Greek with whiter skin,
　　The flat-faced Mongol's roving crowd,
The Moslem Arab, swart and spare,
The daring Briton—all were there.

Upon the maid by turns they fell,
　　Each rent his share of gauds away;
But as he turned his gains to tell,
　　Another came to wrest the prey;
And she sat by and watched the strife—
The robber's prize, the victor's wife.

Wife of a bed still wet with tears:
　　Cursed or caressed, the slave of scorn;
The gold wrenched from her bleeding ears;
　　From her bruised wrists the bangles torn:
Her gems and gem-like shawls a prize,
For grasping hands and hungry eyes.

What if poor India groaned and gasped
　　Beneath each ruffian plund'rer's knee?
Enough for him that he had grasped,
　　His bough of the Pagoda Tree,
And shook and shook its golden shower—
Poor India's fair and fatal dower.

The Briton too has played *his* part
　　Of plund'rer, 'mong the Pagan horde,
As keen of hand, as hard of heart,
　　As proud and pitiless a Lord;
Hath turn'd from India's prayer and plea,
To grasp at the Pagoda Tree.

None shook so long; none shook so well;
　　No stronger hand e'er grasped its bough;
But less and less the fruit that fell,
　　Though flushed the shaker's knitted brow—
His sweat flows fast, his gripe is grim;
But the tree yields no more for *him*!

Enough—too much—of work like this:
　　Work ill-repaid as ill-begun;
'Tis time to right what is amiss;
　　Time India's wrong should be undone:
Time to admit, if hers the soil,
'Tis ours to save, as well as spoil.

Ours as we boast a Christian creed,
   Ours as a righteous law we own,
To trample down usurping Greed,
   And set up Justice on its throne;
The poor Pagoda Tree to spare,
Or in its crop let India share.

To act the truth we speak—that fruit
   Comes not by shaking of the tree,
But digging deep about its root,
   Manuring wisely, pruning free;
So shall poor India's woeful dower,
To her be joy, to us be power;
So full of fruitage we shall see,
For aye, the broad Pagoda Tree!

GERALD MASSEY

From *HAVELOCK'S MARCH*, 1860

———

Massey (1828–1907) was a working-class poet, the self-educated
son of a canal boatman, and much of his early poetry was
written in support of the Chartist movement. This radicalism,
increasingly tempered after 1850 by Christian Socialism, seems
not to have diminished Massey's support for British interests
overseas, for he wrote patriotic poems about both the Crimean
War and the Indian Mutiny. Among these latter, *Havelock's
March* was the most ambitious, and was one of the few poems
contemporary to the Mutiny that attempted to give it an epic
dimension. The story of the long march to relieve Cawnpore and
Lucknow, here supposedly told by the father of one of the
participants, became a heroic set-piece of imperialist history,
and Sir Henry Havelock one of the martyrs of Empire. The
poem also captures something of the brutality that characterized
both sides during the Mutiny, though the slaughter perpetrated
by British troops is excused as retributive justice.

As the Mutiny breaks out, British soldiers and civilians, wholly
unprepared, are massacred.

"The stillness of a brooding storm lay on that Eastern land;
The dark death-circle narrowed round our little English band:
The false Sepoy stooped lower for his spring, and in his eye
A bloody light was burning on them, as he glided by:
Old Horrors rose, and leered at them, from out the tide of time,—
The peering peaks of War's old world, whose brows were stained
    with crime!
The conscious Silence was but dumb, a cursèd Plot to hide;
The darkness only a mask of Death, ready to slip aside.
Under the leafy palms they lay, and through their gay green crown
Our English saw no Storm roll up: no Fate swift-flaming down.

"At last it came. The Rebel drum was heard at dead of night:
They dashed in dust the only torch that showed the face of Right!
Once more the Devil clutches at his lost throne of the earth,
And sends a people, smit with plague of madness, howling forth.

As in a Demon's dream they swarm from horrible hiding-nooks;
Red Murder stabs the air, and lights their way with maddening
    looks!
Snuffing the smell of human blood, the cruel Moloch stands;
Hearing the cry of '*Kill! Kill! Kill!*' and claps his gory hands.
At dead of night, while England slept, the fearful vision came,
She looked, and with a dawn of hell the East was all aflame. ...

"They slew the grizzled Warrior, who to them had been so true;
The ruddy stripling with frank eyes of bonny northern blue;
They slew the Maiden as she slept; the Mother great with child;
The Babe, that smiled up in their face, they stabbed it as it smiled!
The piteous, pleading, hoary hair they draggled in red mire;
And mocked the dying as they dashed out, frantic from the fire,
To fall upon their Tulwars, hacked to Death; the bayonet
Held up some child; the demons danced around it writhing yet:
Warm flesh, that kindled so with life, was torn, and slowly hewn,
To daintiest morsels for the feast where Death began too soon.

"Our English girls, whose sweet red blood went dancing on
    its way,
A merry marriage-maker quick for its near wedding-day,—
All life awaiting for the breath of Love's sweet south to blow,
And budding bridal roses ripe with secret balms to flow,—
They stripped them naked as they were born; naked along the
    street,
In their own blood they made them dip their delicate white feet:
With some last rag of shelter the poor helpless darling tries
To hide her from the cruel hell of those devouring eyes;
Then, plucking at the skirts of Death, she prayerfully doth cling,
To hide her from the eyes that still gloat round her in a ring. ...

Havelock addresses his troops and begins the march to relieve
Cawnpore.

" 'Now, Soldiers of our England, let your love arise in power;
For never yet was greater need than in this awful hour:
Together stand like old true hearts that never fear nor flinch;
With feet that have been shod for death, never to yield an inch.
Our Empire is a Ship on fire, before a howling wind,
With such a smoke of torment, as might make high heaven blind!
Wild Ruin waves his flag of flame, and ye must spring on deck,
And quench the fire in blood, and save our treasures from the wreck.'
Many a time has England thought she sent her bravest forth;
But never went more gallant men of more heroic worth.

"Hungry and lean, through rain and mire, our War-wolves
      ravening go
On their long march, that shall not mete the red grave of the foe:
Like winter trees stripped to their naked strength of heart and arm,
That glory in their grimness as they tussle with the storm!
Only a handful few and stern, and few and stern their words;
Strange meaning in their eyes that meet and strike out sparks
      like swords!
And there goes Havelock, leading the Forlorn Hope of our land:
The quick heart spurring at their side; the banner of their band:
Kindled, but calm, along their ranks his steady eye doth run,
As Marksman seeks the death-line down the level of his gun. . . .

Arriving in Cawnpore, Havelock's soldiers find the city fallen,
discover the scene of the massacre of the women and children,
and vow revenge.

"Cawnpore was ghastly silent, as into it they stepped;
There stood the blackened Ruin that the brave old Soldier kept!
Where strained each ear for the English cheer, and stretched the
      wan wide eyes,
Through all that awful night to see the signal-rocket rise;
No tramp, no cheer of Brothers near; no distant Cannon's boom;
Nothing but death goes to and fro betwixt the glare and gloom.
The living remnant try to hold their bit of blood-stained ground;
Dark gaps continual in their midst; the dead all lying round;
And saddest corpses still are those that die, and do not die:
With just a little glimmering light of life to show them by.

"Each drop of water cost a wound to fetch it from the well;
The father heard his crying child and went, but surely fell.
They had drunk all their tears, and now dry agony drank their
      blood;
The sand was killing in their souls; the wind a fiery flood;
Oh, for one waft of heather-breath from off a Scottish wold!
One shower that makes our English leaves smile greener for its
      gold!
Then life drops inward from the eyes; turns upward with last
      prayer,
To look for its deliverance; the only way lies there:
And then triumphant Treachery made leap each trusting heart,
Like some poor Bird called from the nest, up-poising for the dart.

"'*Come, let us pray*,' their Chaplain said. No other boon was
 craved:
No pleading word for mercy sued; no face the white flag waved;
But all grasped hands and prayed, till peace their souls serenely
 filled;
Then like our noble Martyrs, there they stood up, and were killed.
Only One Saved!
 He led our soldiers to the House of Blood;
An eager, panting, cursing crew! but stricken dumb they stood
In silence that was breathlessness of vengeance infinite;
A-many wept like women who were fiercest in the fight:
There grew a look in human eyes as though a wild beast came
Up in them at that scent of blood and glared devouring flame.

"All the Babes and Women butchered! all the dear ones dead;
The story of their martyrdom in lines of awful red!
The blood-black floor, the clotted gore, fair tresses, deep
 sword-dints;
Last message-scrawl upon the wall; and tiny finger-prints:
Gathered in one were all strange sights of horror and despair,
That make the vision blood-shot, freeze the life, or lift the hair.
Faces to faces flashed hell-fire!   Oh, but they felt 'twould take
The very cup of God's own wrath, that gasping thirst to slake:
For many a day '*Cawnpore*' was hissed, and, at its word of guilt,
The slaying sword went merciless, right ruddy to the hilt. ...

The British troops storm Lucknow and fight their way to the
garrison besieged in the Residency.

"The masked artillery raked the road, and ploughed them front
 and flank;
Some gallant fellow every step was stricken from the rank;
But, as he staggered, in his place another sternly stepped;
And, firing fast as they could load, their onward way they kept.
Now, give them the good bayonet! with England's sternest foes,
Strong arm, cold steel has done it, in the wildest, bloodiest close:
And now their Bayonets flash in forks of Lightning up the ridge,
And with a cheer they take the guns, another, clear the bridge.
One good home-thrust! and surely, as the dead in doom are sure,
They send them where that British cheer can trouble them no
 more.

"The fire is biting bitterly; onward the battle rolls;
Grim Death is glaring at them, from ten thousand hiding-holes;
Death stretches up from earth to heaven, spreading his darkness
        round;
Death piles the heaps of helplessness face downward to the ground;
Death flames from sudden Ambuscades, where all was still and
        dark;
Death swiftly speeds on whizzing wings the bullets to their mark;
Death from the doors and windows, all around and overhead,
Darts, with his cloven fiery tongues, incessant, quick, and red:
Death everywhere, Death in all sounds, and, through its smoke of
        breath,
Victory beckons at the end of long dark lanes of death.

"Another charge, another cheer, another Battery won!
And in a whirlwind of fierce fire the fight went roaring on
Into the very heart of hell: with Comrades falling fast,
Through all that tempest terrible, the glorious remnant passed.
No time to help a dear old friend: but where the wounded fell,
They knew it was all over, and they looked a last farewell.
And dying eyes, slow-setting in a cold and stony stare,
Turned upward, saw a map of murder scribbled on the air
With crossing flames; and others read their fiery fearful fate,
In dark, swart faces waiting for them, whitening with their hate.

"But, proudly men will march to death, when Havelock leads
        them on:
Through all the storm he sat his horse as he were cut in stone!
But now his look grows dark; his eye gleams with uneasy flash:
'On, for the Residency, we must make a last brave dash.'
And on dashed Highlander and Sikh through a sea of fire and
        steel,
On, with the lion of their strength, our first in glory, Niel!
It seemed the face of heaven grew black, so close it held its breath,
Through all the glorious agony of that long march of death.
The round shot tears, the bullets rain; dear God, outspread Thy
        shield!
Put forth Thy red right arm, for them, Thy sword of sharpness
        wield!

Following the relief of Lucknow, Havelock dies as a Christian
martyr whose example, with that of his troops, will be an inspira-
tion to all future soldiers of the Empire.

"The Warrior may be ripe for rest, and laurelled with great deeds,
But till their work be done, no rest for those whom God yet needs:
Whether in rivers of ruin their onward way they tear,
Or healing waters trembling with the beauty that they bear;
Blasting or blessing they must on: on, on, for ever on!
Divine unrest is in their breast, until their work is done.
Nor is it all a pleasant path the sacred band must tread,
With life a summer holiday, and death a downy bed!
They wear away with noble use, they drink the tearful cup;
And they must bear the Cross who are bidden with the Christ
      to sup.

"Each day his face grew thinner, and sweeter, saintlier grew
The smiling soul that every day was burning keenlier through.
And higher, each day higher, did the life-flame heavenward climb,
Like sad sweet sunshine up the wall, that for the sunset time
Seems watching till the signal that shall call it hence is given;
Even so his spirit kept the watch, till beckoned home to heaven.
His work was done, his eyes with peace were soft and satisfied;
War-worn and wasted, in the arms of Victory he died.
'Havelock's dead,' and darkness fell on every upturned face;
The shadow of an Angel passing from its earthly place.

"In the red pass of peril, with a fame shall never dim,
Died Havelock, the Good Soldier: who would not die like him?
In grandest strength he fell, full-length; and now our hero climbs
To those who stood up in their day and spoke with after times:
There on the battlements of Heaven, they watch us, looking back
To see the blessing flow for those who follow in their track.
He smileth from his heaven now; the Martyr with his palm;
The wary warrior's tired life is crowned with starry calm.
On many sailing through the storm another star shall shine,
And they shall look up through the night and conquer at the
      sign. ...

"Joy to old England! she has stuff for storm-sail and for stay,
While she can breed such heroes, in her quiet, homely way:
Such martial souls that go with grim, war-figured brows pulled
      down,
As men that are resolved to bear Death's heavy, iron crown.

So long as she has sons like these, no foe shall make her bow,
While Ocean washes her white feet; Heaven kisses her fair brow.
If India's fate had rested on each single saviour soul,
They would have kept their grasp of it till we regained the whole.
The Lightnings of that bursting Cloud, which were to blast our
    might,
But served to show its majesty clear in the sterner light.

"Our England towers up beautiful with her dilating form,
To greater stature in the strife, and glory in the storm;
Her wrath's great wine-press trodden on so many vintage fields,
With crush and strain, and press of pain, a ripened spirit yields,
To warm us in our winter, when the times are coward and cold,
And work divinely in young veins: wake boyhood in the old.
Behold her flame from field to field on Victory's chariot wheels,
Till to its den, bleeding to death, Rebellion backwards reels.
Her Martyrs are avenged! ye may search that Indian land,
And scarcely find a single soul of all the traitor band.

"We've many a nameless Hero lying in his unknown grave,
Their life's gold fragment glinting but a sun-fleck on the wave.
But rest, you unknown, noble dead! our Living are one hand
Of England's power; but, with her Dead she grasps into the land.
The flower of our Race shall make that Indian desert bud,
Its shifting sands drench firm, and fertilize with English blood.
In many a country they sleep crowned, our conquering, faithful
    Dead:
They pave our path where shines her sun of empire overhead;
They circle in a glorious ring, with which the world is wed,
And where their blood has turned to bloom, our England's Rose
    is red.

WILLIAM ALLINGHAM

From *LAWRENCE BLOOMFIELD IN IRELAND*, 1864

Born into the Protestant minority at Ballyshannon, County
Donegal, Allingham (1824–89) spent his early life in Ireland,
working for the Customs Service. But his chief allegiance was to
English literature, particularly poetry, and after moving to
England in 1863 he became a central figure in London literary
circles. He was well placed to observe the increasingly bitter
struggle between landlords and tenants in Ireland, the subject of
this poem. The Irish land question greatly exercised Gladstone,
who quoted Allingham's poem approvingly in the House of
Commons. Sections I and VIII are included here.

I LORD CRASHTON

Joining Sir Ulick's at the river's bend,
Lord Crashton's acres east and west extend;
Great owner here, in England greater still.
As poor folk say, 'The world's divided ill.'
On every pleasure men can buy with gold
He surfeited, and now, diseased and old,
He lives abroad; a firm in Molesworth Street
Doing what their attorneyship thinks meet.
The rule of seventy properties have they.
Wide waves the meadow on a summer day,
Far spread the sheep across the swelling hill,
And horns and hooves the daisied pasture fill;
A stout and high enclosure girdles all,
Built up with stones from many a cottage wall;
And, thanks to Phinn and Wedgely's thrifty pains,
Not one unsightly ruin there remains.
Phinn comes half-yearly, sometimes with a friend,
Who writes to Mail or Warder to commend
These vast improvements, and bestows the term
Of 'Ireland's benefactors' on the firm,
A well-earn'd title, in the firm's own mind.
Twice only in the memory of mankind
Lord Crashton's proud and noble self appear'd;
Up-river, last time, in his yacht he steer'd,
With Maltese valet and Parisian cook,
And one on whom askance the gentry look,

Altho' a pretty, well-dress'd demoiselle—
Not Lady Crashton, who as gossips tell,
Goes her own wicked way. They stopp'd a week;
Then, with gay ribbons fluttering from the peak,
And snowy skirts spread wide, on either hand
The Aphrodite curtsied to the land,
And glided off. My Lord, with gouty legs,
Drinks Baden-Baden water, and life's dreg's,
With cynic jest inlays his black despair,
And curses all things from his easy chair.

VIII   THE EVICTION

In early morning twilight, raw and chill,
Damp vapours brooding on the barren hill,
Through miles of mire in steady grave array
Threescore well arm'd police pursue their way;
Each tall and bearded man a rifle swings,
And under each greatcoat a bayonet clings;
The Sheriff on his sturdy cob astride
Talks with the chief, who marches by their side,
And, creeping on behind them, Paudeen Dhu
Pretends his needful duty much to rue.
Six big-boned labourers, clad in common frieze,
Walk in the midst, the Sheriff's staunch allies;
Six crowbar men, from distant county brought,—
Orange, and glorying in their work, 'tis thought,
But wrongly,—churls of Catholics are they,
And merely hired at half a crown a day.

The hamlet clustering on its hill is seen,
A score of petty homesteads, dark and mean;
Poor always, not despairing until now;
Long used, as well as poverty knows how,
With life's oppressive trifles to contend.
This day will bring its history to an end.
Moveless and grim against the cottage walls
Lean a few silent men: but some one calls
Far off; and then a child 'without a stitch'
Runs out of doors, flies back with piercing screech,
And soon from house to house is heard the cry
Of female sorrow, swelling loud and high,
Which makes the men blaspheme between their teeth.

Meanwhile, o'er fence and watery field beneath,
The little army moves through drizzling rain;
A 'Crowbar' leads the Sheriff's nag; the lane
Is enter'd, and their plashing tramp draws near:
One instant, outcry holds its breath to hear;
'Halt!'—at the doors they form in double line,
And ranks of polish'd rifles wetly shine.

The Sheriff's painful duty must be done;
He begs for quiet—and the work's begun.
The strong stand ready; now appear the rest,
Girl, matron, grandsire, baby on the breast,
And Rosy's thin face on a pallet borne;
A motley concourse, feeble and forlorn.
One old man, tears upon his wrinkled cheek,
Stands trembling on a threshold, tries to speak,
But, in defect of any word for this,
Mutely upon the doorpost prints a kiss.
Then passes out for ever. Through the crowd
The children run bewilder'd, wailing loud;
Where needed most, the men combine their aid;
And, last of all, is Oona forth convey'd,
Reclined in her accustom'd strawen chair,
Her aged eyelids closed, her thick white hair
Escaping from her cap; she feels the chill,
Looks round and murmurs, then again is still.
Now bring the remnants of each household fire.
On the wet grounds the hissing coals expire;
And Paudeen Dhu, with meekly dismal face,
Receives the full possession of the place.

Whereon the Sheriff, 'We have legal hold.
'Return to shelter with the sick and old.
'Time shall be given; and there are carts below
'If any to the workhouse choose to go.'
A young man makes him answer, grave and clear,
'We're thankful to you! but there's no one here
'Goin' back into them houses: do your part.
'Nor we won't trouble Pigot's horse and cart.'
At which name, rushing into th' open space,
A woman flings her hood from off her face,
Falls on her knees upon the miry ground,
Lifts hands and eyes, and voice of thrilling sound,—

'Vengeance of God Almighty fall on you,
'James Pigot!—may the poor man's curse pursue,
'The widow's and the orphan's curse, I pray,
'Hang heavy round you at your dying day!'
Breathless and fix'd one moment stands the crowd
To hear this malediction fierce and loud.

But now (our neighbour Neal is busy there)
On steady poles he lifted Oona's chair,
Well-heap'd with borrow'd mantles; gently bear
The sick girl in her litter, bed and all;
Whilst others hug the children weak and small
In careful arms, or hoist them pick-a-back;
And, 'midst the unrelenting clink and thwack
Of iron bar on stone, let creep away
The sad procession from that hill-side gray,
Through the slow-falling rain. In three hours more
You find, where Ballytullagh stood before,
Mere shatter'd walls, and doors with useless latch,
And firesides buried under fallen thatch.

FRANCIS HASTINGS DOYLE

'THE PRIVATE OF THE BUFFS', 1866

Doyle (1810–88) came of a military family but had a career in the Customs Service, as well as publishing a good deal of poetry. The occasion of this famous poem, mythologizing plucky Englishness and racial superiority, was an incident during the Chinese War of 1859–60, in the course of which a joint Anglo-French force occupied Peking. Captured by the Chinese, Private Moyse of the East Kent Regiment, known as 'The Buffs', refused to prostrate himself—the traditional Chinese gesture of homage—before his captors and was immediately killed. The war itself was just one episode in the long European campaign to open up China to Western commerce—in particular, from Britain's point of view, the lucrative opium trade with India.

LAST night, among his fellow roughs,
    He jested, quaffed, and swore;
A drunken private of the Buffs,
    Who never looked before.
To-day, beneath the foeman's frown,
    He stands in Elgin's place,
Ambassador from Britain's crown
    And type of all her race.

Poor, reckless, rude, low-born, untaught,
    Bewildered, and alone,
A heart with English instinct fraught
    He yet can call his own.
Aye, tear his body limb from limb,
    Bring cord, or axe, or flame:
He only knows, that not through him
    Shall England come to shame.

Far Kentish hop-fields round him seemed,
  Like dreams, to come and go;
Bright leagues of cherry-blossom gleamed,
  One sheet of living snow;
The smoke above his father's door
  In grey soft eddyings hung:
Must he then watch it rise no more,
  Doomed by himself, so young?

Yes, honour calls!—with strength like steel
  He put the vision by.
Let dusky Indians whine and kneel;
  An English lad must die.
And thus with eyes that would not shrink,
  With knee to man unbent,
Unfaltering on its dreadful brink,
  To his red grave he went.

Vain, mightiest fleets of iron framed;
  Vain, those all-shattering guns;
Unless proud England keep, untamed,
  The strong heart of her sons.
So, let his name through Europe ring—
  A man of mean estate,
Who died, as firm as Sparta's king,
  Because his soul was great.

PUNCH

In 1865–6 a localized rising of black workers in Jamaica was
harshly put down by the Governor, Edward Eyre. Progressive
opinion in Britain was outraged, Eyre was recalled, and his
prosecution was pursued by the so-called Jamaica Committee,
chaired for a time by John Stuart Mill. With memories of the
Indian Mutiny still fresh and in the context of a campaign of
political violence by Fenians (Irish Nationalists), the charges
against Eyre were thrown out by a Grand Jury. Law and order
issues, whether domestic or imperial, always brought out the
most reactionary side of *Punch*, as in this poem welcoming the
failure of the prosecution.

> YE savages thirsting for bloodshed and plunder,
>   Ye miscreants burning for rapine and prey,
> By the fear of the lash and the gallows kept under,
>   Henceforth who shall venture to stand in your way?
> Run riot, destroy, ravage, kill without pity,
>   Let any man how he molests you beware.
> Beholding how hard the Jamaica Committee
>   To ruin are trying to hunt gallant EYRE.
>
> Our mob-leaders suffered, in fancy, with others,
>   Of stamped-out rebellion who felt the strong heel,
> They are touched by the hemp that chastised their black
>   brothers,
>   And their feelings are hurt by the lead and the steel.
> A set ever ranged on the side of sedition,
>   To mutinous negroes, now, hands they extend,
> And, now, with their names back a Fenian petition—
>   The foe of the Ruler is always their Friend.
>
> They are doing their worst to make certain that, never
>   Again, shall rebellion encounter a check;
> That the chief who to crush a revolt may endeavour,
>   Shall his duty perform with a rope round his neck.
> Conspiring against one, from maddened brutes' fury
>   Who saved Englishwomen, and Englishmen's lives,
> Their fangs may they gnash while they curse a Grand Jury
>   Of Britons who value their daughters and wives.

CHARLES KINGSLEY

'THE MANGO-TREE', 1870

Novelist, poet, historian, religious writer and controvertialist, and one of the founders of Christian Socialism, the Revd Charles Kingsley (1819–75) was a major figure in mid-Victorian cultural life. In this unusually angled poem, he reworks the experience of regular colonial soldiering into a domestic tragedy that owes much to the early manner of Wordsworth.

HE wiled me through the furzy croft;
   He wiled me down the sandy lane.
He told his boy's love, soft and oft,
   Until I told him mine again.

We married, and we sailed the main;
   A soldier, and a soldier's wife.
We marched through many a burning plain;
   We sighed for many a gallant life.

But his—God kept it safe from harm.
   He toiled, and dared, and earned command;
And those three stripes upon his arm
   Were more to me than gold or land.

Sure he would win some great renown:
   Our lives were strong, our hearts were high.
One night the fever struck him down.
   I sat, and stared, and saw him die.

I had his children—one, two, three.
   One week I had them, blithe and sound.
The next—beneath this mango-tree,
   By him in barrack burying-ground.

I sit beneath the mango-shade;
   I live my five years' life all o'er—
Round yonder stems his children played;
   He mounted guard at yonder door.

'Tis I, not they, am gone and dead.
  They live; they know; they feel; they see.
Their spirits light the golden shade
  Beneath the giant mango-tree.

All things, save I, are full of life:
  The minas, pluming velvet breasts;
The monkeys, in their foolish strife;
  The swooping hawks, the swinging nests;

The lizards basking on the soil,
  The butterflies who sun their wings;
The bees about their household toil,
  They live, they love, the blissful things.

Each tender purple mango-shoot,
  That folds and droops so bashful down;
It lives; it sucks some hidden root;
  It rears at last a broad green crown.

It blossoms; and the children cry—
  'Watch when the mango-apples fall.'
It lives: but rootless, fruitless, I—
  I breathe and dream;—and that is all.

Thus am I dead: yet cannot die:
  But still within my foolish brain
There hangs a pale blue evening sky;
  A furzy croft; a sandy lane.

'ALIPH CHEEM'

'TO A GRIFFIN', 1871

———

'Aliph Cheem' was the pen-name of Walter Yeldham, an Anglo-Indian whose collection of comic and satiric poems, *Lays of Ind*, went through numerous editions in both India and Britain after its first publication in Bombay in 1871. Here he wryly comments on the home country's ignorance about its Indian empire. In Anglo-Indian slang a 'griffin' was a new arrival from Britain.

So YOU'RE bound for the country of curry and rice, sir?
Well, take on one point an old stager's advice, sir!
Just purge from your mind every English-formed notion
Of Ind, ere you get to the Indian Ocean.
The English are people—what thinker can doubt it?—
Who know and who care very little about it.
Just look at the way Members, even the best, shun,
In Lords or in Commons, an Indian Question.
They're bound, once a year, to look into the budget;
They spare it one sitting, and most of them grudge it;
But talk about opening a park or a gutter,
The benches are crowded, and all in a flutter.
M.P.s, as you know, are our ablest and best!!!
So what do you think we can say of the rest?
Why, there's hardly a schoolboy to whom Indian history,
Bar a few facts, isn't next to a mystery.
There's scarcely a man, if you ask unexpectedly,
Can tell how it's governed at present, connectedly.
You've heard the old jokes about truculent dhoolies,
The wild tribe of Hadjees, and ice-machine coolies,
Of paddy-fields, meaning an Irish location?
They're samples of what is believed by the nation.
It wouldn't surprise me to hear that they've told yer
You'll live like a prince on your pay as a soldier;
A sub—and you'll save something under a million.
Ah me! what a pity you're not a civilian.
It wouldn't surprise me to find you believing
That magnates still spend half their coin in receiving;
Keep house in a style of Nabob prodigality,
And rival each other's profuse hospitality.

I'd venture a wager you think every native
Is either a toady or blood-thirsty caitiff;
Uncov'nanted-wallahs some shady profession,
And Ind for Bengal but another expression;
That cobras are found every day in your slippers;
That horses are cheap, and all Arabs are clippers;
That life in a Station's all romping and riot,
And curry and rice is your principal diet;
That missionary hardships would move you to pity;
That tigers are common, and ayahs are pretty;
That sweet English girls, by the P. and O. carried
By hundreds, are no sooner landed than married;
Et cæt'ra, et cæt'ra—all rank fal-the-lal, sir:
Just drop such ideas in the Suez Canal, sir!

ALFRED TENNYSON

'ENGLAND AND AMERICA IN 1872', written 1832-4

Tennyson did not publish this poem when it was written in the early 1830s. Its publication was occasioned by the arousal of British public indignation in 1872 over the so-called *Alabama* Affair. The *Alabama* was a British-built Confederate warship that had done considerable damage to Union shipping during the American Civil War; the American claim for compensation, thought excessive in Britain, was eventually settled in 1873 after international arbitration. Tennyson's poem offers a convenient revision of imperial history, with the paradoxical argument that the American colonists showed their true Englishness by defeating the mother country in the War of Independence.

O thou, that sendest out the man
    To rule by land and sea,
Strong mother of a Lion-line,
Be proud of those strong sons of thine
    Who wrenched their rights from thee!

What wonder, if in noble heat
    Those men thine arms withstood,
Retaught the lesson thou hadst taught,
And in thy spirit with thee fought—
    Who sprang from English blood!

But Thou rejoice with liberal joy,
    Lift up thy rocky face,
And shatter, when the storms are black,
In many a streaming torrent back,
    The seas that shock thy base!

Whatever harmonies of law
    The growing world assume,
Thy work is thine—The single note
From that deep chord which Hampden smote
    Will vibrate to the doom.

PUNCH

'BA! BA! BLACK SHEEP! A LAY OF ASHANTEE',
20 DECEMBER 1873

The warlike West African kingdom of Ashanti periodically threatened imperial interests on the Gold Coast, now Ghana. In 1873–4, after a series of Ashanti raids, an expeditionary force led by Sir Garnet Wolseley, the late Victorian Empire's most successful soldier, defeated the Ashantis under Kofi Karikari— 'King Coffee' to the British public. Although the war achieved peace for a while and Kofi Karikari was deposed, *Punch* thought it a costly and largely unnecessary exercise. In this poem guying civilian enthusiasm for the conflict, *Punch* looks sceptically at both the material and moral bases of the expedition.

> Ho! Newsboy! bring the paper!
>   It is all the same to me—
> *Times*, *Telegraph*, or *Standard*.
>   What's the news from Ashantee?
> For Politics I care not—
>   Hang the Trial of BAZAINE!
> Home Rule! and DISRAELI!
>   And the Telegrams from Spain!
> This is no time for trifling:—
>   All our prices may increase;
> All my friends be smashed on Railways,
>   Or abused by the Police!
> I am one whose business habits
>   Cannot dull his martial soul;
> And my ardour burns within me—
>   It's a substitute for Coal!
> Though my scuttle may be empty,
>   I imagine in my glee
> A vicarious perspiration
>   When I read of Ashantee!
>
> For there no dreaded enemy
>   Brings Science to the fight;
> No needle-guns to shoot our sons
>   Before they are in sight;

But cheap and nasty weapons
   (How I love to think of *them!*)
Bad powder, and worse barrels
   Of time-serving Brummagem!
And the greatest satisfaction
   In our modern British eyes
Is, to think we're only hitting
   At a man not half our size.
So our Valour is Discretion;
   We can boldly cross the sea,
Send out our Cracks to make the Blacks
   Behave in Ashantee!

Through the land the tale is thrilling
   Of the Stores so thickly sent
(Let the cargoes all be useless,
   But our money must be spent)—
Many thousand bales of blankets
   Are suggested by the wise,
And unnumbered pairs of trousers,
   To impede our bare Allies;
Traction-Engines, that with whistle
   Shall strike terror to our foes,
And some fifty tons of pokers
   Are thrown in by "One Who Knows."
Twice a hundred miles of Railway,
   When our Troops would onward push,
Neatly packed in pic-nic baskets,
   To be laid down in the Bush.
A small fleet of patent lifeboats
   To be used across the plains,
If advance should be retarded
   By the unexpected rains.
Worsted comforters, goloshes,
   Strapless skates of newest plan,
Kalydor to give our soldiers
   An immunity from tan!
Of all that Art can furnish,
   Of all that Wealth can buy,
We'll have no lack—against the Black
   We'll not work *nigger*dly;
Load all our ships to fulness!
   Send out any one but me!
At home in bed I'll back the Red
   To win in Ashantee!

Twaddle not to me of fevers,
   Of malaria on the plains;
Even here in modern London
   We have trouble with our drains.
You may prate of savage cunning,
   Urge KING COFFEE is no fool,
Make much cry about this Black sheep,
   And respect his Royal wool;
It is easy (from this distance,
   Which lends strength to all my views)
To upset his pig-stye palace,
   Burn his city of bamboos—
Where this grand Imperial Savage
   Boasts Palm-oil his end in life—
And for sceptre wields a thigh-bone
   Of a late lamented wife;
Where his babies ply for rattle
   Fantee ribs, as ready toys,
And the skulls of conquered chieftains
   Are the footballs of his boys!
Is the picture black I've painted?
   Do you doubt the likeness true?
Go! and judge yourselves, my heroes!
   That's the work I leave to you.
For Improvement is the motto
   That rules mankind to-day
(We've published Maps, that no mishaps
   May make you lose your way).
Go! improve this noble Savage.
   I can prophesy his lot.
What's in a name?   But all the same
   KING COFFEE goes to pot!

ALFRED TENNYSON

'EPILOGUE TO THE QUEEN', 1873

Tennyson placed this poem as an epilogue to *Idylls of the King* in the Imperial Library Edition of his works. Its specific contemporary references are to the recent recovery from illness of the Prince of Wales, and the calls being made, on financial grounds, for the separation of Canada from Britain. But these are made the occasion for a far wider reflection on the nature of the imperial enterprise, on its heroic history and possible future—this last touched with characteristically Tennysonian foreboding.

O LOYAL to the royal in thyself,
And loyal to thy land, as this to thee—
Bear witness, that rememberable day,
When, pale as yet, and fever-worn, the Prince
Who scarce had plucked his flickering life again
From halfway down the shadow of the grave,
Past with thee through thy people and their love,
And London rolled one tide of joy through all
Her trebled millions, and loud leagues of man
And welcome! witness, too, the silent cry,
The prayer of many a race and creed, and clime—
Thunderless lightnings striking under sea
From sunset and sunrise of all thy realm,
And that true North, whereof we lately heard
A strain to shame us 'keep you to yourselves;
So loyal is too costly! friends—your love
Is but a burthen: loose the bond, and go.'
Is this the tone of empire? here the faith
That made us rulers? this, indeed, her voice
And meaning, whom the roar of Hougoumont
Left mightiest of all peoples under heaven?
What shock has fooled her since, that she should speak
So feebly? wealthier—wealthier—hour by hour!
The voice of Britain, or a sinking land,
Some third-rate isle half-lost among her seas?
There rang her voice, when the full city pealed
Thee and thy Prince! The loyal to their crown
Are loyal to their own far sons, who love
Our ocean-empire with her boundless homes

For ever-broadening England, and her throne
In our vast Orient, and one isle, one isle,
That knows not her own greatness: if she knows
And dreads it we are fallen.—But thou, my Queen,
Not for itself, but through thy living love
For one to whom I made it o'er his grave
Sacred, accept this old imperfect tale,
New-old, and shadowing Sense at war with Soul,
Ideal manhood closed in real man,
Rather than that gray king, whose name, a ghost,
Streams like a cloud, man-shaped, from mountain peak,
And cleaves to cairn and cromlech still; or him
Of Geoffrey's book, or him of Malleor's, one
Touched by the adulterous finger of a time
That hovered between war and wantonness,
And crownings and dethronements: take withal
Thy poet's blessing, and his trust that Heaven
Will blow the tempest in the distance back
From thine and ours: for some are scared, who mark,
Or wisely or unwisely, signs of storm,
Waverings of every vane with every wind,
And wordy trucklings to the transient hour,
And fierce or careless looseners of the faith,
And Softness breeding scorn of simple life,
Or Cowardice, the child of lust for gold,
Or Labour, with a groan and not a voice,
Or Art with poisonous honey stolen from France,
And that which knows, but careful for itself,
And that which knows not, ruling that which knows
To its own harm: the goal of this great world
Lies beyond sight: yet—if our slowly-grown
And crowned Republic's crowning common-sense,
That saved her many times, not fail—their fears
Are morning shadows huger than the shapes
That cast them, not those gloomier which forego
The darkness of that battle in the West,
Where all of high and holy dies away.

PUNCH

'DAVID LIVINGSTONE', 25 APRIL 1874

Between 1841 and his death on the shores of Lake Bemba, David Livingstone made three great journeys of African exploration. Livingstone's courage, his missionary zeal, his belief in the benefits of Western progress, and his battle against East African slaving, combined with the mysterious glamour of the 'Dark Continent' to make him a legend. Ironically, that legend also helped justify Britian's eager participation in the 'scramble for Africa' that began soon after his death. This elegy was written to mark the return of Livingstone's body for burial in Westminster Abbey.

DROOP half-mast colours, bow, bare-headed crowds,
    As this plain coffin o'er the side is slung,
To pass by woods of masts and ratlined shrouds,
    As erst by Afric's trunks liana-hung.

'Tis the last mile, of many thousands trod
    With failing strength, but never-failing will,
By the worn frame, now at its rest with God,
    That never rested from its fight with ill.

Or if the ache of travel and of toil
    Would sometimes wring a short sharp cry of pain,
From agony of fever, blain, and boil,
    'Twas but to crush it down, and on again!

He knew not that the trumpet he had blown,
    Out of the darkness of that dismal land,
Had reached, and roused an army of its own,
    To strike the chains from the Slave's fettered hand.

Now, we believe, he knows, sees all is well:
    How God had stayed his will, and shaped his way,
To bring the light to those that darkling dwell,
    With gains that life's devotion well repay.

Open the Abbey doors, and bear him in
   To sleep with king and statesman, chief, and sage,
The Missionary, come of weaver-kin,
   But great by work that brooks no lower wage.

He needs no epitaph to guard a name
   Which men shall prize while worthy work is known;
He lived and died for good—be that his fame:
   Let marble crumble: this is Living-stone.

PUNCH

'VICTORIA', 15 MAY 1875

The successful development of Australia and New Zealand as colonies of white settlement was increasingly a cause of imperialist satisfaction, proof of the civilizing mission of the British Empire—whatever the indigenous peoples may have thought. Here *Punch* celebrates the prosperity of Victoria; the occasion was a speech by the Governor, Sir George Bowen, then on a tour of England and America.

HAIL, far colonial Commonwealth,
Where a young giant, full of health,
Sprung from the loins of England, grows
To greatness in a calm repose;
Where wealth that comes from crowded mart
Is spent on Letters and on Art;
Where Englishmen work well together
Under divine Italian weather;
Worthy you are to bear the name
Of the great Queen whose dearest aim
Is peace to all beneath her sway—
      VICTORIA!

Australian waters shall not feel
The cleavage of a hostile keel,
Nor foeman's flag from Europe toss
Beneath the silver Southern Cross:
There terrors of invasion cease,
And all men learn the Arts of Peace;
There poets of a newer type
Shall greet us, when the Age is ripe,
And Melbourne, strong and youthful town,
Shall share Athenæ's Violet Crown,
Ere many decades pass away—
      VICTORIA!

Shame to the dullards who desire
To quench our colonising fire,
To keep the imperial instinct down,
And make a fool's cap of the Crown.
It shall not be: while ocean rolls,
And Englishmen have gallant souls,
And court the strong heroic hour,
While Freedom is a word of power,
While great colonial nations rise
In alien seas, 'neath unseen skies,
We do not dread that servile day—
VICTORIA!

ALFRED COMYN LYALL

'BADMINTON', 1876

One of two 'Studies at Delhi', this offers a laconic view of the
Raj at peace, with the great Mutiny just a memory—to the
British at least. The main gate at Delhi was the scene of some of
the fiercest fighting when the city was taken back from the
mutineers in 1857.

HARDLY a shot from the gate we stormed,
  Under the Moree battlement's shade;
Close to the glacis our game was formed,
  There had the fight been, and there we played.

Lightly the demoiselles tittered and leapt,
  Merrily capered the players all;
North, was the garden where Nicholson slept,
  South, was the sweep of a battered wall.

Near me a Musalmán, civil and mild,
  Watched as the shuttlecocks rose and fell;
And he said, as he counted his beads and smiled,
  "God smite their souls to the depths of hell."

PUNCH

'KAISER-I-HIND', 13 JANUARY 1877

Largely to serve the political calculations of the British Prime
Minister Benjamin Disraeli, Queen Victoria was proclaimed
Empress of India on 1 January 1877. *Punch* regarded the whole
proceedings as un-English, hence the consciously foreign title to
this poem on the proclamation—which is also the occasion for a
rehearsal of what was for *Punch* the true paternalist mission of
the British in India.

ROAR, cannon, to the brass-bands' blare, and elephantine trump;
Big drums, make all the noise you can, and native *tom-toms* thump!
While VICEROY LYTTON changes gilt howdah for gilt throne,
And VICTORIA's Indian titles are to India's corners blown!

Prank yourselves, SCINDIAH, GAEKWAR, NIZAM, RAM,
    JAM, & CO.,
Rear your new-broidered banners, your new-coined medals show;
Own that Old England, when she likes, can turn out a parade,
Almost as well as if such pomp were *her*, as 'tis *your*, trade.

Think not of cost, nor of the needs that call for it elsewhere;
The cloud of coming scarcity that darkens the parched air:
Let not the whiff unmannerly of cyclone-swallowed dead
Come 'twixt your new nobility, and attar freely shed.

Lay your nuzzers down in homage at the courteous Viceroy's feet;
Drink the sweet powder of salutes, increased new ranks to greet:
Nor ask if all this tinsel, these gewgaws, bind the band
More close betwixt your weakness and the strength of England's
    hand.

'Twas not *thus* England spread her rule, from CHARNOCK's
    narrow sway
To the days of CLIVE and Plassy, of WELLESLEY and Assaye;
But, first, by sharp swords in strong hands, and when their work
    was done,
By proving she knew how to rule the Empire these had won.

And if some stains of force or fraud deface that record long,
The force is used, the fraud condoned, she *now* is just as strong:
The baser greeds of gold and rule a higher power o'er-rides,
By purer law than yours directs, to ends more worthy guides.

She holds your swarming millions now, but as a trust of Heaven,
To civilise and educate to her best teaching given:
A nursery for her Statesmen, for her Warriors a school,
To show men how a wiser West a wider East can rule.

Till India, as she bows before her Empress-Queen to-day,
Can offer *her* a gift for all the blessings of her sway—
Governors wise in council, and Christian soldiers, bold,
If need were, a more troubled East to take into their hold.

PUNCH

Russia's growing influence in Afghanistan following success in the Russo-Turkish War of 1877–8 appeared to threaten the security of British India. Populist imperialism, stirred up by parts of the press and exploited by Disraeli, urged action in a way that fell little short of advocating all-out war; despite this, a diplomatic solution was eventually reached. In this deft villanelle *Punch* uses the mock cockney of Dickens's character Betsy Prig, who speaks the poem, to parody war-mongering patriotism.

A Villanelle of Vexations.   By B***y P**g.

In wain would I the British Lion wake!
　　In wain I'd rouge the brute to wilent springing;
His tail won't wag, his mane declines to shake.

In wain my daily 'larum-bell I take,
　　Till his ears tingle with its brazen ringing;
In wain would I the British Lion wake!

In wain I warn him of that Northern snake,
　　Who midst our Injun grass will soon be stinging;
His tail won't wag, his mane declines to shake.

In wain to GLADSTONE I my gingham take,
　　And spatter all his lot with free mud-flinging;
In wain would I the British Lion wake!

In wain I shriek out "Hinterests at stake!"
　　Shout "Hup and at 'em! for the hours is winging!"
His tail won't wag, his mane declines to shake.

In wain are all the noisy pains I take,
　　My fierce tongue-wagging and my sore hand-wringing,
In wain would I the British Lion wake!

He sleeps as placid as a windless lake;
　　Cold water on my fire his calm is flinging.
His tail *won't* wag, his mane declines to shake;
　　In wain would I the British Lion wake!

[224]

PUNCH

The word 'jingo' was first used in 1878 to label a supporter of the blustering nationalism and imperialism that Disraeli was often accused of encouraging. *Punch* heartily disliked jingoism, which was offensive to its own sense of the higher moral purpose of empire. In this close parody of Eliza Cook's 'The Englishman', the bellicose rhetoric of the jingo is presented as a thin cover for greed and bullying.

THERE's a Land that's Cock of Creation's walk,
    Though it is but a tiny isle,
And to hear its brag, and its tall tall talk,
    Might make e'en *Bombastes* smile.
It holds itself holiest, first in fight,
    Most brave, most wise, most strong,
And will n'er admit what it fancies right
    Can by any chance be wrong.
'Tis the pink of perfection, deny it who can,
The Home of the Jingo Englishman!

There's a Flag that floats o'er every sea,
    And claims to control the brine;
And if any dare hint that it makes too free,
    The result is a deuce of a shine.
For the bouncing boys who walk the deck
    Deem the Ocean their own little lot,
And if foreign fools at their pride should check,
    They will catch it exceedingly hot.
Right-divine's in its bunting, deny it who can,
Is the Flag of the Jingo-Englishman!

There's a Heart that leaps with a generous glow
 A paying cause to defend,
Lets interest rule it in fixing a foe,
 And profit in choosing a friend.
It nurtures a deep and abiding love
 For possession of power and pelf,
And deems that the duty all others above
 Is enshrined in that sweet word "self."
'Tis a rare tough organ, deny it who can,
The Heart of your Jingo-Englishman!

The Briton may traverse the Pole or the Zone,
 And annex on sea or shore;
He calls an immense domain his own,
 But he means going in for more.
Let the wandering stranger seek to know
 To what charter such "rights" are owed,
And a flush will rise to the Briton's brow
 As he answers—"You be blowed!"
There's no end of a pull, deny it who can,
In the words, "I'm a Jingo-Englishman!"

Alfred Tennyson

'THE REVENGE. A BALLAD OF THE FLEET', 1878

Central to the Victorian consciousness of empire was the construction of the imperial story, not only a narrative of the Empire's historical origins but also an account of the moral qualities by which it was sustained and—it was to be hoped—justified. Tennyson made many contributions to this process, none more telling than this celebration of the heroic age of English sea power. In 1591 *The Revenge*, commanded by Sir Richard Grenville, was caught by a Spanish fleet; though hopelessly outnumbered, Grenville and his crew fought a final, epic battle rather than surrender. While acknowledging the heroism of the action, Elizabethan contemporaries blamed the loss of *The Revenge* on Grenville's inexperience, his flagrant disobedience of orders, and his 'wilful rashness'; Tennyson's poem ignores such historical inconveniences.

I

At Flores in the Azores Sir Richard Grenville lay,
And a pinnace, like a fluttered bird, came flying from far away:
'Spanish ships of war at sea! we have sighted fifty-three!'
Then sware Lord Thomas Howard: ''Fore God I am no coward;
But I cannot meet them here, for my ships are out of gear,
And the half my men are sick. I must fly, but follow quick.
We are six ships of the line; can we fight with fifty-three?'

II

Then spake Sir Richard Grenville: 'I know you are no coward;
You fly them for a moment to fight with them again.
But I've ninety men and more that are lying sick ashore.
I should count myself the coward if I left them, my Lord Howard,
To these Inquisition dogs and the devlildoms of Spain.'

III

So Lord Howard past away with five ships of war that day,
Till he melted like a cloud in the silent summer heaven;
But Sir Richard bore in hand all his sick men from the land
Very carefully and slow,
Men of Bideford in Devon,
And we laid them on the ballast down below;
For we brought them all aboard,
And they blest him in their pain, that they were not left to Spain,
To the thumbscrew and the stake, for the glory of the Lord.

IV

He had only a hundred seamen to work the ship and to fight,
And he sailed away from Flores till the Spaniard came in sight,
With his huge sea-castles heaving upon the weather bow.
'Shall we fight or shall we fly?
Good Sir Richard, tell us now,
For to fight is but to die!
There'll be little of us left by the time this sun be set.'
And Sir Richard said again: 'We be all good English men.
Let us bang these dogs of Seville, the children of the devil,
For I never turned my back upon Don or devil yet.'

V

Sir Richard spoke and he laughed, and we roared a hurrah, and so
The little Revenge ran on sheer into the heart of the foe,
With her hundred fighters on deck, and her ninety sick below;
For half of their fleet to the right and half to the left were seen,
And the little Revenge ran on through the long sea-lane between.

VI

Thousands of their soldiers looked down from the decks and
    laughed,
Thousands of their seamen made mock at the mad little craft
Running on and on, till delayed
By their mountain-like San Philip that, of fifteen hundred tons,
And up-shadowing high above us with her yawning tiers of guns,
Took the breath from our sails, and we stayed.

VII

And while now the great San Philip hung above us like a cloud
Whence the thunderbolt will fall
Long and loud,
Four galleons drew away
From the Spanish fleet that day,
And two upon the larboard and two upon the starboard lay,
And the battle-thunder broke from them all.

VIII

But anon the great San Philip, she bethought herself and went
Having that within her womb that had left her ill content;
And the rest they came aboard us, and they fought us hand to
    hand,
For a dozen times they came with their pikes and musqueteers,
And a dozen times we shook 'em off as a dog that shakes his ears
When he leaps from the water to the land.

IX

And the sun went down, and the stars came out far over the
    summer sea,
But never a moment ceased the fight of the one and the fifty-three.
Ship after ship, the whole night long, their high-built galleons
    came,
Ship after ship, the whole night long, with her battle-thunder and
    flame;
Ship after ship, the whole night long, drew back with her dead
    and her shame.
For some were sunk and many were shattered, and so could fight
    us no more—
God of battles, was ever a battle like this in the world before?

X

For he said 'Fight on! fight on!'
Though his vessel was all but a wreck;
And it chanced that, when half of the short summer night was
    gone,
With a grisly wound to be drest he had left the deck,
But a bullet struck him that was dressing it suddenly dead,
And himself he was wounded again in the side and the head,
And he said 'Fight on! fight on!'

XI

And the night went down, and the sun smiled out far over the
    summer sea,
And the Spanish fleet with broken sides lay round us all in a ring;
But they dared not touch us again, for they feared that we still
    could sting,
So they watched what the end would be.
And we had not fought them in vain,
But in perilous plight were we,
Seeing forty of our poor hundred were slain,
And half of the rest of us maimed for life
In the crash of the cannonades and the desperate strife;
And the sick men down in the hold were most of them stark and
    cold,
And the pikes were all broken or bent, and the powder was all of
    it spent;
And the masts and the rigging were lying over the side;
But Sir Richard cried in his English pride,
'We have fought such a fight for a day and a night
As may never be fought again!
We have won great glory, my men!
And a day less or more
At sea or ashore,
We die—does it matter when?
Sink me the ship, Master Gunner—sink her, split her in twain!
Fall into the hands of God, not into the hands of Spain!'

XII

And the gunner said 'Ay, ay,' but the seamen made reply:
'We have children, we have wives,
And the Lord hath spared our lives.
We will make the Spaniard promise, if we yield, to let us go;
We shall live to fight again and to strike another blow.'
And the lion there lay dying, and they yielded to the foe.

XIII

And the stately Spanish men to their flagship bore him then,
Where they laid him by the mast, old Sir Richard caught at last,
And they praised him to his face with their courtly foreign grace;
But he rose upon their decks, and he cried:
'I have fought for Queen and Faith like a valiant man and true;
I have only done my duty as a man is bound to do:
With a joyful spirit I Sir Richard Grenville die!'
And he fell upon their decks, and he died.

XIV

And they stared at the dead that had been so valiant and true,
And had holden the power and glory of Spain so cheap
That he dared her with one little ship and his English few;
Was he devil or man? He was devil for aught they knew,
But they sank his body with honour down ino the deep,
And they manned the Revenge with a swarthier alien crew,
And away she sailed with her loss and longed for her own;
When a wind from the lands they had ruined awoke from sleep,
And the water began to heave and the weather to moan,
And or ever that evening ended a great gale blew,
And a wave like the wave that is raised by an earthquake grew,
Till it smote on their hulls and their sails and their masts and
     their flags,
And the whole sea plunged and fell on the shot-shattered navy of
     Spain,
And the little Revenge herself went down by the island crags
To be lost evermore in the main.

Alfred Tennyson

'THE DEFENCE OF LUCKNOW', 1878

The siege of Lucknow during the Indian Mutiny, like Havelock's march to relieve the city, became part of imperial mythology. Tennyson's dramatic monologue, supposedly spoken by one of the defenders, is a story of stubborn and courageous resistance in the face of overwhelming odds—a Victorian parallel, in fact, the Elizabethan heroics of 'The Revenge'. The British never forgot, or really forgave, the Mutiny. The 'Banner of England', the poem's central motif, continued to fly, day and night, over the ruins of the Lucknow Residency from the ending of the siege in 1857 until midnight on 14 August 1947, when British rule in India came to an end.

I

Banner of England, not for a season, O banner of Britain, hast thou
Floated in conquering battle or flapt to the battle-cry!
Never with mightier glory than when we had reared thee on high
Flying at top of the roofs in the ghastly siege of Lucknow—
Shot through the staff or the halyard, but ever we raised thee anew,
And ever upon the topmost roof our banner of England blew.

II

Frail were the works that defended the hold that we held with our
    lives—
Women and children among us, God help them, our children and
    wives!
Hold it we might—and for fifteen days or for twenty at most.
'Never surrender, I charge you, but every man die at his post!'
Voice of the dead whom we loved, our Lawrence the best of the
    brave:
Cold were his brows when we kissed him—we laid him that night
    in his grave.
'Every man die at his post!' and there hailed on our houses and
    halls
Death from their rifle-bullets, and death from their cannon-balls,
Death in our innermost chamber, and death at our slight barricade,
Death while we stood with the musket, and death while we stoopt
    to the spade,

Death to the dying, and wounds to the wounded, for often there
    fell,
Striking the hospital wall, crashing through it, their shot and their
    shell,
Death—for their spies were among us, their marksmen were told
    of our best,
So that the brute bullet broke through the brain that could think
    for the rest;
Bullets would sing by our foreheads, and bullets would rain at our
    feet—
Fire from ten thousand at once of the rebels that girdled us
    round—
Death at the glimpse of a finger from over the breadth of a street,
Death from the heights of the mosque and the palace, and death
    in the ground!
Mine? yes, a mine! Countermine! down, down! and creep
    through the hole!
Keep the revolver in hand! you can hear him—the murderous mole!
Quiet, ah! quiet—wait till the point of the pickaxe be through!
Click with the pick, coming nearer and nearer again than before—
Now let it speak, and you fire, and the dark pioneer is no more;
And ever upon the topmost roof our banner of England blew!

III

Ay, but the foe sprung his mine many times, and it chanced on
    a day
Soon as the blast of that underground thunderclap echoed away,
Dark through the smoke and the sulphur like so many fiends in
    their hell—
Cannon-shot, musket-shot, volley on volley, and yell upon yell—
Fiercely on all the defences our myriad enemy fell.
What have they done? where is it? Out yonder. Guard the Redan!
Storm at the Water-gate! storm at the Bailey-gate! storm, and it ran
Surging and swaying all round us, as ocean on every side
Plunges and heaves at a bank that is daily devoured by the tide—
So many thousands that if they be bold enough, who shall escape?
Kill or be killed, live or die, they shall know we are soldiers and
    men!
Ready! take aim at their leaders—their masses are gapped with
    our grape—
Backward they reel like the wave, like the wave flinging forward
    again,
Flying and foiled at the last by the handful they could not subdue;
And ever upon the topmost roof our banner of England blew.

IV

Handful of men as we were, we were English in heart and in limb,
Strong with the strength of the race to command, to obey, to
    endure,
Each of us fought as if hope for the garrison hung but on him;
Still—could we watch at all points? we were every day fewer and
    fewer.
There was a whisper among us, but only a whisper that past:
'Children and wives—if the tigers leap into the fold unawares—
Every man die at his post—and the foe may outlive us at last—
Better to fall by the hands that they love, than to fall into theirs!'
Roar upon roar in a moment two mines by the enemy sprung
Clove into perilous chasms our walls and our poor palisades.
Rifleman, true is your heart, but be sure that your hand be as true!
Sharp is the fire of assault, better aimed are your flank fusillades—
Twice do we hurl them to earth from the ladders to which they
    had clung,
Twice from the ditch where they shelter we drive them with
    hand-grenades;
And ever upon the topmost roof our banner of England blew.

V

Then on another wild morning another wild earthquake out-tore
Clean from our lines of defence ten or twelve good paces or more.
Rifleman, high on the roof, hidden there from the light of the
    sun—
One has leapt up on the breach, crying out: 'Follow me, follow
    me!'—
Mark him—he falls! then another, and *him* too, and down goes he.
Had they been bold enough then, who can tell but the traitors
    had won?
Boardings and rafters and doors—an embrasure! make way for
    the gun!
Now double-charge it with grape! It is charged and we fire, and
    they run.
Praise to our Indian brothers, and let the dark face have his due!
Thanks to the kindly dark faces who fought with us, faithful and
    few,
Fought with the bravest among us, and drove them, and smote
    them, and slew,
That ever upon the topmost roof our banner in India blew.

VI

Men will forget what we suffer and not what we do. We can fight!
But to be soldier all day and be sentinel all through the night—
Ever the mine and assault, our sallies, their lying alarms,
Bugles and drums in the darkness, and shoutings and soundings
    to arms,
Ever the labour of fifty that had to be done by five,
Ever the marvel among us that one should be left alive,
Ever the day with its traitorous death from the loop-holes around,
Ever the night with its coffinless corpse to be laid in the ground,
Heat like the mouth of a hell, or a deluge of cataract skies,
Stench of old offal decaying, and infinite torment of flies,
Thoughts of the breezes of May blowing over an English field,
Cholera, scurvy, and fever, the wound that *would* not be healed,
Lopping away of the limb by the pitiful-pitiless knife,—
Torture and trouble in vain,—for it never could save us a life.
Valour of delicate women who tended the hospital bed,
Horror of women in travail among the dying and dead,
Grief for our perishing children, and never a moment for grief,
Toil and ineffable weariness, faltering hopes of relief,
Havelock baffled, or beaten, or butchered for all that we knew—
Then day and night, day and night, coming down on the
    still-shattered walls
Millions of musket-bullets, and thousands of cannon-balls—
But ever upon the topmost roof our banner of England blew.

VII

Hark cannonade, fusillade! is it true what was told by the scout,
Outram and Havelock breaking their way through the fell
    mutineers?
Surely the pibroch of Europe is ringing again in our ears!
All on a sudden the garrison utter a jubilant shout,
Havelock's glorious Highlanders answer with conquering cheers,
Sick from the hospital echo them, women and children come out,
Blessing the wholesome white faces of Havelock's good fusileers,
Kissing the war-hardened hand of the Highlander wet with their
    tears!
Dance to the pibroch!—saved! we are saved!—is it you? is it you?
Saved by the valour of Havelock, saved by the blessing of Heaven!
'Hold it for fifteen days!' we have held it for eighty-seven!
And ever aloft on the palace roof the old banner of England blew.

WILLIAM ROSSETTI

'EMIGRATION', written c.1881

The brother of the more famous Dante and Christina, William Rossetti (1829–1919) wrote widely on art and literature. As one of the original founders of the Pre-Raphaelite Brotherhood, and later as a close friend of Swinburne, he became a leading advocate of both first and second generation Pre-Raphaelitism. Perhaps rather uneasily, this sonnet on emigration presents the mythology of racial progress that became one of the justifications for imperial expansion.

WEAVE o'er the world your weft, yea weave yourselves,
   Imperial races weave the warp thereof.
   Swift like your shuttle speed the ships, and scoff
At wind and wave.   And, as a miner delves
For hidden treasure bedded deep in stone,
   So seek ye and find the treasure patriotism
   In lands remote and dipped with alien chrism,
And make those new lands heart-dear and your own.
Weave o'er the world yourselves.   Half-human man
   Wanes from before your faces like a cloud
   Sun-stricken, and his soil becomes his shroud.
    But of your souls and bodies ye shall make
The sov'reign vesture of its leagueless span,
   Clothing with history cliff and wild and lake.

WILLIAM MCGONAGALL

'THE BATTLE OF TEL-EL-KEBIR', written 1882

McGonagall (1830–1902) is famous as the best bad poet in English. From a poor Scottish family he struggled heroically for much of his life to establish himself as a literary figure, first through readings from Shakespeare, then through performances of his own work. He specialized in verse commemorating events of historical moment—from railway disasters to royal visits. Here, in his inimitable way, he celebrates Tel-el-Kebir, where forces under the ubiquitous Sir Garnet Wolseley ended an Egyptian nationalist rising led by Arabi Pasha.

YE sons of Great Britain, come join with me,
And sing in praise of Sir Garnet Wolseley;
Sound drums and trumpets cheerfully,
For he has acted most heroically.

Therefore loudly his praises sing
Until the hills their echoes back doth ring;
For he is a noble hero bold,
And an honour to his Queen and country, be it told.

He has gained for himself fame and renown,
Which to posterity will be handed down;
Because he has defeated Arabi by land and by sea,
And from the battle of Tel-el-Kebir he made him to flee.

With an army about fourteen thousand strong,
Through Egypt he did fearlessly march along,
With the gallant and brave Highland brigade,
To whom honour is due, be it said.

Arabi's army was about seventy thousand in all,
And, virtually speaking, it wasn't very small;
But if they had been as numerous again,
The Irish and Highland brigades would have beaten them,
        it is plain.

'Twas on the 13th day of September, in the year of 1882,
Which Arabi and his rebel horde long will rue;
Because Sir Garnet Wolseley and his brave little band
Fought and conquered them on Kebir land.

[237]

He marched upon the enemy with his gallant band
O'er the wild and lonely desert sand,
And attacked them before daylight,
And in twenty minutes he put them to flight.

The first shock of the attack was borne by the Second Brigade,
Who behaved most manfully, it is said,
Under the command of brave General Grahame,
And have gained a lasting honour to their name.

But Major Hart and the 18th Royal Irish, conjoint,
Carried the trenches at the bayonet's point;
Then the Marines chased them about four miles away,
At the charge of the bayonet, without dismay!

General Sir Archibald Alison led on the Highland Brigade,
Who never were the least afraid.
And such has been the case in this Egyptian war,
For at the charge of the bayonet they ran from them afar!

With their bagpipes playing, and one ringing cheer,
And the 42nd soon did the trenches clear;
Then hand to hand they did engage,
And fought like tigers in a cage.

Oh! it must have been a glorious sight
To see Sir Garnet Wolseley in the thickest of the fight!
In the midst of shot and shell, and the cannon's roar,
Whilst the dead and the dying lay weltering in their gore.

Then the Egyptians were forced to yield,
And the British were left masters of the field;
Then Arabi he did fret and frown
To see his army thus cut down.

Then Arabi the rebel took to flight,
And spurred his Arab steed with all his might;
With his heart full of despair and woe,
And never halted till he reached Cairo.

Now since the Egyptian war is at an end,
Let us thank God! Who did send
Sir Garnet Wolseley to crush and kill
Arabi and his rebel army at Kebir hill.

WILFRED SCAWEN BLUNT

From 'THE WIND AND THE WHIRLWIND', 1883

Blunt (1840–1922) began life as a diplomat, but soon retired and
devoted himself to travel in the Middle East and India, to numer-
ous love affairs, and to politics. He was strongly and courage-
ously anti-imperialist, supporting both Arab and Irish nationalists
against British policies: in 1888 he was actually imprisoned for
opposing coercion in Ireland. 'The Wind and the Whirlwind'
describes recent events in Egypt, in particular the rebellion led
by Arabi Pasha, the demise of which at Tel-el-Kebir elicited so
very different a response from McGonagall.

> Oh insolence of strength!   Oh boast of wisdom!
>   Oh poverty in all things truly wise!
> Thinkest thou, England, God can be outwitted
>   For ever thus by him who sells and buys?
>
> Thou sellest the sad nations to their ruin.
>   What hast thou bought?   The child within the womb,
> The son of him thou slayest to thy hurting,
>   Shall answer thee, "An Empire for thy tomb."
>
> Thou hast joined house to house for thy perdition.
>   Thou hast done evil in the name of right.
> Thou hast made bitter sweet and the sweet bitter,
>   And called light darkness and the darkness light.
>
> Thou art become a by-word for dissembling,
>   A beacon to thy neighbours for all fraud.
> Thy deeds of violence men count and reckon.
>   Who takes the sword shall perish by the sword.
>
> Thou hast deserved men's hatred.   They shall hate thee.
>   Thou hast deserved men's fear.   Their fear shall kill.
> Thou hast thy foot upon the weak.   The weakèst
>   With his bruised head shall strike thee on the heel.
>
> Thou wentest to this Egypt for thy pleasure.
>   Thou shalt remain with her for thy sore pain.
> Thou hast possessed her beauty.   Thou wouldst leave her.
>   Nay.   Thou shalt lie with her as thou hast lain.

She shall bring shame upon thy face with all men.
   She shall disease thee with her grief and fear.
Thou shalt grow sick and feeble in her ruin.
   Thou shalt repay her to the last sad tear.

Her kindred shall surround thee with strange clamours,
   Dogging thy steps till thou shalt loathe their din.
The friends thou hast deceived shall watch in anger.
   Thy children shall upbraid thee with thy sin.

All shall be counted thee a crime,—thy patience
   With thy impatience. Thy best thought shall wound.
Thou shalt grow weary of thy work thus fashioned,
   And walk in fear with eyes upon the ground.

The Empire thou didst build shall be divided.
   Thou shalt be weighed in thine own balances
Of usury to peoples and to princes,
   And be found wanting by the world and these.

They shall possess the lands by thee forsaken
   And not regret thee. On their seas no more
Thy ships shall bear destruction to the nations,
   Or thy guns thunder on a fenceless shore.

Thou hadst no pity in thy day of triumph.
   These shall not pity thee. The world shall move
On its high course and leave thee to thy silence,
   Scorned by the creatures that thou couldst not love.

Thy Empire shall be parted, and thy kingdom.
   At thy own doors a kingdom shall arise,
Where freedom shall be preached and the wrong righted
   Which thy unwisdom wrought in days unwise.

DOUGLAS SLADEN

'MRS WATSON. A QUEENSLAND HERO', 1883

Sladen (1856–1946) was a belletrist and one of the best known
literary hosts in late Victorian London. Between 1879 and 1884
he lived in Australia, and subsequently published a number of
anthologies of poetry by Australian writers. In this extraordin-
ary effort of his own, and with a sublime disregard for bathos,
Sladen commemorates the bravery and suffering of Mrs Watson,
an otherwise obscure settler in the far north of Queensland. The
quotations in the poem are from her diary, discovered after
her death.

YES! bury this woman as heroes are buried—
    A daughter and type of the conquering race—
With bayonets sheathed and with ranks unserried;
    For she fought with the savages face to face,
And conquered. There's many a chapter in story
    With heroines' names writ in characters fair,
But never a one that outglitters in glory
    The wife of the fisher of Bêche-de-mer.

The Maid of Arc, had she not chivalrous Frenchmen
    Impatient to follow wherever she led?
The Countess of Brittany, had she no henchmen?
    And Hennebon Castle was battlemented.
Brave Mary Ambree had a company merry
    Of roystering English, one thousand and three;
And Grace Darling pulled in a good stout wherry
    In her perilous feat on the wild North Sea.

This wife, just a mother, had little to aid her—
    No fosse or escarpment or rampart of stone
To shelter her breast from the savage invader,
    With a babe and two Chinamen living alone
Within weatherboard walls on a desolate island
    Off the far away northerly Queensland coast;
While the wild blacks were swarming from delta and
       highland
    To swell and to aid the beleaguering host.

She left us her diary. Let it be printed:
  Let the heroine tell, in her own brave words,
How this one fell speared, and the other, sore-dinted,
  Could only just crawl to the sheltering boards.
She fought as her countrymen fought at Gibraltar
  The armies and navies of France and of Spain,
And made the fierce savages stagger and falter,
  And oft as they rallied repulsed them again.

They fled: but she knew what the flight of the foe meant,
  A ruse or a pause reinforcements to hail,
That if they withdrew it was but for the moment,
  That sooner or later her powder must fail.
So she stored a ship's boiler, her tank, with provision,
  And water enough, as she thought, for the while,
And, taking the firearms and ammunition,
  Launched out on the deep for a fostering isle.

This woman was born of a nation of freemen,—
  Their birthright to dare and to die on the wave;
Yet even to Britain's adventurous seamen
  'Twere hardly disgrace if they seemed not as brave.
What wonder if Gilbert who sank in the "Squirrel,"
  Or Davis, or Baffin, or Frobisher shrank
From facing the strange supernatural peril
  Of crossing the sea in a worn water-tank?

A pitiful story!—this valiant woman
  Who tempted the sea (here a dozen leagues wide),
Thus shipped, after routing the barbarous foeman,
  When she came to a haven to shelter her, died.
Eight days on the waves in a rust-eaten boiler—
  (She had better by half have been slaughtered at first),
And the foe that outflanked her, her only one foiler,
  Stands dim in her diary—"Dead with thirst!"

No drain left to drink!—yet she would not be fearful,
  But in painful and feeble handwriting had writ
That her baby "was better and more cheerful,
  And condensed milk appeared to agree with it."
Not even the steamer when passing so near her,
  Unheeding the signals she hoisted in vain,
Could sicken the hope from her heart, or dis-cheer her;
  She noted it down, but she did not complain.

If only a watch had been kept on that steamer!
   What has not that captain to answer for,
Sent hither by Heaven to be her redeemer?
   He will surely be haunted for evermore.
Were she living who fought then and wrought then so well,
      sons
   Might perchance have been born in our own far north
To match with the Drakes, and the Cooks and the Nelsons
   Whom the Mother of Continents has brought forth.

GEORGE ROBERT SIMS

'ODE AND PAID TO KAHU, THE FIGHTING CHRISTIAN OF TAPITAWA', 1883

———

Sims (1847–1922) was a journalist, short story writer and poet, best known for his campaigning and frequently lachrymose ballads about working-class life, social conditions and poverty, including 'It is Christmas Day in the Workhouse'. His work is rarely concerned with Britain overseas, but 'Kahu' is an exception, the occasion of a notably vigorous attack upon the hypocrisy that gave Christian sanction to imperialist rapacity. Kahu was a local chieftain on the large Pacific island of Tapitua in the Gilbert and Ellice group, eventually annexed to the Empire in 1892. Apparently converted to Christianity, Kahu massacred a neighbouring tribe and claimed that, in so doing, he was clearing the path for their conversion as well. Aggressive evangelism in the South Seas frequently found itself caught up in such long-standing tribal rivalries, with similarly bloody consequences.

> MY poor Kahu—my green Kahu,
> Who twice five hundred heathen slew,
> To make them Christians like yourself,
> And not for bloodshed or for pelf,—
> How could you think a savage had
> The right to make the heathen glad—
> To give their souls the Christian creed
> On spears that made their bodies bleed?
> This sort of thing is only right
> In Christian chieftains who are white.
>
> You've doubtless read, mayhap been told,
> How white kings never fight for gold;
> But when they filch a neighbour's land
> The motive is intensely grand.
> We English never fight unless
> It is that we the foe may bless
> By teaching them our laws and ways—
> 'Tis all for good that England slays.
> So much the stranger's good we prize,
> We kill that we may civilise.

'Tis true we carry fire and sword
'Gainst many a far-off savage horde.
'Tis true we've taken far and wide
Our neighbours' land on every side.
And when the natives we have slain
Ourselves have filled the void again.
But always has't been understood
We did it for our neighbours' good.
We found they were a wicked race,
And killed them off by Heaven's grace.

But you, Kahu—O shocking, sad!
Your conduct is extremely bad,
To go and strew the land with dead
That Christian precepts might be spread;
The right to do such deeds you lack—
I fear, Kahu, you'll get the sack.
The journals here across the sea
Are cross with you as cross can be.
To slaughter men in Heaven's name
Is Christian England's private game.

PUNCH

In the early 1880s the militant Islamic leader known as the Mahdi united the scattered tribes of the Sudan and inflicted a series of defeats upon the Egyptian army. Although the British at first refused to intervene, General Charles Gordon, a former Governor-General of the Sudan and already one of the Empire's favourite Christian warriors, was sent to evacuate the important Nile base of Khartoum, where he promptly found himself besieged and cut off. The imperial epic of Gordon of Khartoum then began, protracted by government indecision that fatally delayed the dispatch of a relief column. When the rescuers eventually arrived in the city in January 1885, they found that it had fallen to the Mahdi's forces only two days before. The death of Gordon was widely mourned and almost as widely versified. Here, in what is possibly the earliest poem in the whole saga, *Punch* imagines Gordon faithfully at his post awaiting rescue.

THE Spring is round us with its budding green
    And brightening sun-shafts under English skies;
But 'tis not April shifts of shade and sheen
        That draw all English eyes.
Our thoughts are in the Desert, where there stands
    Alone, o'erlooking the unpeopled waste,
The scattered sun-bleached rocks and barren sands,
    One at whose cry a people's feet would haste.
That cry comes not,—so calm official lips
    With comfortable certainty protest;
    Yet fail to still the tumult of unrest
In many hearts; word-clouds will not eclipse
    The vision of that lonely watcher, lone
    'Midst alien hordes, on England's business gone;
Followed by England's eyes, and followed not
By England's arms!   A wolfhound on the slot
    Held tight in leash, less eagerly looks out
After the unseen quarry, than we gaze,
Phrase-checked, through Policy's confusing haze
        Toward that watcher stout!

What are his thoughts?   His glance,
Clear as the glitter of an Arab lance,
Cleaves the dim desert-haze.   What does he see?
The vanguard of his country's chivalry?
   She was not wont to leave her bravest sons
With cool deliberate forecast to their doom;
Her rescuing onset not the dread simoom,
   Spear jungles, huge array of hostile guns,
Or mountain gorge, or black miasma-breath,
Would check; nay, nor the bodily menace of Pale Death
   With all his horsemen!
                True, no hot appeal
   Flashed through the wires for her avenging steel.
But since she knows him—and her honour, well,
   What need of that?   *He* has no wish to point
All-marring Faction's calculated yell
   Of simulated horror, or unjoint
State-armour for his safety.   Make *his* name
   A stalking-horse for the sham patriot troop
   Of mean place-hunters, who with howl and whoop
Pursue their quarry?   'Twere too great a shame!
   His life is but a light-held gift, to yield
   With cheery ease upon the stricken field,
Or at the gate of danger, where to stand
   Like that Pompeian sentinel, and die,
   Not called upon to strike, scorning to fly,
            Is duty simple, unexciting, grand
With a calm grandeur that's beyond the reach
Of furious strugglers in the perilous breach.
   Yet—yet—one man, much hampered, here as there,
   By Party shifts, by philanthropic prayer
Purblind in narrow zeal, 'midst ceaseless change
Of circumstance and policy whose range
   None can forecast, one man, and he not free,
   May need,—
            "*What* is it that I seem to see
Across the sand waste?   Is it the quick gleam
Of English steel, or but a desert-dream?
   Help—or, that last illusion of distress,
   The mocking *Mirage* of the Wilderness?"

ALFRED AUSTIN

'HENRY BARTLE EDWARD FRERE.
BORN 1815 DIED 1884', 1884

Tennyson's successor as Poet Laureate, Austin (1835–1913) wrote widely on political and colonial issues, both in verse and prose, and he owed his elevation to the Laureateship as much to his support for conservatism as to his literary abilities. The subject of this elegy, Sir Bartle Frere, was a highly successful and enlightened colonial administrator in India for most of his career, but as Governor of the Cape he was blamed for the failures of British policy that led to the disasters of the Zulu War in 1878–9. Austin sees him as an imperial hero wronged by the indecision and self-seeking of politicians at home—a role similar to that more frequently given to Gordon.

BEND down and read—the birth, the death, the name.
Born in the year that Waterloo was won,
And died in this, whose days are not yet run,
But which, because a year conceived in shame,
No noble need will christen or will claim.
And yet this dead man, England, was Thy son,
And at his grave we ask what had he done,
Bred to be famous, to be foiled of Fame.
Be the reply his epitaph: That he,
In years as youth, the unyielding spirit bore
He got from Thee, but Thou hast got no more;
And that it is a bane and bar to be
A child of Thine, now the adventurous sea
All vainly beckons to a shrinking shore.

Therefore, great soul, within your marble bed
Sleep sound, nor hear the useless tears we weep.
Why should you wake, when England is asleep,
Or care to live, since England now is dead?
Forbidden are the steeps where Glory led;
No more from furrowed danger of the deep
We harvest greatness; to our hearths we creep,
Count and recount our coin, and nurse our dread.

The sophist's craft hath grown a prosperous trade,
And womanish Tribunes hush the manly drum:
The very fear of Empire strikes us numb,
Fumbling with pens, who brandished once the blade.
Therefore, great soul, sleep sound where you are laid,
Blest in being deaf when Honour now is dumb.

ANDREW LANG

'COLONEL BURNABY', 1885

Lang (1844–1912) was a prolific writer whose work ranged from poems and literary essays to folklore and collections of fairy tales. Colonel Frederick Augustus Burnaby, commemorated here, was one of the most dashing of the Empire's soldiers—a famous traveller, a contributor to *Vanity Fair*, and an intimate of the Prince of Wales. Lang's elegy reflects on the irony of Burnaby's death at Abu Klea during the Khartoum relief expedition, at a time when—as well as the Sudan crisis—Britain seemed to be on the brink of war with Russia over Afghanistan. The poem first appeared in *Punch* in January 1885, a week after Burnaby was killed.

BRAVE BURNABY down!   Wheresoever 'tis spoken
    The news leaves the lips with a wistful regret.
We picture that square in the desert, shocked, broken,
    Yet packed with stout hearts, and impregnable yet.
And there fell, at last, in close *mêlée*, the fighter,
    Who Death had so often affronted before,
One deemed he'd no dart for his valorous slighter
    Who such a gay heart to the battle-front bore.
But alas! for the spear-thrust that ended a story
    Romantic as ROLAND's, as Lion-Heart's brief!
Yet crowded with incident, gilded with glory,
    And crowned by a laurel that's verdant of leaf.
A latter-day Paladin, prone to adventure,
    With little enough of the spirit that sways
The man of the market, the shop, the indenture!
    Yet grief-drops will glitter on BURNABY's bays.
Fast friend as keen fighter, the strife-glow preferring,
    Yet cheery all round with his friends and his foes;
Content through a life-story short, yet soul-stirring
    And happy, as doubtless he'd deem, in its close.

Thou that in every field of earth and sky
   Didst hunt for Death, who seemed to flee and fear,
How great and greatly fallen dost thou lie,
   Slain in the desert by a nameless spear!
   "Not here, alas!" may England say, "not here,
In such a quarrel was it meet to die;
But in that dreadful battle drawing nigh,
   To shake the Afghan mountains lone and sere!"
Like Aias by the ships, shouldst thou have stood.
   And in some pass have stayed the stream of fight,
     The bulwark of thy people and their shield,
Till Helmund or till Lora ran with blood,
   And back, towards the Northlands and the Night,
     The stricken Eagles scattered from the field!

George MacDonald

'GENERAL GORDON', 1885

Now best remembered for his fantasy stories and children's fiction, particularly *At the Back of the North Wind*, MacDonald (1824–1905) also wrote a number of powerful novels, principally set in Scotland, and a substantial body of poetry. In these two sonnets on the death of Gordon, he contributes to the Victorian construction of Gordon as imperial martyr and Christian warrior.

I

Victorious through failure! faithful Lord,
Who for twelve angel legions wouldst not pray
From thine own country of eternal day,
To shield thee from the lanterned traitor horde,
Making thy one rash servant sheath his sword!—
Our long retarded legions, on their way,
Toiling through sands, and shouldering Nile's downsway,
To reach thy soldier, keeping at thy word,
Thou sawest foiled—but glorifiedst him,
Over ten cities giving him thy rule!
We will not mourn a star that grew not dim,
A soldier-child of God gone home from school!
A dregless cup, with life brimmed, he did quaff,
And quaffs it now with Christ's imperial staff!

II

Another to the witnesses' roll-call
Hath answered, "Here I am!" and so stept out—
With willingness crowned everywhere about,
Not the head only, but the body all,
In one great nimbus of obedient fall,
His heart's blood dashing in the face of doubt—
Love's last victorious stand amid the rout!
—Silence is left, and the untasted gall.
No chariot with ramping steeds of fire
The Father sent to fetch his man-child home;
His brother only called, "My Gordon, come!"
And like a dove to heaven he did aspire,
His one wing Death, his other, Heart's-desire.
—Farewell a while! we climb where thou has clomb!

[252]

Andrew Lang

'THE WHITE PACHA', 1885

Gordon's body was never found and for a time there was some
speculation that he might have escaped from Khartoum. Lang's
poem dismisses these hopes and, in an extraordinary and
ominous analogy, aligns the dead Gordon with Arthur and Char-
lemagne, the warrior-heroes of vanished Christian empires.

VAIN is the dream! However Hope may rave,
He perished with the folk he could not save,
And though none surely told us he is dead,
And though perchance another in his stead,
Another, not less brave, when all was done,
Had fled unto the southward and the sun,
Had urged a way by force, or won by guile
To streams remotest of the secret Nile,
Had raised an army of the Desert men,
And, waiting for his hour, had turned again
And fallen on that False Prophet, yet we know
GORDON is dead, and these things are not so!
Nay, not for England's cause, nor to restore
Her trampled flag—for he loved Honour more—
Nay, not for Life, Revenge, or Victory,
Would he have fled, whose hour had dawned to die.
He will not come again, what'er our need,
He will not come, who is happy, being freed
From the deathly flesh, and perishable things,
And lies of statesmen, and rewards of kings.
Nay, somewhere by the sacred River's shore
He sleeps like those who shall return no more,
No more return for all the prayers of men—
Arthur and Charles—they never come again!
They shall not wake, though fair the vision seem:
Whate'er sick Hope may whisper, vain the dream!

Alfred Tennyson

'OPENING OF THE INDIAN AND COLONIAL EXHIBITION BY THE QUEEN', 1886

According to the subtitle of the poem, Tennyson wrote it 'at the Request of the Prince of Wales', the future Edward VII; it was set to music by Sir Arthur Sullivan. The exhibition was held at South Kensington in London, and its state opening on 4 May 1886—according to a contemporary source—was attended 'by delegates from one-fourth of the human race'. A glittering display of the achievements and products of the Empire, the exhibition was a huge success, visited by some five and a half million people.

WELCOME, welcome with one voice!
In your welfare we rejoice,
Sons and brothers that have sent,
From isle and cape and continent,
Produce of your field and flood,
Mount and mine, and primal wood;
Works of subtle brain and hand,
And splendours of the morning land,
Gifts from every British zone;
    Britons, hold your own!

May we find, as ages run,
The mother featured in the son;
And may yours for ever be
That old strength and constancy
Which has made your fathers great
In our ancient island State,
And wherever her flag fly,
Glorying between sea and sky,
Makes the might of Britain known;
    Britons, hold your own!

Britain fought her sons of yore—
Britain failed; and never more,
Careless of our growing kin,
Shall we sin our fathers' sin,
Men that in a narrower day—
Unprophetic rulers they—
Drove from out the mother's nest
That young eagle of the West
To forage for herself alone;
      Britons, hold your own!

Sharers of our glorious past,
Brothers, must we part at last?
Shall we not through good and ill
Cleave to one another still?
Britain's myriad voices call,
'Sons, be welded each and all,
Into one imperial whole,
One with Britain, heart and soul!
One life, one flag, one fleet, one Throne!'
      Britons, hold your own!

RUDYARD KIPLING

'THE STORY OF URIAH', 1886

Born in Bombay and sent to school in England, Kipling (1865–1936) returned to the subcontinent in 1882, establishing his reputation as the outstanding writer on British India firstly through his journalism, then through the poetry of *Departmental Ditties* (1886), and then through the brilliant short stories collected, most notably, in *Plain Tales from the Hills* (1888) and *Soldiers Three* (1888). Settling finally in England in the 1890s, he continued to produce a prodigious amount of work, much of it centred on national and imperial issues. Contemporaries identified Kipling as the principal literary spokesman for imperialism, which he certainly promoted directly at times. Nevertheless, Kipling understood the diversity of empire, and the attitudes embodied in his writings are not only far from consistent but also frequently problematized by irony and ambiguity.

'The Story of Uriah', from *Departmental Ditties*, parallels the biblical narrative in 2 Samuel 11, in which King David, lusting after Bathsheba, sends her husband Uriah to certain death in battle. During the summer months the officials of the Raj and their families moved to Himalayan hill stations like Simla to escape the heat and disease of the plains and of cities like Quetta.

JACK BARRETT went to Quetta
    Because they told him to.
He left his wife at Simla
    On three-fourths his monthly screw.
Jack Barrett died at Quetta
    Ere the next month's pay he drew.

Jack Barrett went to Quetta.
    He didn't understand
The reason for his transfer
    From the pleasant mountain-land.
The season was September,
    And it killed him out of hand.

Jack Barrett went to Quetta
  And there gave up the ghost,
Attempting two men's duty
  In that very healthy post;
And Mrs Barrett mourned for him
  Five lively months at most.

Jack Barrett's bones at Quetta
  Enjoy profound repose;
But I shouldn't be astonished
  If *now* his spirit knows
The reason of his transfer
  From the Himalayan snows.

And, when the Last Great Bugle Call
  Adown the Hurnai throbs,
And the last grim joke is entered
  In the big black Book of Jobs,
And Quetta graveyards give again
  Their victims to the air,
I shouldn't like to be the man
  Who sent Jack Barrett there.

Rudyard Kipling

'ARITHMETIC ON THE FRONTIER', 1886

———

The focus for this sceptical appraisal of imperial logistics is the North West Frontier between the Punjab and Afghanistan, notoriously restless and inhabited by tribesmen with a formidable reputation as snipers.

A GREAT and glorious thing it is
  To learn, for seven years or so,
The Lord knows what of that and this,
  Ere reckoned fit to face the foe—
The flying bullet down the Pass,
That whistles clear: "All flesh is grass."

Three hundred pounds per annum spent
  On making brain and body meeter
For all the murderous intent
  Comprised in "villainous saltpetre!"
And after?—Ask the Yusufzaies
What comes of all our 'ologies.

A scrimmage in a Border Station—
  A canter down some dark defile—
Two thousand pounds of education
  Drops to a ten-rupee *jezail*—
The Crammer's boast, the Squadron's pride,
Shot like a rabbit in a ride!

No proposition Euclid wrote
  No formulæ the text-books know,
Will turn the bullet from your coat,
  Or ward the tulwar's downward blow.
Strike hard who cares—shoot straight who can—
The odds are on the cheaper man.

One sword-knot stolen from the camp
  Will pay for all the school expenses
Of any Kurrum Valley scamp
  Who knows no word of moods and tenses,
But, being blessed with perfect sight,
Picks off our messmates left and right.

With home-bred hordes the hillsides teem,
  The troopships bring us one by one,
At vast expense of time and steam,
  To slay Afridis where they run.
The "captives of our bow and spear"
Are cheap, alas! as we are dear.

LEWIS MORRIS

From 'A SONG OF EMPIRE', 1887

A prolific Welsh poet whose *Epic of Hades* (1876–7) was celeb-
rated in its day, Morris (1833–1907) was sufficiently eminent to
be a serious contender for the Laureateship after Tennyson's
death. In 1895 he was knighted, largely for his important work
in the cause of Welsh education and culture. Morris's 'A Song
of Empire', written for Victoria's Golden Jubilee, was one of the
more ambitious of the many poetic effusions that greeted the
official day of celebration on 20 June 1887. In the first half of
the poem, given here, Victoria is apotheosized as the Imperial
Mother, her children thronging back to greet here from the
'Greater England' that is spread over the continents of the world.

FIRST Lady of our English race,
In Royal dignity and grace
Higher than all in old ancestral blood,
But higher still in love of good,
And care for ordered Freedom, grown
To a great tree where'er
In either hemisphere,
Its vital seeds are blown;
Where'er with every day begun
Thy English bugles greet the coming sun!

Thy life is England's.   All these fifty years
Thou from thy lonely Queenly place
Hast watched the clouds and sunshine on her face;
Hast marked her changing hopes and fears;
Her joys and sorrows have been always thine;
Always thy quick and Royal sympathy
Has gone out swiftly to the humblest home,
Wherever grief and pain and suffering come.

Therefore it is that we
Take thee for head and symbol of our name.
For fifty years of reign thou wert the same,
Therefore to-day we make our jubilee.

Firm set on ancient right, as on thy people's love,
Unchecked thy wheels of empire onward move.
Not as theirs is thy throne
Who, though their hapless subjects groan,
Sit selfish, caring not at all,
Until the fierce mob surges and they fall,
Or the assassin sets the down-trod free.
Not such thy fate on this thy jubilee,
But love and reverence in the hearts of all.

Oh England! Empire wide and great
As ever from the shaping hand of fate
Did issue on the earth, august, large grown!
What were the Empires of the past to thine,
The old old Empires ruled by kings divine—
Egypt, Assyria, Rome? What rule was like thine own,
Who over all the round world bearest sway?
Not those alone who thy commands obey
Thy subjects are; but in the boundless West
Our grandsires lost, still is thy reign confest.
"The Queen" they call thee, the young People strong,
Who, being Britons, might not suffer wrong,
But are reknit with us in reverence for thee;
Therefore it is we make our jubilee.

See what a glorious throng they come,
Turned to their ancient home,
The children of our England! See
What vigorous company
Thou sendest, Greater England of the Southern Sea!
Thy stately cities, thick with domes and spires,
Chase the illumined night with festal fires
In honour of their Queen, whose happy reign
Began when, 'mid their central roar,
The naked savage trod the pathless plain.
Thousands of miles, North, South, East, West, to-day,
Their countless herds and flocks unnumbered stray.
Theirs are the vast primæval forest depths profound;
Yet everywhere are found
The English laws, the English accents fair,
'Mid burning North or cooler Southern air.
A world within themselves, and with them blent
Island with continent.
The green isles, jewels on the tropic blue,
Where flower and tree and bird are strange and new;

Or that which lies within a temperate air
As summer-England fair;
Or those, our Southern Britain that shall be,
Set in the lonely sea.
Lands of deep fiord and snow-clad soaring hill,
Wherethrough the ocean-currents ebb and fill,
And craters vast, wherefrom the prisoned force
Of the great earth-fires runs its dreadful course.
And vales of fern and palm, whence rising like a dream
High in mid-heaven, the ghostly ice-fields gleam.

And from her far and wintry North
The great Dominion issues forth,
Fit nurse of stalwart British hearts and strong;
From her black pine woods, deep in snow,
Her billowy prairies boundless as the sea,
Where on the sweet untroubled soil
Yearly the unnoticed, countless wild-flowers blow,
And by men's fruitful and compelling toil
Yearly the deep and bounteous harvests grow;
From the lone plains, wherethrough the icy wind
Sweeps from the North, leaving the Pole behind;
In whose brief summer suns, so fierce they shine,
Flourish alike the apple and the vine;
From teeming ancient cities bright and fair,
Whether in summer's heat or frosty wintry air,
Stamped with the nameless charm and grace
Of a more joyous race;
Or on the rounding prairie nestling down
Homestead and frequent new-built town.
Even to those ultimate wilds where comes to be
Another Westminster on the Pacific Sea.

Nor shall thy Western Isles
Be wanting, where the high green breakers fall
Upon the torrid shore, and nature smiles;
And yet sometimes broods over all,
Thick woods and hot lagunes with steaming breath,
A nameless presence with a face of death.
Fair balmy Isles, where never wintry air
Ruffles the scentless tropic blossoms fair,
Upon whose sun-warmed fruitful soil
Our father's dusky freedmen toil.

Lands of bright plumes that flash from tree to tree,
Long creepers trailing thick with brilliant bloom,
And loud upon the forest's silent gloom
The plunging surges of the encircling sea.

   And from the ancient land
Scorching beneath the strong unfailing sun,
Round thee thy unnumbered subject millions stand;
From many a storied city fair,
Old ere our England, first begun,
From marble tomb and temple white,
Built ere our far forefathers were,
And still a miracle defying Time;
Palaces gray with age and dark with crime,
Fierce superstitions, only quenched in blood,
And sweet flower-fancies yearning towards the light,
And lustral cleansings in the sacred flood,
Where by dim temple cool, or shaded street,
From hill or parchèd plain the wayworm pilgrims meet.

   And from the unhappy Continent
Which breeds the savage and the slave—
From our enormous South, there shall be sent
A scanty band of strong self-governed men.
And from those poisoned swamps, to-day a grave,
But which one day shall smile with plenty, when
The onward foot of Knowledge, slow, sublime,
Has traversed her and set her children free
From ocean to her fabulous inland sea,
And the fierce savage, full of kingly grace,
Is father of a gentler race,
And peaceful commerce heals the wounds of Time,
And the long history of blood and pain
Comes nevermore again.

   And nearest to thee, and of all most dear,
Thy people of these little Northern Isles,
Who never shall their Queen forget,
Nor be forgotten, whether Fortune smiles
Or armèd Europe storm around,
Whom none assail, beyond the waves' deep sound,
Behind their surge-struck ramparts safe and free
These are thy closest subjects, these

The brain and heart of Empire, as thy Rose
Within its close-ranged petals comes to hold
A perfumed heart of gold,
Wherein the seed of the miraculous flower,
Safe hid, defies Fate's power.
And most of all thy wondrous mother-town
Upon our broad Thames sitting like a crown,
Who, 'mid her healthful labour-laden air,
Grows every day more fair;
Whom not for fairness do her children prize,
But for her gracious homely memories—
A nation, not a city, the loved home
Whereto the longing thoughts of exiled Britons come!

OSCAR WILDE

'AVE IMPERATRIX', 1887

The brilliant career that Wilde (1854–1900) enjoyed as a playwright, fashionable wit, and leader of the aesthetic avant-garde, was brought to a brutally abrupt end in 1895 when he was sentenced to two years' hard labour for his homosexual relationship with Lord Alfred Douglas, the son of the Marquis of Queensberry. 'Ave Imperatrix' ('Hail Empress') was written for the 1887 Jubilee and seems to reveal a wholly different aspect of Wilde's creative personality. Sensuousness and evocative orientalism here contrast with the impassioned self-sacrifice of Britain's imperial mission, a destiny that the final stanzas equate with Christ's crucifixion.

Set in this stormy sea,
    Queen of these restless fields of tide,
England! what shall men say of thee,
    Before whose feet the worlds divide?

The earth, a brittle globe of glass,
    Lies in the hollow of thy hand,
And through its heart of crystal pass,
    Like shadows through a twilight land,

The spears of crimson-suited war,
    The long white-crested waves of fight,
And all the deadly fires which are
    The torches of the Lords of Night.

The yellow leopards, strained and lean,
    The treacherous Russian knows so well,
With gaping blackened jaws are seen
    Leap through the hail of screaming shell.

The strong sea-lion of England's wars
    Hath left his sapphire cave of sea,
To battle with the storm that mars
    The stars of England's chivalry.

The brazen-throated clarion blows
  Across the Pathan's reedy fen,
And the high steeps of Indian snows
  Shake to the tread of armèd men.

And many an Afghan chief, who lies
  Beneath his cool pomegranate-trees,
Clutches his sword in fierce surmise
  When on the mountain-side he sees

The fleet-foot Marri scout, who comes
  To tell how he hath heard afar
The measured roll of English drums
  Beat at the gates of Kandahar.

For southern wind and east wind meet
  Where, girt and crowned by sword and fire,
England with bare and bloody feet
  Climbs the steep road of wide empire.

O lonely Himalayan height,
  Grey pillar of the Indian sky,
Where saw'st thou last in clanging flight
  Our wingèd dogs of Victory!

The almond groves of Samarcand,
  Bokhara, where red lilies blow,
And Oxus, by whose yellow sand
  The grave white-turbaned merchants go:

And on from thence to Ispahan,
  The gilded garden of the sun,
Whence the long dusty caravan
  Brings cedar wood and vermilion;

And that dread city of Cabool
  Set at the mountain's scarpèd feet,
Whose marble tanks are ever full
  With water for the noonday heat:

Where through the narrow straight Bazaar
  A little maid Circassian
Is led, a present from the Czar
  Unto some old and bearded khan,—

Here have our wild war-eagles flown,
    And flapped wide wings in fiery fight;
But the sad dove, that sits alone
    In England—she hath no delight.

In vain the laughing girl will lean
    To greet her love with love-lit eyes:
Down in some treacherous black ravine,
    Clutching his flag, the dead boy lies.

And many a moon and sun will see
    The lingering wistful children wait
To climb upon their father's knee;
    And in each house made desolate.

Pale women who have lost their lord
    Will kiss the relics of the slain—
Some tarnished epaulette—some sword—
    Poor toys to soothe such anguished pain.

For not in quiet English fields
    Are these, our brothers, lain to rest,
Where we might deck their broken shields
    With all the flowers the dead love best.

For some are by the Delhi walls,
    And many in the Afghan land,
And many where the Ganges falls
    Through seven mouths of shifting sand.

And some in Russian waters lie,
    And others in the seas which are
The portals to the East, or by
    The wind-swept heights of Trafalgar.

O wandering graves! O restless sleep!
    O silences of the sunless day!
O still ravine! O stormy deep!
    Give up your prey! Give up your prey!

And thou whose wounds are never healed,
    Whose weary race is never won,
O Cromwell's England! must thou yield
    For every inch of ground a son?

Go! crown with thorns thy gold-crowned head,
   Change thy glad song to song of pain;
Wind and wild wave have got thy dead,
   And will not yield them back again.

Wave and wild wind and foreign shore
   Possess the flower of English land—
Lips that thy lips shall kiss no more,
   Hands that shall never clasp thy hand.

What profit now that we have bound
   The whole round world with nets of gold,
If hidden in our heart is found
   The care that groweth never old?

What profit that our galleys ride,
   Pine-forest-like, on every main?
Ruin and wreck are at our side,
   Grim warders of the House of pain.

Where are the brave, the strong, the fleet?
   Where is our English chivalry?
Wild grasses are their burial-sheet,
   And sobbing waves their threnody.

O loved ones lying far away,
   What word of love can dead lips send!
O wasted dust! O senseless clay!
   Is this the end! is this the end!

Peace, peace! we wrong the noble dead
   To vex their solemn slumber so;
Though childless, and with thorn-crowned head,
   Up the steep road must England go,

Yet when this fiery web is spun,
   Her watchmen shall descry from far
The young Republic like a sun
   Rise from these crimson seas of war.

PUNCH

' "ADVANCE AUSTRALIA!" ', 4 FEBRUARY 1888

Punch offers paternal, and rather patronizing, congratulations to New South Wales on the centenary of its foundation. Characteristically 'the wandering black-fellow', the pre-colonial inhabitant, is seen as a mere bystander in the inevitable march of progress.

ADVANCE Australia!   Yes, my boys,
　　And this seems something *like* advancing!
In this great day all England joys;
　　It sets our slowest pulses dancing.
The echoes of your ringing cheers,
　　From Sydney Cove the wide sea over,
Sound welcome on our elder ears,
　　Far as the old white walls of Dover.
Winter's with us, and summer shine
　　Graces your Austral January;
But warm hearts greet across the brine,
　　　　Your Centenary.

A hundred years!   At Time's old pace
　　The merest day's march, little changing;
But now the measure's new, the race
　　Fares even faster, forward ranging.
What cycle of Cathay e'er saw
　　Your Century's wondrous transformation?
From wandering waifs to wards of Law!
　　From nomads to a mighty nation!
Belated dreamers moan and wail;
　　What scenes for croakers of that kidney,
Since first the *Sirius* furled her sail
　　　　Where now is Sydney!

A hundred years!   Let Fancy fly—
　　She has a flight that nothing hinders,
Not e'en reaction's raven cry—
　　Back to the days of MATTHEW FLINDERS;
Stout slip of Anglo-Saxon stock
　　Who gave the new-found land its nomen.
Faith, memory-fired, may proudly mock
　　At dismal doubt, at owlish omen.
Five sister-colonies spread now
　　Where then the wandering black-fellow
Alone enjoyed day's golden glow
　　　　Night's moonlight mellow.

Adelaide, Sydney, Brisbane, Perth,
　　And merry Melbourne!   There's a cluster
Of towns that you may challenge earth
　　In swifter braver show to muster.
Out of that hundred scarce a year
　　But saw some new quick-spreading settlement,
To prove to moody thralls of fear
　　What youth and Anglo-Saxon mettle meant.
And now your century to its close
　　Rounds amidst joy and jubilation,
And faith in your fair future flows
　　　　Through all the nation.

"The Island-Continent!   Hooray!"
　　Punch drinks your health in honest liquor
On this your great Centennial day,
　　Whose advent makes his blood flow quicker.
We know what you can do, dear boys
　　In City-founding—and in Cricket.
A fig for flattery!—it cloys;
　　Frank truth, true friendship,—that's the ticket!
Land of rare climate, stalwart men,
　　And pretty girls, and queer mammalia,
All England cries, through *Punch*'s pen,
　　　　"Advance, Australia!"

WILFRED SCAWEN BLUNT

From 'THE CANON OF AUGHRIM', 1888

―――

Blunt based this dramatic monologue on a conversation he had
with the Roman Catholic Bishop of Clonfert when he visited
Ireland in 1885 in support of the Irish Land League.

THERE! You asked for the truth. You have it plain from my lips.
   Scientists tell us the world has no direction or plan,
Only a struggle of Nature, each beast and nation at grips,
   Still the fittest surviving and he the fittest who can.

You are that fittest, the lion to-day in your strength. To-morrow?
   Well, who knows what other will come with a wider jaw?
Justly, you say, the nations give place and yield in their sorrow;
   Vainly, you say, Christ died in face of the natural law.

Would you have me believe it? I tell you, if it were so,
   If I were not what I am, a priest instructed in grace,
Knowing the truth of the Gospel and holding firm what I know,
   Where should I be at this hour? Nay, surely not in this place.

Granted your creed of destruction, your right of the strong to
     devour,
   Granted your law of Nature that he shall live who can kill,
Find me the law of submission shall stay the weak in his hour,
   His single hour of vengeance, or set a rein on his will.

Where should I be, even I? Not surely here with my tears,
   Weeping an old man's grief at wrongs which are past regret,
Healing here a little and helping there with my prayers,
   All for the sake of Nature, to fill the teeth she has whet!

Not a priest at Aughrim. My place would be down with those
   Poor lost souls of Ireland, who, loving her far away,
Not too wisely but well, deep down in your docks lie close,
   Waiting the night of ruin which needs must follow your day.

England's lion is fat. Full-bellied with fortune he sleeps;
   Why disturb his slumber with ominous news of ill?
Softly from under his paw the prey he has mangled creeps,
   Deals his blow in the back, and all the carcase is still.

Logic and counter-logic.   You talk of cowardice rarely!
   Dynamite under your ships might make even your cheek white.
Treacherous?   Oh, you are jesting.   The natural law works fairly,
   He that has cunning shall live, and he that has poison bite.

Only I dare not believe it.   I hold the justice of Heaven
   Larger than all the science, and welled from a purer fount;
God as greater than Nature, His law than the wonders seven,
   Darwin's sermon on Man redeemed by that on the Mount.

———

Thus spoke the Canon of Aughrim, and raised in silence his hands,
   Seeming to bless the battle his eyes had seen on the plain.
Order and law, he murmered, a Nation's track in the sands,
   Ridge and furrow of grass, the graves of our women and men.

PUNCH

'ASK A WHITE MAN!', 14 JUNE 1890

———

Despite casual racism of its own, *Punch* not infrequently attacked imperialist assumptions about white superiority, particularly in the context of the 'scramble for Africa'. The occasion of this poem—based on the popular song 'Ask a Policeman!'—was a speech by the explorer Henry Morton Stanley in which he smugly recalled the King of Uganda's admiration for the knowledgeability of white men.

THE White Men are a noble band
    (Though TIPPOO swears they're not),
Their valour is tremendous, and
    They know an awful lot,
If anything you'd learn, and meet
    A White Man on the way,
Ask *him*. You'll find him a complete
    En-cy-clo-pæ-di-a.

Chorus.

If you want to know, you know,
    Ask a White Man!
Near Nyanza or Congo,
    Ask a White Man!
In Uganda I am King,
Yet *I* don't know everything.
If you want to know, you know,
    Ask a White Man!

If you would learn how best to fight
    Your way through regions queer,
Thread forest mazes dark as night,
    And deserts dim and drear!
If you your rival's roads would shut,
    And get his in your grip;
You go to him, he's artful, but
    He'll give you the straight tip.

Chorus.

If you'd know your way about,
      Ask a White Man!
He knows every in and out
      Does a White Man!
He will tell you like a shot
If the roads are good or not;
He can open up the lot,
      Ask a White Man!

And if about the Angels you
  Feel cu-ri-os-i-ty,
For information prompt and true,
  To a White Man apply.
He knows 'em, and, indeed, 'tis said
  Himself is *almost* such.
His "words of wisdom" on this head
  Will interest you much.

Chorus.

If you want to shoot and drink,
      Ask a White Man!
He can help you there, I think.
      Ask a White Man!
If you'll learn to grab and fight,
And be mutually polite,
And observe the laws of Right,
      Ask a White Man!

WILLIAM WATSON

'ENGLAND AND HER COLONIES', written 1890

Watson (1858–1935) is one of the most interesting late Victorian poets who wrote on imperial themes. Starting from a liberal position that regarded the Empire as a largely positive and civilizing force, he was disillusioned by the clearly self-interested nature of imperialism in the 1890s, and subsequently took the unpopular stance of opposing the Boer War. His anti-imperialism probably cost him the Laureateship in succession to Tennyson. In this relatively early poem the metaphor of organic growth supports a benign view of colonial expansion.

SHE stands a thousand-wintered tree,
  By countless morns impearled;
Her broad roots coil beneath the sea,
  Her branches sweep the world;
Her seeds, by careless winds conveyed,
  Clothe the remotest strand
With forests from her scatterings made,
New nations fostered in her shade,
  And linking land with land.

O ye by wandering tempest sown
  'Neath every alien star,
Forget not whence the breath was blown
  That wafted you afar!
For ye are still her ancient seed
  On younger soil let fall—
Children of Britain's island-breed,
To whom the Mother in her need
  Perchance may one day call.

SARAH GERALDINE STOCK
'LET THE SONG GO ROUND THE EARTH',
written *c*.1890

The expansion of the Empire in the later nineteenth century was accompanied by an increasingly well-organized missionary campaign, of which Stock (1838–98) was an enthusiastic supporter. She wrote several accounts of the missions that went to Central Africa in the 1880s and 1890s, as well as poems and hymns, of which this, subsequently included in *Hymns Ancient and Modern*, is the best known.

LET the song go round the earth,
    JESUS CHRIST is LORD;
Sound His praises, tell His worth,
    Be His Name adored;
Every clime and every tongue
Join the grand, the glorious song.

Let the song go round the earth
    From the eastern sea,
Where the daylight has its birth,
    Glad, and bright, and free;
China's millions join the strains,
Waft them on to India's plains.

Let the song go round the earth!
    Lands, where Islam's sway
Darkly broods o'er home and hearth,
    Cast their bonds away;
Let His praise from Afric's shore
Rise and swell her wide lands o'er.

Let the song go round the earth,
   Where the summer smiles;
Let the notes of holy mirth
   Break from distant isles;
Inland forests, dark and dim,
Snow-bound coasts give back the hymn.

Let the song go round the earth!
   JESUS CHRIST is King!
With the story of His worth
   Let the whole world ring;
Him creation all adore
Evermore and evermore.

WILLIAM ERNEST HENLEY

'PRO REGE NOSTRO', 1892

As well as being a poet whose early work, particularly *Hospital Verses* (1875), has considerable originality, Henley (1849–1903) was a leading literary editor and art critic, championing the then avant-garde work of Whistler and Rodin. He also held advanced imperialist, even jingoist, views, which he promoted through his editorship of the *National Observer*. This poem, often known as 'England, my England', was a particular favourite among public school patriots; it acquired its more elevated Latin title—'For Our Kingdom'—during the Boer War.

WHAT have I done for you,
   England, my England?
What is there I would not do,
   England, my own?
With your glorious eyes austere,
As the Lord were walking near,
Whispering terrible things and dear
     As the Song on your bugles blown,
       England—
     Round the world on your bugles blown!

Where shall the watchful sun,
   England, my England,
Match the master-work you've done,
   England, my own?
When shall he rejoice agen
Such a breed of mighty men
As come forward, one to ten,
     To the Song on your bugles blown,
       England—
     Down the years on your bugles blown?

Ever the faith endures,
   England, my England:—
'Take and break us: we are yours,
   England, my own!
Life is good, and joy runs high
Between English earth and sky:
Death is death; but we shall die
   To the Song on your bugles blown,
      England—
   To the stars on your bugles blown!'

They call you proud and hard,
   England, my England:
You with worlds to watch and ward,
   England, my own!
You whose mailed hand keeps the keys
Of such teeming destinies,
You could know nor dread nor ease
   Were the Song on your bugles blown,
      England,
   Round the Pit on your bugles blown!

Mother of Ships whose might,
   England, my England,
Is the fierce old Sea's delight,
   England, my own,
Chosen daughter of the Lord,
Spouse-in-Chief of the ancient Sword,
There's the menace of the Word
   In the Song on your bugles blown,
      England—
   Out of heaven on your bugles blown!

RUDYARD KIPLING

'THE WIDOW AT WINDSOR', 1892

———

Like the other poems in *Barrack Room Ballads*, this purports to be spoken by a soldier of the regular army; here, his sense of the extent of Victoria's—'the Widow's'—great empire is ironically balanced by his awareness of being one of the 'poor beggars in red' whose job is to keep it intact.

'AVE you 'eard o' the Widow at Windsor
  With a hairy gold crown on 'er 'ead?
She 'as ships on the foam—she 'as millions at 'ome,
  An' she pays us poor beggars in red.
    (Ow, poor beggars in red!)

There's 'er nick on the cavalry 'orses,
  There's 'er mark on the medical stores—
An' 'er troopers you'll find with a fair wind be'ind
  That takes us to various wars.
    (Poor beggars!—barbarious wars!)
      Then 'ere 's to the Widow at Windsor,
        An' 'ere 's to the stores an' the guns,
      The men an' the 'orses what makes up the forces
        O' Missis Victorier's sons.
    (Poor beggars!   Victorier's sons!)

Walk wide o' the Widow at Windsor,
  For 'alf o' Creation she owns:
We 'ave bought 'er the same with the sword an' the flame,
  An' we've salted it down with our bones.
    (Poor beggars!—it's blue with our bones!)
Hands off o' the sons o' the widow,
  Hands off o' the goods in 'er shop,
For the Kings must come down an' the Emperors frown
  When the Widow at Windsor says "Stop!"
    (Poor beggars!—we're sent to say "Stop!")
      Then 'ere 's to the Lodge o' the Widow,
        From the Pole to the Tropics it runs—
      To the Lodge that we tile with the rank an' the file,
        An' open in form with the guns.
    (Poor beggars!—it's always they guns!)

We 'ave 'eard o' the Widow at Windsor,
  It's safest to leave 'er alone:
For 'er sentries we stand by the sea an' the land
  Wherever the bugles are blown.
      (Poor beggars!—an' don't we get blown!)
Take 'old o' the Wings o' the Mornin',
  An' flop round the earth till you're dead;
But you won't get away from the tune that they play
  To the bloomin' old rag over'ead.
      (Poor beggars!—it's 'ot over'ead!)
      Then 'ere 's to the sons o' the Widow,
        Wherever, 'owever they roam.
      'Ere 's all they desire, an' if they require
        A speedy return to their 'ome.
      (Poor beggars!—they'll never see 'ome!)

RUDYARD KIPLING

'MANDALAY', 1892

From *Barrack Room Ballads*; an ex-soldier, caught in the tedium
of working-class civilian life, remembers the exotic experience
of colonial soldiering in the Far East. Mandalay, the Burmese
capital, was occupied by British troops under General Prender-
gast in the Burma War of 1885; following the deposition of King
Thebau, the whole country was annexed to the Empire.

By the old Moulmein Pagoda, lookin' eastward to the sea,
There's a Burma girl a-settin', and I know she thinks o' me;
For the wind is in the palm-trees, and the temple-bells they say:
"Come you back, you British soldier; come you back to
    Mandalay!"
        Come you back to Mandalay,
        Where the old Flotilla lay:
        Can't you 'ear their paddles chunkin' from Rangoon to
           Mandalay?
        On the road to Mandalay,
        Where the flyin'-fishes play,
        An' the dawn comes up like thunder outer China 'crost
           the Bay!

'Er petticoat was yaller an' 'er little cap was green,
An' 'er name was Supi-yaw-lat—jes' the same as Theebaw's Queen,
An' I seed her first a-smokin' of a whackin' white cheroot,
An' a-wastin' Christian kisses on an 'eathen idol's foot:
        Bloomin' idol made o' mud—
        Wot they called the Great Gawd Budd—
        Plucky lot she cared for idols when I kissed 'er where
           she stud!
        On the road to Mandalay ...

When the mist was on the rice-fields an' the sun was droppin' slow,
She'd git 'er little banjo an' she'd sing *"Kulla-lo-lo!"*
With 'er arm upon my shoulder an' 'er cheek agin my cheek
We useter watch the steamers an' the *hathis* pilin' teak.
       Elephints a-pilin' teak
       In the sludgy, squdgy creek,
       Where the silence 'ung that 'eavy you was 'arf afraid to
          speak!
       On the road to Mandalay ...

But that's all shove be'ind me—long ago an' fur away,
An' there ain't no 'busses runnin' from the Bank to Mandalay;
An' I'm learnin' 'ere in London what the ten-year soldier tells:
"If you've 'eard the East a-callin', you won't never 'eed naught
    else."
       No! you won't 'eed nothin' else
       But them spicy garlic smells,
       An' the sunshine an' the palm-trees an' the tinkly
          temple-bells;
       On the road to Mandalay ...

I am sick o' wastin' leather on these gritty pavin'-stones,
An' the blasted Henglish drizzle wakes the fever in my bones;
'Tho' I walks with fifty 'ousemaids outer Chelsea to the Strand,
An' they talks a lot o' lovin', but wot do they understand?
       Beefy face an' grubby 'and—
       Law! wot do they understand?
       I've a neater, sweeter maiden in a cleaner, greener land!
       On the road to Mandalay ...

Ship me somewheres east of Suez, where the best is like the worst,
Where there are n't no Ten Commandments an' a man can raise a
    thirst;
For the temple-bells are callin', an' it's there that I would be—
By the old Moulmein Pagoda, looking lazy at the sea;
       On the road to Mandalay,
       Where the old Flotilla lay,
       With our sick beneath the awnings when we went to
          Mandalay!
       O the road to Mandalay,
       Where the flyin'-fishes play,
       An' the dawn comes up like thunder outer China 'crost
          the Bay!

RUDYARD KIPLING

'SHILLIN' A DAY', 1892

Again from *Barrack Room Ballads*, and another ex-soldier, on the standard army pension of a shilling a day, running errands for his social betters in London after a lifetime of service to the Empire.

My Name is O'Kelly, I've heard the Revelly
From Birr to Bareilly, from Leeds to Lahore,
Hong-Kong and Peshawur.
Lucknow and Etawah,
And fifty-five more all endin' in "pore."
Black Death and his quickness, the depth and the thickness,
Of sorrow and sickness I've known on my way,
But I'm old and I'm nervis,
I'm cast from the Service,
And all I deserve is a shillin' a day.

> (*Chorus*)   Shillin' a day,
> Bloomin' good pay—
> Lucky to touch it, a shillin' a day!

Oh, it drives me half crazy to think of the days I
Went slap for the Ghazi, my sword at my side,
When we rode Hell-for-leather,
Both squadrons together,
That didn't care whether we lived or we died.
But it's no use despairin', my wife must go charin'
An' me commissairin', the pay-bills to better,
So if me you be'old
In the wet and the cold,
By the Grand Metropold won't you give me a letter?

> (*Full chorus*)   Give 'im a letter—
> 'Can't do no better,
> Late Troop-Sergeant-Major an'—runs with a letter!
> Think what 'e's been,
> Think what 'e's seen.
> Think of his pension an'—
> GAWD SAVE THE QUEEN!

LEWIS MORRIS

'THE IMPERIAL INSTITUTE. AN ODE', 1893

The Imperial Institute of the Colonies and India was an ambitious foundation in South Kensington, proposed by the Prince of Wales as a permanent memorial to the 1887 Jubilee, and intended to promote the arts, manufactures and commerce of the Empire. Morris's ode was written to mark its official opening by the Queen on 10 May 1893.

WITH soaring voice and solemn music sing!
High to Heaven's gate let pealing trumpets ring!
To-day our hands consolidate
The Empire of a thousand years:
Delusive hopes, distracting fears,
Have passed and left her great.
For Britain, Britain, we our jubilant anthems raise.
Uplift your voices all: worthy is she of praise!

Our Britain, issuing at the call of Fate
From her lone islets in the Northern Sea,
Donned her Imperial robe, assumed her crownèd state,
Took the sole sceptre of the Free;
'Mid clang of arms her crescent glory rose,
By shattered fleet and flaming town:
Victorious at the last o'er all her foes,
Embattled rolls her splendid story down.

Soldier and seaman, side by side,
Her strong sons, greatly dared and bravely died.
Close on their steps her dauntless toilers went
O'er unknown sea and pathless continent,
Till when the centuries of strife were done
They left the greatest Realm beneath the sun.
Praise them and her; your grateful voices raise.
Mother of Freedom! thou art worthy of our praise!

No more we seek our Realm's increase
By War's red rapine, but by white-winged Peace;
To-day we seek to bind in one,
Till all our Britain's work be done—

Through wider knowledge closer grown,
As each fair sister by the rest is known,
And mutual Commerce, mighty to efface
The envious bars of Time and Place,
Deep-pulsing from a common heart
And through a common speech expressed,—
From North to South, from East to West,
Our great World Empire's every part;
A universal Britain, strong
To raise up right and beat down Wrong.
Let this thing be! who shall our Realm divide?
Ever we stand together, Kinsmen, side by side!

To-day we would make free
Our millions of their glorious heritage.
Here, Labour crowds in hopeless misery,—
There, is unbounded work and ready wage.
The salt breeze, calling, stirs our Northern blood,—
Lead we the toilers to their certain good;
Guide we their feet to where
Is spread for those who dare
A happier Britain 'neath an ampler air.
Uprise, O Palace fair!
With ordered knowledge of each far-off land
For all to understand!
Uprise, O Palace fair, where for the Poor shall be
Wise thought and love to guide o'er the dividing sea.

First Lady of our British race!
'Tis well that with thy peaceful Jubilee
This glorious dream begins to be.
This thy lost Consort would; this would thy Son,
Who has seen all thy Empire face to face
And fain would leave it One.
Oh, may the Hand which rules our Fate
Keep this our Britain great!
We cannot tell, we can but pray
Heaven's blessing on our work to-day.
Uprise, O Palace fair, where every eye may see
This proud embodied Unity!
For Britain and our Queen one voice we raise,—
Laud them, rejoice, peal forth: worthy are they of praise!

OWEN SEAMAN

'THE SPACIOUS TIMES', 1896

An accomplished parodist and writer of light and satirical verse, Seaman (1861–1936) became a regular contributor to *Punch*, joined the staff in 1897, and was editor from 1906 to 1932. His no-nonsense imperialism and increasingly reactionary views largely determined the magazine's political complexion over the early decades of this century. Here, characteristically, he contrasts contemporary ethical anxieties about the legitimacy of imperial expansion with the buccaneering spirit that laid the basis of empire.

I WISH that I had flourished then,
　　When ruffs and raids were in the fashion,
When Shakespeare's art and Raleigh's pen
　　Encouraged patriotic passion;
For though I draw my happy breath
　　Beneath a Queen as good and gracious,
The times of Great Elizabeth
　　Were more conveniently spacious.

Large-hearted age of cakes and ale!
　　When, undeterred by nice conditions,
Good Master Drake would lightly sail
　　On little privateer commissions;
Careering round with sword and flame
　　And no pretence of polished manners,
He planted out in England's name
　　A most refreshing lot of banners.

Blest era, when the reckless tar,
　　Elated by a sense of duty,
Feared not to face his country's Bar
　　But freely helped himself to booty;
Returning home with bulging hold
　　The Queen would meet him, much excited,
Pronounce him worth his weight in gold
　　And promptly have the hero knighted.

No Extra Special, piping hot,
   Broke out in unexpected Pyrrhics;
No Poet Laureate on the spot
   Composed apologetic lyrics;
Transpiring slowly by-and-by,
   The act was voted one of loyalty;
The nation winked the other eye,
   And pocketed the usual royalty. ...

No Member had the hardy nerve
   To criticise our depredations
As unadapted to preserve
   The perfect comity of nations;
No High Commissioner would doubt
   If brigandage was quite judicial;
Indeed we mostly did without
   This rather eminent Official.

No Ministry would care a rap
   For theoretic arbitration;
They simply modified the map
   To meet the latest annexation;
And so without appeal to law,
   Or other needless waste of tissue,
The Lion, where he put his paw,
   Remained and propagated issue.

To-day we wax exceeding fat
   On lands our roving fathers raided;
And blush with holy horror at
   Their lawless sons who do as they did;
No doubt the age improves a lot,
   It grows more honest, more veracious;
But, as I said, the times are not
   Quite so conveniently spacious.

Rudyard Kipling

'A SONG OF THE ENGLISH', 1896

The opening sequence from the collection *The Seven Seas*, 'A Song of the English' was occasioned by efforts over a number of years to establish a formal Imperial Federation, based on naval power, throughout the Empire. It is one of Kipling's most sustained pieces of imperialist advocacy, and one of his most elaborate. In its panoramic quality, its fusion of racial myth and religious invocation, and in the semi-mystical relationship it seeks to establish between Britain and the colonies, the poem exemplifies many of the key components in the imperialist ideology that developed in the late nineteenth and early twentieth centuries.

Fair is our lot—O goodly is our heritage!
(Humble ye, my people, and be fearful in your mirth!)
  For the Lord our God Most High
  He hath made the deep as dry,
He hath smote for us a pathway to the ends of all the Earth!

Yea, though we sinned—and our rulers went from righteousness—
Deep in all dishonour though we stained our garments' hem.
  Oh be ye not dismayed,
  Though we stumbled and we strayed,
We were led by evil counsellors—the Lord shall deal with them!

Hold ye the Faith—the Faith our Fathers sealèd us;
Whoring not with visions—overwise and overstale.
  Except ye pay the Lord
  Single heart and single sword,
Of your children in their bondage shall He ask them treble-tale!

Keep ye the Law—be swift in all obedience—
Clear the land of evil, drive the road and bridge the ford.
  Make ye sure to each his own
  That he reap where he hath sown;
By the peace among Our peoples let men know we serve the Lord!

Hear now a song—a song of broken interludes—
A song of little cunning; of a singer nothing worth.
  Through the naked words and mean
  May ye see the truth between
As the singer knew and touched it in the ends of all the Earth!

THE COASTWISE LIGHTS

Our brows are bound with spindrift and the weed is on our knees;
Our loins are battered 'neath us by the swinging, smoking seas.
From reef and rock and skerry—over headland, ness, and voe—
The Coastwise Lights of England watch the ships of England go!

Through the endless summer evenings, on the lineless, level floors;
Through the yelling Channel tempest when the siren hoots and
    roars—
By day the dipping house-flag and by night the rocket's trail—
As the sheep that graze behind us so we know them where they
    hail.

We bridge across the dark and bid the helmsman have a care,
The flash that wheeling inland wakes his sleeping wife to prayer;
From our vexed eyries, head to gale, we bind in burning chains
The lover from the sea-rim drawn—his love in English lanes.

We greet the clippers wing-and-wing that race the Southern wool;
We warn the crawling cargo-tanks of Bremen, Leith, and Hull;
To each and all our equal lamp at peril of the sea—
The white wall-sided warships or the whalers of Dundee!

Come up, come in from Eastward, from the guard-ports of the
    Morn!
Beat up, beat in from Southerly, O gipsies of the Horn!
Swift shuttles of an Empire's loom that weave us, main to main,
The Coastwise Lights of England give you welcome back again!

Go, get you gone up-Channel with the sea-crust on your plates;
Go, get you into London with the burden of your freights!
Haste, for they talk of Empire there, and say, if any seek,
The Lights of England sent you and by silence shall ye speak!

KIPLING (1896)

THE SONG OF THE DEAD

Hear now the Song of the Dead—in the North by the torn berg-edges—
They that look still to the Pole, asleep by their hide-stripped sledges.
Song of the Dead in the South—in the sun by their skeleton horses,
Where the warrigal whimpers and bays through the dust of the sere
    river-courses.

Song of the Dead in the East—in the heat-rotted jungle hollows,
Where the dog-ape barks in the kloof—in the brake of the
    buffalo-wallows.
Song of the Dead in the West—in the Barrens, the waste that
    betrayed them,
Where the wolverine tumbles their packs from the camp and the
    grave-mound they made them;
          Hear now the Song of the Dead!

I

We were dreamers, dreaming gently, in the man-stifled town;
We yearned beyond the sky-line where the strange roads go down.
Came the Whisper, came the Vision, came the Power with the
    Need,
Till the Soul that is not man's soul was lent us to lead.
As the deer breaks—as the steer breaks—from the herd where
    they graze,
In the faith of little children we went on our ways.
Then the wood failed—then the food failed—then the last water
    dried—
In the faith of little children we lay down and died.
On the sand-drift—one the veldt-side—in the fern-scrub we lay,
That our sons might follow after by the bones on the way.
Follow after—follow after! We have watered the root,
And the bud has come to blossom that ripens for fruit!
Follow after—we are waiting, by the trails that we lost,
For the sounds of many footsteps, for the tread of a host.
Follow after—follow after—for the harvest is sown:
By the bones about the wayside ye shall come to your own!

        When Drake went down to the Horn
         And England was crowned thereby,
       'Twixt seas unsailed and shores unhailed
         Our Lodge—our Lodge was born
         (And England was crowned thereby!)

Which never shall close again
  By day nor yet by night,
While man shall take his life to stake
  At risk of shoal or main
  (By day nor yet by night)

But standeth even so
  As now we witness here,
While men depart, of joyful heart,
  Adventure for to know
  (As now bear witness here!)

II

We have fed our sea for a thousand years
  And she calls us, still unfed,
Though there's never a wave of all her waves
  But marks our English dead:
We have strawed our best to the weed's unrest
  To the shark and the sheering gull.
If blood be the price of admiralty,
  Lord God, we ha' paid in full!

There's never a flood goes shoreward now
  But lifts a keel we manned;
There's never an ebb goes seaward now
  But drops our dead on the sand—
But slinks our dead on the sands forlore,
  From the Ducies to the Swin.
If blood be the price of admiralty,
If blood be the price of admiralty,
  Lord God, we ha' paid it in!

We must feed our sea for a thousand years,
  For that is our doom and pride,
As it was when they sailed with the *Golden Hind*,
Or the wreck that struck last tide—
  Or the wreck that lies on the spouting reef
  Where the ghastly blue-lights flare.
If blood be the price of admiralty,
If blood be the price of admiralty,
If blood be the price of admiralty,
  Lord God, we ha' bought it fair!

THE DEEP-SEA CABLES

The wrecks dissolve above us; their dust drops down from afar—
Down to the dark, to the utter dark, where the blind white
    sea-snakes are.
There is no sound, no echo of sound, in the deserts of the deep,
Or the great grey level plains of ooze where the shell-burred
    cables creep.

Here in the womb of the world—here on the tie-ribs of earth
    Words, and the words of men, flicker and flutter and beat—
Warning, sorrow and gain, salutation and mirth—
    For a Power troubles the Still that has neither voice nor feet.

They have wakened the timeless Things; they have killed their
    father Time;
    Joining hands in the gloom, a league from the last of the sun.
Hush! Men talk to-day o'er the waste of the ultimate slime,
    And a new Word runs between: whispering, 'Let us be one!'

THE SONG OF THE SONS

One from the ends of the earth—gifts at an open door—
Treason has much, but we, Mother, thy sons have more!
From the whine of a dying man, from the snarl of a wolf-pack
    freed,
Turn, and the world is thine. Mother, be proud of thy seed!
Count, are we feeble or few? Hear, is our speech so rude?
Look, are we poor in the land? Judge, are we men of The Blood?
Those that have stayed at thy knees, Mother, go call them in—
We that were bred overseas wait and would speak with our kin.
Not in the dark do we fight—haggle and flout and gibe;
Selling our love for a price, loaning our hearts for a bribe.
Gifts have we only to-day—Love without promise or fee—
Hear, for thy children speak, from the uttermost parts of the sea!

THE SONG OF THE CITIES

BOMBAY

Royal and Dower-royal, I the Queen
    Fronting thy richest sea with richer hands—
A thousand mills roar through me where I glean
    All races from all lands.

CALCUTTA

Me the Sea-captain loved, the River built,
  Wealth sought and Kings adventured life to hold.
Hail, England!   I am Asia—Power on silt,
  Death in my hands, but Gold!

MADRAS

Clive kissed me on the mouth and eyes and brow,
  Wonderful kisses, so that I became
Crowned above Queens—a withered beldame now,
  Brooding on ancient fame.

RANGOON

Hail, Mother!   Do they call me rich in trade?
  Little care I, but hear the shorn priest drone,
And watch my silk-clad lovers, man by maid,
  Laugh 'neath my Shwe Dagon.

SINGAPORE

Hail, Mother!   East and West must seek my aid
  Ere the spent gear may dare the ports afar.
The second doorway of the wide world's trade
  Is mine to loose or bar.

HONG-KONG

Hail, Mother!   Hold me fast; my Praya sleeps
  Under innumerable keels to-day.
Yet guard (and landward), or to-morrow sweeps
  Thy warships down·the bay!

HALIFAX

Into the mist my guardian prows put forth,
  Behind the mist my virgin ramparts lie,
The Warden of the Honour of the North,
  Sleepless and veiled am I!

QUEBEC AND MONTREAL

Peace is our portion.   Yet a whisper rose,
  Foolish and causeless, half in jest, half hate.
Now wake we and remember mighty blows,
  And, fearing no man, wait!

KIPLING (1896)

VICTORIA

From East to West the circling word has passed,
  Till West is East beside our land-locked blue;
From East to West the tested chain holds fast,
  The well-forged link rings true!

CAPETOWN

Hail! Snatched and bartered oft from hand to hand,
  I dream my dream, by rock and heath and pine,
Of Empire to the northward. Ay, one land
  From Lion's Head to Line!

MELBOURNE

Greeting! Nor fear nor favour won us place,
  Got between greed of gold and dread of drouth,
Loud-voiced and reckless as the wild tide-race
  That whips our harbour-mouth!

SYDNEY

Greeting! My birth-stain have I turned to good;
  Forcing strong wills perverse to steadfastness:
The first flush of the tropics in my blood,
  And at my feet Success!

BRISBANE

The northern stirp beneath the southern skies—
  I build a Nation for an Empire's need,
Suffer a little, and my land shall rise,
  Queen over lands indeed!

HOBART

Man's love first found me; man's hate made me Hell;
  For my babes' sake I cleansed those infamies.
Earnest for leave to live and labour well,
  God flung me peace and ease.

AUCKLAND

Last, loneliest, loveliest, exquisite, apart—
  On us, on us the unswerving season smiles,
Who wonder 'mid our fern why men depart
  To seek the Happy Isles!

ENGLAND'S ANSWER

Truly ye come of The Blood; slower to bless than to ban;
Little used to lie down at the bidding of any man.
Flesh of the flesh that I bred, bone of the bone that I bare;
Stark as your sons shall be—stern as your fathers were.
Deeper than speech our love, stronger than life our tether,
But we do not fall on the neck nor kiss when we come together.
My arm is nothing weak, my strength is not gone by;
Sons, I have borne many sons, but my dugs are not dry.
Look, I have made ye a place and opened wide the doors,
That ye may talk together, your Barons and Councillors—
Wards of the Outer March, Lords of the Lower Seas,
Ay, talk to your grey mother that bore you on her knees!—
That ye may talk together, brother to brother's face—
Thus for the good of your peoples—thus for the Pride of the Race.
Also, we will make promise. So long as The Blood endures,
I shall know that your good is mine: ye shall feel that my
     strength is yours:
In the day of Armageddon, at the last great fight of all,
That Our House stand together and the pillars do not fall.
Draw now the threefold knot firm on the ninefold bands,
And the Law that ye make shall be law after the rule of your lands.
This for the waxen Heath, and that for the Wattle-bloom,
This for the Maple-leaf, and that for the southern Broom.
The Law that ye make shall be law and I do not press my will,
Because ye are Sons of The Blood and call me Mother still.
Now must ye speak to your kinsmen and they must speak to you,
After the use of the English, in straight-flung words and few.
Go to your work and be strong, halting not in your ways,
Baulking the end half-won for an instant dole of praise.
Stand to your work and be wise—certain of sword and pen,
Who are neither children nor Gods, but men in a world of men!

WILLIAM WATSON

———

Between 1895 and 1897 recurrent massacres of Armenian Christians by the Turks led to international outrage, but the European powers refused to intervene directly. For Watson this was an abdication of responsibility that exposed the hypocrisy of claiming a Christian and civilizing mission for British imperialism. His 1897 collection *The Year of Shame*, from which this poem is taken, is wholly given over to the Armenian situation and the moral bankruptcy of the British position.

OF kings and courts; of kingly, courtly ways
In which the life of man is bought and sold;
How weary is our heart these many days!

Of ceremonious embassies that hold
Parley with Hell in fine and silken phrase,
How weary is our heart these many days!

Of wavering counsellors neither hot nor cold,
Whom from His mouth God speweth, be it told
How weary is our heart these many days!

Yea, for the ravelled night is round the lands,
And sick are we of all the imperial story.
The tramp of Power, and its long trail of pain;
The mighty brows in meanest arts grown hoary;
The mighty hands,
That in the dear, affronted name of Peace
Bind down a people to be racked and slain;
The emulous armies waxing without cease,
All-puissant all in vain;
The pacts and leagues to murder by delays,
And the dumb throngs that on the deaf thrones gaze;
The common loveless lust of territory;
The lips that only babble of their mart,
While to the night the shrieking hamlets blaze;
The bought allegiance, and the purchased praise,
False honour, and shameful glory;—
Of all the evil whereof this is part,
How weary is our heart,
How weary is our heart these many days!

Rudyard Kipling

'RECESSIONAL', 1897

———

The sombre, monitory quality of Kipling's response to Victoria's
Diamond Jubilee strikes a tellingly different note from the self-
congratulatory celebration of monarchy and empire produced by
many of his contemporaries.

> God of our fathers, known of old,
>   Lord of our far-flung battle-line,
> Beneath whose awful Hand we hold
>   Dominion over palm and pine—
> Lord God of Hosts, be with us yet,
> Lest we forget—lest we forget!
>
> The tumult and the shouting dies;
>   The Captains and the Kings depart:
> Still stands Thine ancient sacrifice,
>   An humble and a contrite heart.
> Lord God of Hosts, be with us yet,
> Lest we forget—lest we forget!
>
> Far-called, our navies melt away;
>   On dune and headland sinks the fire:
> Lo, all our pomp of yesterday
>   Is one with Nineveh and Tyre!
> Judge of the Nations, spare us yet,
> Lest we forget—lest we forget!
>
> If, drunk with sight of power, we loose
>   Wild tongues that have not Thee in awe,
> Such boastings as the Gentiles use,
>   Or lesser breeds without the Law—
> Lord God of Hosts, be with us yet,
> Lest we forget—lest we forget!
>
> For heathen heart that puts her trust
>   In reeking tube and iron shard,
> All valiant dust that builds on dust,
>   And guarding, calls not Thee to guard,
> For frantic boast and foolish word—
> Thy mercy on Thy People, Lord!

HENRY NEWBOLT

'VITAÏ LAMPADA', 1898

Newbolt (1862–1938) was made famous by his poem 'Drake's Drum', first published in 1896 and then included in his first collection of verse, *Admirals All*, in 1897. Subsequent volumes, *The Island Race* of 1898 and *Songs of the Sea* of 1904, continued to promote patriotism, heroic history, and service to the Empire. The public school ethos provided the background to much of his liberal imperialism, as in this well-known celebration of school-boy pluck on games field and battlefield, 'The Lamp of Life'.

THERE's a breathless hush in the Close to-night—
    Ten to make and the match to win—
A bumping pitch and a blinding light,
    An hour to play and the last man in.
And it's not for the sake of a ribboned coat,
    Or the selfish hope of a season's fame,
But his Captain's hand on his shoulder smote—
"Play up! play up! and play the game!"

The sand of the desert is sodden red,—
    Red with the wreck of a square that broke;
The Gatling's jammed and the Colonel dead,
    And the regiment blind with dust and smoke.
The river of death has brimmed his banks,
    And England's far, and Honour a name,
But the voice of a schoolboy rallies the ranks:
"Play up! play up! and play the game!"

This is the word that year by year,
    While in her place the School is set,
Every one of her sons must hear,
    And none that hears it dare forget.
This they all with joyful mind
    Bear through life like a torch in flame,
And falling fling to the host behind—
"Play up! play up! and play the game!"

Henry Newbolt

'HE FELL AMONG THIEVES', 1898

The solitary death on the distant margins of the Empire was a potent theme for imperialist poets. Here, Newbolt's images of a traditionally and aristocratically ordered England are deployed against the final lonely reckoning on the North West Frontier.

"Ye have robbed," said he, "ye have slaughtered and made an end,
   Take your ill-got plunder, and bury the dead:
What will ye more of your guest and sometime friend?"
   "Blood for our blood," they said.

He laughed: "If one may settle the score for five,
   I am ready; but let the reckoning stand till day:
I have loved the sunlight as dearly as any alive."
   "You shall die at dawn," said they.

He flung his empty revolver down the slope,
   He climbed alone to the Eastward edge of the trees;
All night long in a dream untroubled of hope
   He brooded, clasping his knees.

He did not hear the monotonous roar that fills
   The ravine where the Yassin river sullenly flows;
He did not see the starlight on the Laspur hills,
   Or the far Afghan snows.

He saw the April noon on his books aglow,
   The wistaria trailing in at the window wide;
He heard his father's voice from the terrace below
   Calling him down to ride.

He saw the gray little church across the park,
   The mounds that hide the loved and honoured dead;
The Norman arch, the chancel softly dark,
   The brasses black and red.

He saw the School Close, sunny and green,
   The runner beside him, the stand by the parapet wall,
The distant tape, and the crowd roaring between
   His own name over all.

He saw the dark wainscot and timbered roof,
    The long tables, and the faces merry and keen;
The College Eight and their trainer dining aloof,
    The Dons on the daïs serene.

He watched the liner's stem ploughing the foam,
    He felt her trembling speed and the thrash of her screw;
He heard her passengers' voices talking of home,
    He saw the flag she flew.

And now it was dawn. He rose strong on his feet,
    And strode to his ruined camp below the wood;
He drank the breath of the morning cool and sweet;
    His murderers round him stood.

Light on the Laspur hills was broadening fast,
    The blood-red snow-peaks chilled to a dazzling white:
He turned, and saw the golden circle at last,
    Cut by the Eastern height.

"O glorious Life, Who dwellest in earth and sun,
    I have lived, I praise and adore Thee."
                               A sword swept.
Over the pass the voices one by one
    Faded, and the hill slept.

HILAIRE BELLOC

From *THE MODERN TRAVELLER*, 1898

Belloc (1870–1953) was one of the most industrious and wide-ranging authors of the first half of the twentieth century—historian, biographer, travel writer, novelist, essayist and poet. His wryly subversive poems for children, particularly the *Cautionary Tales* of 1907, are still widely known. *The Modern Traveller* is an early work that burlesques the late Victorian vogue for stories of imperial exploration and adventure, combining broad parody with a sharp satiric consciousness of the brutality and commercial chicanery that lay just below the surface of so much colonial enterprise. The poem is narrated by Mr Rooter, the author of a lying book of West African travels and, with his companions Commander Henry Sin and Captain William Blood, the projector of a fraudulent speculative company. The specific target of the satire was Goldie's Royal Niger Company, engaged in 'opening up' West Africa in the 1890s. In the following extracts the travellers arrive in Africa, learn how the whites manage to control the native population, and spy out the land they will market to speculators.

V

Oh! Africa, mysterious Land!
Surrounded by a lot of sand
    And full of grass and trees,
And elephants and Afrikanders,
And politics and Salamanders,
And Germans seeking to annoy,
And horrible rhinoceroi,
And native rum in little kegs,
And savages call Touaregs
    (A kind of Soudanese).
And tons of diamonds, and lots
Of nasty, dirty Hottentots,
And coolies coming from the East;
And serpents, seven yards long at least,
    And lions, that retain
Their vigour, appetites and rage
Intact to an extreme old age,

And never lose their mane.
Far Land of Ophir! Mined for gold
By lordly Solomon of old,
Who sailing northward to Perim
Took all the gold away with him,
    And left a lot of holes;
Vacuities that bring despair
    To those confiding souls
Who find that they have bought a share
In marvellous horizons, where
The Desert terrible and bare
    Interminably rolls. ...

VI

In getting up our Caravan
We met a most obliging man,
The Lord Chief Justice of Liberia,
And Minister of the Interior;
Cain Abolition Beecher Boz,
Worked like a Nigger—which he was—
    And in a single day
Procured us Porters, Guides, and kit,
And would not take a sou for it
    Until we went away.[1]
We wondered how this fellow made
Himself so readily obeyed,
And why the natives were so meek;
Until by chance we heard him speak,
And then we clearly understood
How great a Power for Social Good
    The African can be.
He said with a determined air:
'You are not what your fathers were;
Liberians, you are Free!
Of course, if you refuse to go—'
And here he made a gesture.
He also gave us good advice
Concerning Labour and its Price.
'In dealing wid de Native Scum,
Yo' cannot pick an' choose;
Yo' hab to promise um a sum
Ob wages, paid in Cloth and Rum.

---

[1] But when we went away, we found
A deficit of several pound.

But, Lordy! that's a ruse!
Yo' get yo' well on de Adventure,
And.change de wages to Indenture.'

We did the thing that he projected,
The Caravan grew disaffected,
    And Sin and I consulted;
Blood understood the Native mind,
He said: 'We must be firm but kind.'
    A Mutiny resulted.
I never shall forget the way
That Blood upon this awful day
Preserved us all from death.
He stood upon a little mound,
Cast his lethargic eyes around,
And said beneath his breath:
'Whatever happens we have got
The Maxim Gun, and they have not.'

He marked them in their rude advance,
He hushed their rebel cheers;
With one extremely vulgar glance
He broke the Mutineers.
(I have a picture in my book
Of how he quelled them with a look.)
We shot and hanged a few, and then
The rest became devoted men.
And here I wish to say a word
Upon the way my heart was stirred
    By those pathetic faces.
Surely our simple duty here
Is both imperative and clear;
While they support us, we should lend
Our every effort to defend,
And from a higher point of view
To give the full direction due
    To all the native races.
And I, throughout the expedition,
Insisted upon this position.

VII

Well, after that we toiled away
At drawing maps, and day by day
Blood made an accurate survey
    Of all that seemed to lend

A chance, no matter how remote,
Of letting our financier float
That triumph of Imagination,
'The Libyan Association.'
    In this the 'Negroes' friend,
Was much concerned to show the way
Of making Missionaries pay.

At night our leader and our friend
    Would deal in long discourses
Upon this meritorious end,
And how he would arrange it.
'The present way is an abuse
    Of Economic Forces;
They Preach, but they do not Produce.
Observe how I would change it.
I'd have the Missionary lent,
Upon a plot of land,
A sum at twenty-five percent;
And (if I understand
The kind of people I should get)
An ever-present risk of debt
Would make them work like horses,
And form the spur, or motive spring,
In what I call "developing
    The Natural resources";
While people who subscribe will find
Profit and Piety combined.'

Imagine how the Mighty Scheme,
The Goal, the Vision, and the Dream,
Developed in his hands!
With such a purpose, such a mind
Could easily become inclined
To use the worst of lands!
Thus once we found him standing still,
Enraptured, on a rocky hill;
Beneath his feet there stank
A swamp immeasurably wide,
Wherein a kind of foetid tide
Rose rhythmical and sank,
Brackish and pestilent with weeds
And absolutely useless reeds,
It lay; but nothing daunted
At seeing how it heaved and steamed

He stood triumphant, and he seemed
Like one possessed or haunted.

With arms that welcome and rejoice,
We heard him gasping, in a voice
By strong emotion rendered harsh:
'That Marsh—that Admirable Marsh!'
The Tears of Avarice that rise
In purely visionary eyes
Were rolling down his nose.
He was no longer Blood the Bold,
The Terror of his foes;
But Blood inflamed with greed of gold.

He saw us, and at once became
The Blood we knew, the very same
Whom we had loved so long.
He looked affectionately sly,
And said, 'Perhaps you wonder why
My feelings are so strong?
You only see a swamp, but I—
My friends, I will explain it.
I know some gentlemen in town
Will give me fifty thousand down,
Merely for leave to drain it.'

A little later on we found
A piece of gently rolling ground
That showed above the flat.
Such a protuberance or rise
As wearies European eyes.
To common men, like Sin and me,
The Eminence appeared to be
As purposeless as that.
Blood saw another meaning there,
He turned with a portentous glare,
And shouted for the Native Name.
The Black interpreter in shame
Replied: 'The native name I fear
Is something signifying Mud.'
        Then, with the gay bravado
That suits your jolly Pioneer,
In his prospectus Captain Blood
        Baptized it 'Eldorado'.
He also said the Summit rose
Majestic with Eternal Snows.

Rudyard Kipling

'THE WHITE MAN'S BURDEN', 1898

This (in)famous poem promoting the ideology of a white mission to civilize the world was addressed less perhaps to Britain and more to the United States, where Kipling lived for a number of years with his American wife. Significantly, though it outraged American liberals, the poem was enthusiastically received by Theodore Roosevelt and the large section of the population that supported him.

Take up the White Man's burden—
　　Send forth the best ye breed—
Go bind your sons to exile
　　To serve your captives' need;
To wait in heavy harness,
　　On fluttered folk and wild—
Your new-caught, sullen peoples,
　　Half-devil and half-child.

Take up the White Man's burden—
　　In patience to abide,
To veil the threat of terror
　　And check the show of pride;
By open speech and simple,
　　An hundred times made plain,
To seek another's profit,
　　And work another's gain.

Take up the White Man's burden—
　　The savage wars of peace—
Fill full the mouth of Famine
　　And bid the sickness cease;
And when your goal is nearest
　　The end for others sought,
Watch Sloth and heathen Folly
　　Bring all your hope to nought.

[307]

Take up the White Man's burden—
　　No tawdry rule of kings,
But toil of serf and sweeper—
　　The tale of common things.
The ports ye shall not enter,
　　The roads ye shall not tread,
Go make them with your living,
　　And mark them with your dead.

Take up the White Man's burden—
　　And reap his old reward:
The blame of those ye better,
　　The hate of those ye guard—
The cry of hosts ye humour
　　(Ah, slowly!) toward the light:—
"Why brought ye us from bondage,
　　"Our loved Egyptian night?"

Take up the White Man's burden—
　　Ye dare not stoop to less—
Nor call too loud on Freedom
　　To cloak your weariness;
By all ye cry or whisper,
　　By all ye leave or do,
The silent, sullen peoples
　　Shall weigh your Gods and you.

Take up the White Man's burden—
　　Have done with childish days—
The lightly proffered laurel,
　　The easy, ungrudged praise.
Comes now, to search your manhood
　　Through all the thankless years,
Cold, edged with dear-bought wisdom,
　　The judgment of your peers!

ROBERT WILLIAMS BUCHANAN

From *THE NEW ROME:*
POEMS AND BALLADS OF OUR EMPIRE, 1899

A novelist and dramatist as well as a poet, Buchanan (1841–1901) was a leading literary figure in London from the 1860s, his career including a notorious row with Swinburne and the Pre-Raphaelites, whom he derided in his essay 'The Fleshly School of Poetry'. Brought up as a socialist, Buchanan retained radical sympathies all his life, and these are nowhere more clear than in *The New Rome*, published as Britain was about to go to war in South Africa. The poems in the collection are loosely based on a parallel between the late Victorian British Empire and Rome in its decadence, and constitute an acerbic attack upon the military aggrandisement and commercial rapacity that Buchanan saw as the driving forces of imperial expansion.

'A SONG OF JUBILEE'

Here, ambiguity of tone and the demythologizing of British imperial history ironically invert the triumphalism and complacency that attended the celebration of Victoria's Diamond Jubilee.

> Ho, heirs of Saxon Alfred
>   And Cœur de Lion bold!
> Mix'd breed of churls and belted earls
>   Who worshipped God of old;
> Who harried East and harried West
>   And gather'd land and gold,
> While from the lips of white-wing'd ships
>   Our battle-thunder rolled!
> With a hey! and a ho!
>   And a British three times three!
> At the will of the Lord of the Cross and Sword
>   We swept from sea to sea!

And lo, our mighty Empire
   Rises like ROME of yore—
Another Rome, that feasts at home
   And hugs its golden store;
Another and a mightier Rome!
   That, growing more and more,
Now reaches from Saint Paul's great dome
   To far Tasmania's shore!
With a hey! and a ho!
   And a British three times three!
True strain and seed of the Ocean-breed,
   We keep this Jubilee!

Liegemen of Bess the Virgin,
   Heirs of the harlot Nell!
Our once bright blood hath mix'd with mud
   More oft than song need tell;
But through each hour of pride and power,
   When free we fought and fell,
What gave us might to face the Fight
   Was—faith in Heaven and Hell!
With a hey! and a ho!
   And a British three times three!
Though the faith hath fled and our Lord lies dead,
   We keep this Jubilee!

Stay!   By the Soul of Milton!
   By Cromwell's battle-cry!
The voice of the Lord of the Cross and Sword
   Still rings beneath our sky!
Our faith lives still in the stubborn Will
   No Priest or Pope could buy—
Ours is the creed of the doughty Deed,
   The strength to do and die!
With a hey! and a ho!
   And a British three times three!
Still sword in hand 'neath the Cross we stand
   And keep this Jubilee!

Lady and Queen and Mother!
  Our long sea-race is run!
Let Love and Peace bless and increase
  What Cross and Sword have won!
The nameless guilt, the red blood spilt,
  The deeds in darkness done,
All these are past, and our souls at last
  Stand shriven in the sun.
With a hey! and a ho!
  And a British three times three!
We Men of the Deep sheathe swords, and keep
  Thy bloodless Jubilee!

Queen of the many races
  That round thy footstool cling,
Take heed lest Cain o'erthrow again
  His brother's offering!
Beyond the waves crawl butchering knaves,
  Now crouching for the spring,
While stolen gold stains, as of old,
  The gift thy legions bring!
With a hey! and a ho!
  And a British three times three!
There are robbers still who are fain to spill
  Blood, on thy Jubilee!

Ghosts of sad Queens departed
  Watch thee from far away:
Not theirs the bliss and calm of this
  Thy peaceful triumph-day!
A faith more fearless and serene,
  A creed less swift to slay,
Are thine, if thou hast found, O QUEEN,
  A gentler God for stay!
With a hey! and a ho!
  And a British three times three!
We thy might proclaim in that one God's Name
  On this thy Jubilee.

'TOMMIE ATKINS'

As so often in *Punch*, the jingoist in this poem is identified as a cockney, which for Buchanan connoted the narrow economic self-interest of the petit bourgeois as well as vulgar prejudice. The poem also seems ironically directed towards the cockney tommies of Kipling, whose poetry Buchanan saw as pandering to jingoism.

SHRIEKING and swinging legs, astride
On his native fence, the Cockney cried:
'Fee faw fum! beware of me!
I am the Lord of Land and Sea!'

Out on the fields, where day and night
The weary warriors strove in fight,
They paused a space to gaze upon
The moat-surrounded fence,—his throne!

And while they heard that war-cry float
From the smug Cockney's raucous throat,
'Come off the fence,' they cried, 'and share
The brunt of battle, if you dare!'

Yet still they heard him shriek and brag
Waving a little schoolboy's Flag,
And angry at his martial mien
They tried to hoot him from the scene!

'Ho ho!' he said, 'if that's your plan,
I'll teach you I'm an Englishman!—
Here, Tommie Atkins,—take your fee,—
Go fight these knaves who flout at me!'

Poor Tommie Atkins waiting stood,
And heard his master's cry for blood,
Then held out hand to take his pay,
And drew his sword, and sprang away!

All day the bloody strife was wrought,
The Cockney shriek'd, while Tommie fought.
Night came, the foe were driven away,—
But Tommie Atkins dying lay.

'Tommie, what cheer?' the Cockney said;
Poor Tommie raised his bleeding head,—
'You've lick'd them, sir!' poor Tommie cried,
And slowly droop'd his head, and died!

Still on his fence the Cockney swings,
Loud in the air the war-cry rings,
And still, in answer to his cries,
Poor Tommie Atkins bleeds and dies.

'THE CHARTER'D COMPANIE'

A major part of the late Victorian land grab in Africa was
managed through chartered companies like Rhodes's British
South Africa Company, and Goldie's Royal Niger Company—
attacked in Belloc's *The Modern Traveller* the year before *The
Modern Rome* appeared. These companies operated for private
profit under charter from the Crown, and had access to military
resources to support their enterprises.

THE Devil's will is the Devil's still, wherever the Devil may be—
He used to delight in the thick of the fight, whether on land
    or sea;
'Twas difficult for mortal men to know what side he took,
When the wrath of the Lord from heaven was poured and the
    whole Creation shook;
Yet for many a day the Devil's way was ever mighty and grand,
'Mid the swift sword's flash and the cannon's crash he boldly took
    his stand:
Such perilous work he has learn'd to shirk, and quiet at home
    sits he,
Having turn'd himself for the love of pelf to a Charter'd
    Companie!

'Ho! better far than the work of War, and the storm and stress
    of strife,
Is to rest at home, while others roam,' he murmurs to Sin, his
    wife!
'Tho' the fiends my sons make Gatling guns, they're Christians to
    the core,
And they love the range of the Stock Exchange far better than
    battle-roar.

They are spared, in truth, much strife uncouth and trouble by
    field and flood,
Since the work of Hell is done so well by creatures of flesh and
    blood;
And I think on the whole,' says the grim old Soul, ''tis better for
    you and me
That I've turned myself, ere laid on the shelf, to a Charter'd
    Companie!

'The thin red line was doubtless fine as it crept across the plain,
While the thick fire ran from the black Redan and broke it again
    and again,
But the hearts of men throbb'd bravely then, and their souls could
    do and dare,
'Mid the thick of the fight, in my despite, God found out Heroes
    there!
The Flag of England waved on high, and the thin red line
    crept on,
And I felt, as it flashed along to die, my occupation gone!
O'er a brave man's soul I had no control in those old days,'
    said he,
'So I've turned myself, ere laid on the shelf, to a Charter'd
    Companie!

'The Flag of England still doth blow and flings the sunlight back,
But the line that creepeth now below is changed to a line of black!
Wherever the Flag of England blows, down go all other flags,
Wherever the line of black print goes, the British Bulldog brags!
The newspaper, my dear, is best to further such work as mine,—
My blessing rest, north, south, east, west, on the thin black
    penny-a-line!
For my work is done 'neath moon or sun, by men and not by me,
Now I've changed myself, in the reign of the Guelph, to a
    Charter'd Companie!

'Of Church and of State let others prate, let martyr'd thousands
    moan,—
I'm responsible, I beg to state, to my shareholders alone!
The Flag of England may rot and fall, both Church and State
    may end,
Whate'er befall, I laugh at it all, if I pay a dividend!
But O my dear, it is very clear that the thing is working well—
When they hunt the black man down like deer, we devils rejoice
    in Hell!

'Tis loot, loot, loot, as they slaughter and shoot out yonder across
    the sea,
Now I've turned myself, like a gamesome elf, to a Charter'd
    Companie!

'Just study, my dear, the record here, of the mighty deeds they've
    done—
Hundreds, *en masse*, mowed down like grass, to an English loss
    of *one!*
Then loot, loot, loot, as they slaughter and shoot, to the shrieks of
    the naked foe,
While murder and greed on the fallen feed, right up my stock
    must go!
And the best of the lark, you'll be pleased to mark, is the
    counter-jumper's cry,
As he clutches his shares and mumbles his prayers to the
    Jingo-God on high!
With Bible and Gun the work is done both here and across the
    sea,
Now I've turned myself, in the reign of the Guelph, to a
    Charter'd Companie!'

The Devil's will is the Devil's still, though wrought in a Christian
    land,
He chuckles low and laughs his fill, with the latest news in hand;
Nor God nor man can mar his plan so long as the markets thrive,
Tho' the Flag be stained and the Creed profaned, he keepeth the
    game alive!
'The Flag of England may rot and fall, both Church and State
    may end,
Whatever befall, I laugh at it all, if I pay a dividend!
Right glad I dwell where I make my Hell, in the white man's
    heart,' cries he,
'Now I've turned myself, for the love of pelf, to a Charter'd
    Companie!'

THOMAS HARDY

From 'WAR POEMS', written 1899–1900

Hardy (1840–1928) was writing poetry by the mid-1860s but turned to fiction, if we are to believe his autobiography, as the only means of making a living from literature: the result was the great series of the Wessex novels. After the publication of *The Well-Beloved* in 1897, with income and reputation secure, Hardy turned back to poetry, which then occupied him almost exclusively for the rest of his long life. The 'War Poems' sequence, written in response to the Boer War, appeared in 1901 in his second collection, *Poems of the Past and the Present*.

The South African War, which began in October 1899 when Boer forces of the Transvaal republic invaded Natal, resulted from decades of hostility between the British colonial authorities and the Dutch Afrikaner settlers: at the core of the conflict was control of the Rand gold mines. Although early British reverses caused considerable alarm, the defeat of the Boers was inevitable once the numerically and technologically superior British forces were fully deployed. Even so, the conflict dragged on until 1902 and eventually cost the lives of more than 22,000 British and colonial troops.

Although public opinion broadly supported the war, it was the first in which there was a considerable and organized civilian anti-war movement. It also generated more poems than any previous British war, among them Hardy's. In those selected here, his emphasis upon the civilian experience of loss, his fascination with the physical and psychological otherness of the war, and his characteristically pervasive irony, produce a reworking of the familiar imperial theme of soldiers fighting and dying far from home.

'EMBARCATION (*SOUTHAMPTON DOCKS: OCTOBER 1899*)'

> HERE, where Vespasian's legions struck the sands,
> And Cerdic with his Saxons entered in,
> And Henry's army leapt afloat to win
> Convincing triumphs over neighbour lands,

Vaster battalions press for further strands,
To argue in the selfsame bloody mode
Which this late age of thought, and pact, and code,
Still fails to mend.—Now deckward tramp the bands,

Yellow as autumn leaves, alive as spring;
And as each host draws out upon the sea
Beyond which lies the tragical To-be,
None dubious of the cause, none murmuring,

Wives, sisters, parents, wave white hands and smile,
As if they knew not that they weep the while.

'DEPARTURE (*SOUTHAMPTON DOCKS: OCTOBER 1899*)'

WHILE the far farewell music thins and fails,
And the broad bottoms rip the bearing brine—
All smalling slowly to the gray sea-line—
And each significant red smoke-shaft pales,
Keen sense of severance everywhere prevails,
Which shapes the late long tramp of mounting men
To seeming words that ask and ask again:
"How long, O striving Teutons, Slavs, and Gaels

Must your wroth reasonings trade on lives like these,
That are as puppets in a playing hand?—
When shall the saner softer polities
Whereof we dream, have sway in each proud land
And patriotism, grown Godlike, scorn to stand
Bondslave to realms, but circle earth and seas?"

'THE GOING OF THE BATTERY.
WIVES' LAMENT (*NOVEMBER 2, 1899*)'

O IT was sad enough, weak enough, mad enough—
Light in their loving as soldiers can be—
First to risk choosing them, leave alone losing them
Now, in far battle, beyond the South Sea! ...

—Rain came down drenchingly; but we unblenchingly
Trudged on beside them through mirk and through mire,
They stepping steadily—only too readily!—
Scarce as if stepping brought parting-time nigher.

[317]

Great guns were gleaming there, living things seeming there,
Cloaked in their tar-cloths, upmouthed to the night;
Wheels wet and yellow from axle to felloe,
Throats blank of sound, but prophetic to sight.

Gas-glimmers drearily, blearily, eerily
Lit our pale faces outstretched for one kiss,
While we stood prest to them, with a last quest to them
Not to court perils that honour could miss.

Sharp were those sighs of ours, blinded these eyes of ours,
When at last moved away under the arch
All we loved. Aid for them each woman prayed for them,
Treading back slowly the track of their march.

Some one said: "Nevermore will they come: evermore
Are they now lost to us."   O it was wrong!
Though may be hard their ways, some Hand will guard
    their ways,
Bear them through safely, in brief time or long.

—Yet, voices haunting us, daunting us, taunting us,
Hint in the night-time when life beats are low
Other and graver things. ... Hold we to braver things,
Wait we, in trust, what Time's fulness shall show.

'A WIFE IN LONDON (*DECEMBER 1899*)'

I

SHE sits in the tawny vapour
    That the Thames-side lanes have uprolled,
    Behind whose webby fold on fold
Like a waning taper
    The street-lamp glimmers cold.

A messenger's knock cracks smartly,
    Flashed news is in her hand
    Of meaning it dazes to understand
Though shaped so shortly:
    He—has fallen—in the far South Land. ...

II

'Tis the morrow; the fog hangs thicker,
    The postman nears and goes:
    A letter is brought whose lines disclose
By the firelight flicker
    His hand, whom the worm now knows:

Fresh—firm—penned in highest feather—
    Page-full of his hoped return,
    And of home-planned jaunts by brake and burn
In the summer weather,
    And of new love that they would learn.

'DRUMMER HODGE'

THEY throw in Drummer Hodge, to rest
    Uncoffined—just as found:
His landmark is a kopje-crest
    That breaks the veldt around;
And foreign constellations west
    Each night above his mound.

Young Hodge the Drummer never knew—
    Fresh from his Wessex home—
The meaning of the broad Karoo,
    The Bush, the dusty loam,
And why uprose to nightly view
    Strange stars amid the gloam.

Yet portion of that unknown plain
    Will Hodge for ever be;
His homely Northern breast and brain
    Grow to some Southern tree,
And strange-eyed constellations reign
    His stars eternally.

ALGERNON CHARLES SWINBURNE

'TRANSVAAL', 1899

———

The patriotic and imperialist themes in much of the verse Swinburne (1837–1909) produced towards the end of his life offer a marked contrast to the lush eroticism and the vehement republican and atheist sentiments that characerized the poetry that made him famous—or infamous—in the 1860s and 1870s. Swinburne himself saw no inconsistency, however, and frequently invoked the Cromwellian Commonwealth as a model and inspiration for the Victorian Empire, as in this typically violent sonnet written at the start of the Boer War.

PATIENCE, long sick to death, is dead. Too long
  Have sloth and doubt and treason bidden us be
  What Cromwell's England was not, when the sea
To him bore witness given of Blake how strong
She stood, a commonweal that brooked no wrong
  From foes less vile than men like wolves set free
  Whose war is waged where none may fight or flee—
With women and with weanlings. Speech and song
Lack utterance now for loathing. Scarce we hear
  Foul tongues that blacken God's dishonoured name
  With prayers turned curses and with praise found shame
Defy the truth whose witness now draws near
  To scourge these dogs, agape with jaws afoam,
  Down out of life. Strike, England, and strike home.

WILFRED SCAWEN BLUNT

From *SATAN ABSOLVED.*
A VICTORIAN MYSTERY, 1899

———

Satan Absolved is an extraordinary poem, an appalled, apocalyptic vision of the devastation wrought by the Western nations, and Britain in particular, in the pursuit of empire. In the following extract, Satan, witheringly dismissive of the ideology of The White Man's Burden, tells God that the Anglo-Saxon races have pillaged the earth in the name of Christianity, and The Angel of Pity catalogues the destruction of the natural world at the hands of white imperialists.

Nay, they have tarred Time's features, pock-marked Nature's face,
Brought all to the same jakes with their own lack of grace.
In all Thy living World there is no sentient thing
Polluteth and defileth as this Saxon king,
This intellectual lord and sage of the new quest,
The only wanton he that fouleth his own nest.
And still his boast goeth forth. Nay, Lord, 'tis shame to Thee
This slave, being what he is, should ape divinity,
The poorest saddest drudge, the least joy-lifted heart
In all a World where tears are sold in open mart,
That he should stand, Thy choice, to preach Thy law, and set
His impress on the Earth in full apostolate,
Thy missioner and priest. He goeth among the nations,
Saith he, to spread Thy truth, to preach Thy law of patience,
To glorify Thy name! Not selfishly, forsooth,
But for their own more good, to open them the truth,
To teach them happiness, to civilise, to save,
To smite down the oppressor and make free the slave.
To bear the "White Man's Burden," which he yearns to take
On his white Saxon back for his white conscience' sake.
Huge impudent imposture!—Lord, there were fair lands
Once on Thy Earth, brave hills, bright isles, sweet coral strands,
Noble savannahs, plains of limitless waving green,
Lakes girt with giant forests, continents unseen,
Unknown by these white thieves, where men lived in the way
Of Thy good natural law with Thy free beasts at play. . . .

Nay Lord, 'tis not a lie, the thing I tell Thee thus.
Their bishops in their Churches lead, incredulous,
The public thanks profane.   They sanctify the sword:
"Te Deum laudamus.   Give peace in our time, O Lord."
Hast Thou not heard their chaunting?   Nay, Thou dost not hear,
Or Thou hadst loosed Thy hand like lightning in the clear
To smite their ribald lips with palsy, these false priests,
These Lords who boast Thine aid at their high civic feasts,
The ignoble shouting crowds, the prophets of their Press,
Pouring their daily flood of bald self-righteousness,
Their poets who write big of the "White Burden."   Trash!
The White Man's Burden, Lord, is the burden of his cash.
—There!   Thou hast heard the truth.   Thy world, Lord God
        of Heaven,
Lieth in the hands of thieves who pillage morn and even.
And Thou still sleepest on!   Nay but Thou needs must hear
Or abdicate Thy name of High Justiciar
Henceforward and for ever.   It o'erwhelmeth Thee
With more than temporal shame.   Thy silence is a Sea
Crying through all the spheres in pain and ceasing not
As blood from out the ground to mark crime's murder spot:
"There is no hope—no truth.   He hath betrayed the trust.
The Lord God is unjust.   The Lord God is unjust."

> [*A cry without.*

This is their cry in Heaven who give Thee service true.
Arise, Lord, and avenge as was Thy wont to do.

> [*The Angels re-enter in disorder, weeping.*

The Lord God.   What tears be these, my Sons?   What ails ye
        that ye weep?
Speak, Shepherds of the flock!   Ye that have cared my sheep!
Ye that are charged with Man!   Is it as this One saith?
Is Satan then no liar who loudly witnesseth
Man's ruin of the World?

The Angel of Pity (*coming forward*).   Lord, it is even so.
Thy Earth is a lost force, Man's lazar-house of woe,
Undone by his lewd will.   We may no longer strive.
The evil hath prevailed.   There is no soul alive
That shall escape his greed.   We spend our days in tears
Mourning Thy world's lost beauty in the night of years.
All pity is departed.   Each once happy thing
That on Thy fair Earth went, how fleet of foot or wing,
How glorious in its strength, how wondrous in design,
How royal in its raiment tinctured opaline,
How rich in joyous life, the inheritor of forms
All noble, all of worth, which had survived the storms,

The chances of decay in the World's living plan
From the remote fair past when still ignoble Man
On his four foot-soles went and howled through the lone hills
In moody bestial wrath, unclassed among Earth's ills:
Each one of them is doomed. From the deep Central Seas
To the white Poles, Man ruleth pitiless Lord of these,
And daily he destroyeth. The great whales he driveth
Beneath the northern ice, and quarter none he giveth,
Who perish there of wounds in their huge agony.
He presseth the white bear on the white frozen sea
And slaughtereth for his pastime. The wise amorous seal
He flayeth big with young; the walrus cubs that kneel
But cannot turn his rage, alive he mangleth them,
Leaveth in breathing heaps, outrooted branch and stem.
In every land he slayeth. He hath new engines made
Which no life may withstand, nor in the forest shade
Nor in the sunlit plain, which wound all from afar,
The timorous with the valiant, waging his false war,
Coward, himself unseen. In pity, Lord, look down
On the blank widowed plains which he hath made his own
By right of solitude. Where, Lord God, are they now,
Thy glorious bison herds, Thy ariels white as snow,
Thy antelopes in troops, the zebras of Thy plain?
Behold their whitened bones on the dull track of men.
Thy elephants, Lord, where? For ages thou didst build
Their frames' capacity, the hide which was their shield
No thorn might pierce, no sting, no violent tooth assail,
The tusks which were their levers, the lithe trunk their flail.
Thou strengthenedst their deep brain. Thou madest them wise
    to know
And wiser to ignore, advised, deliberate, slow,
Conscious of power supreme in right. The manifest token
Of Thy high will on earth, Thy natural peace unbroken,
Unbreakable by fear. For ages did they move
Thus, kings of Thy deep forest swayed by only love.
Where are they now, Lord God? A fugitive spent few
Used as Man's living targets by the ignoble crew
Who boast their coward skill to plant the balls that fly,
Thy work of all time spoiled, their only use to die
That these sad clowns may laugh. Nay, Lord, we weep for *Thee*,
And spend ourselves in tears for Thy marred majesty.
Behold, Lord, what we bring—this last proof in our hands,
Their latest fiendliest spoil from Thy fair tropic lands,
The birds of all the Earth unwinged to deck the heads
Of their unseemly women; plumage of such reds

[323]

As not the sunset hath, such purples as no throne,
Not even in heaven, showeth (hardly, Lord, Thine own),
Such azures as the sea's, such greens as are in Spring
The oak trees' tenderest buds of watched-for blossoming,
Such opalescent pearls as only in thy skies
The lunar bow revealeth to night's sleep-tired eyes.
Behold them, Lord of Beauty, Lord of Reverence,
Lord of Compassion, Thou who metest means to ends,
Nor madest Thy world fair for less than Thine own fame,
Behold Thy birds of joy lost, tortured, put to shame
For these vile strumpets' whim!   Arise, or cease to be
Judge of the quick and dead!   These dead wings cry to Thee!
Arise, Lord, and avenge!

PUNCH

A wry reflection on the much-vaunted relationship between commercial prosperity and the imperial flag. Thomas Cook, the travel agents, had just announced tours of the Boer War battlefields.

> O FLAG! whose benefits so fair
> We would with others freely share—
> Aye, forcing on reluctant nations,
> At bayonet point, their own salvations,
> And bidding them accept our mission
> On pain of instant demolition—
> O flag! howe'er they disagree,
> The sages that have studied thee,
> Alleging, these, that trade must grow
> Beneath thy folds; while those say, "No.
> That is a most mistaken view:
> There's no connection 'twixt the two."
> O flag! however this may be,
> And whether trade doth follow thee,
> I know not, I; but this is true,
> Beyond all question tourists do.
> No matter where thou art unfurled,
> In whatso region of the world,
> They swarm, they flock, and Messrs. COOK
> Interminable tourists book
> To Eland's Laagte, Bloemfontein,
> (Where passengers may stop to dine
> Before proceeding on their way
> To further north Pretoria). .
> In myriads behold they come,
> And almost ere the guns are dumb,
> The picknickers' champagne will pop
> Upon the plains of Spion Kop.
> O flag! O tourist! Powers twain
> That all the world resists in vain,
> When 'neath the one the other picks
> The wings and legs of festive chicks,
> And strews the battlefield with bones,
> Newspapers, orange peel, plum stones—
> Then is the reign of darkness done,
> And Freedom's fight is fought and won.

WILLIAM ERNEST HENLEY

'LAST POST', 1900

Published in Henley's enthusiastically pro-Boer War collection *For England's Sake*, this elegy for the nation's dead goes beyond his normal martial fervour to see the conflict as one stage in the establishment of English racial ascendancy. It was set to music for chorus and orchestra by Charles Villiers Stanford.

The day's high work is over and done,
And these no more will need the sun:
Blow, you bugles of England, blow!
These are gone whither all must go,
Mightily gone from the field they won.
So in the workaday wear of battle,
Touched to glory with God's own red,
Bear we our chosen to their bed.
Settle them lovingly where they fell,
In that good lap they loved so well;
And, their deliveries to the dear Lord said,
And the last desperate volleys ranged and sped,
Blow, you bugles of England, blow
Over the camps of her beaten foe—
Blow glory and pity to the victor Mother,
Sad, O, sad in her sacrificial dead!
Labour, and love, and strife, and mirth,
They gave their part in this goodly Earth—
Blow, you bugles of England, blow!—
That her Name as a sun among stars might glow,
Till the dusk of Time, with honour and worth:
That, stung by the lust and the pain of battle
The One Race ever might starkly spread
And the One Flag eagle it overhead!
In a rapture of wrath and faith and pride,
Thus they felt it, and thus they died;
So to the Maker of homes, to the Giver of bread,
For whose dear sake their triumphing souls they shed,
Blow, you bugles of England, blow
Though you break the heart of her beaten foe,
Glory and praise to the everlasting Mother,
Glory and peace to her lovely and faithful dead!

[326]

HENRY NEWBOLT

'APRIL ON WAGGON HILL', written 1900

Waggon Hill was a key position in the defence of Ladysmith
during the Boer War. In January 1900 a desperately fought
action in which the Devonshire Regiment was prominent even-
tually prevented the Boer forces besieging the town from
capturing the hill. In this elegiac poem, the tone of which owes
much to Housman, Newbolt addresses a Devon soldier killed in
the battle.

LAD, and can you rest now,
　　There beneath your hill!
Your hands are on your breast now
　　But is your heart so still?
'Twas the right death to die, lad,
　　A gift without regret,
But unless truth's a lie, lad,
　　You dream of Devon yet.

Ay, ay, the year's awaking,
　　The fire's among the ling,
The beechen hedge is breaking,
　　The curlew's on the wing;
Primroses are out, lad,
　　On the high banks of Lee,
And the sun stirs the trout, lad,
　　From Brendon to the sea.

I know what's in your heart, lad,—
　　The mare he used to hunt—
And her blue market-cart, lad,
　　With posies tied in front—
We miss them from the moor road,
　　They're getting old to roam,
The road they're on's a sure road
　　And nearer, lad, to home.

Your name, the name they cherish?
  'Twill fade, lad, 'tis true:
But stone and all may perish
  With little loss to you.
While fame's fame you're Devon, lad,
  The Glory of the West;
Till the roll's called in heaven, lad,
  You may well take your rest.

Henry Newbolt

'THE ONLY SON', written *c*.1900

———

Although the aristocratic and patriarchal England invoked by this poem about a soldier killed in South Africa is standard in Newbolt's work, the emphasis it gives to intense maternal loss strikes a more unfamiliar note.

O BITTER wind toward the sunset blowing,
   What of the dales to-night?
In yonder gray old hall what fires are glowing,
   What ring of festal light?

"In the great window as the day was dwindling
   I saw an old man stand;
His head was proudly held and his eyes kindling,
   But the list shook in his hand."

O wind of twilight, was there no word uttered,
   No sound of joy or wail?
"'A great fight and a good death,' he muttered;
   'Trust him, he would not fail.'"

What of the chamber dark where she was lying
   For whom all life is done?
"Within her heart she rocks a dead child, crying
   'My son, my little son.'"

ALFRED EDWARD HOUSMAN

'LANCER', written *c*.1900

One of the greatest English classical scholars, Housman (1859–1936) achieved widespread celebrity with the intense rural melancholy of *A Shropshire Lad*, his first volume of poetry, published in 1896. Most of his other poems were written before 1910, some, like 'Lancer', appearing in *Last Poems* of 1922; its sexual ambiguities give a wry inflection to the martial glamour of the imperial enterprise.

> I 'LISTED at home for a lancer,
>   *Oh who would not sleep with the brave?*
> I 'listed at home for a lancer
>   To ride on a horse to my grave.
>
> And over the seas we were bidden
>   A country to take and to keep;
> And far with the brave I have ridden,
>   And now with the brave I shall sleep.
>
> For round me the men will be lying
>   That learned me the way to behave,
> And showed me my business of dying:
>   *Oh who would not sleep with the brave?*
>
> They ask and there is not an answer;
> Says I, I will 'list for a lancer,
>   *Oh who would not sleep with the brave?*
>
> And I with the brave shall be sleeping
>   At ease on my mattress of loam,
> When back from their taking and keeping
>   The squadron is riding at home.
>
> The wind with the plumes will be playing,
>   The girls will stand watching them wave,
> And eyeing my comrades and saying
>   *Oh who would not sleep with the brave?*
>
> They ask and there is not an answer;
> Says you, I will 'list for a lancer,
>   *Oh who would not sleep with the brave?*

ALFRED EDWARD HOUSMAN

'ASTRONOMY', written *c*.1900

———

First published in *Last Poems*, this delicately managed elegy for
one of the dead of the Boer War compares interestingly with
Hardy's 'Drummer Hodge'.

THE Wain upon the northern steep
   Descends and lifts away.
Oh I will sit me down and weep
   For bones in Africa.

For pay and medals, name and rank,
   Things that he has not found,
He hove the Cross to heaven and sank
   The pole-star underground.

And now he does not even see
   Signs of the nadir roll
At night over the ground where he
   Is buried with the pole.

ARTHUR CHRISTOPHER BENSON

'LAND OF HOPE AND GLORY', 1901

———

One of the three literary sons of Edward White Benson, Archbishop of Canterbury, A.C. Benson (1862–1925) was an influential housemaster at Eton, moving in 1903 to Magdalene College, Cambridge, where he subsequently became Master. He wrote the words of 'Land of Hope and Glory' to fit the main theme of Elgar's first *Pomp and Circumstance March*, which the composer had incorporated in the *Coronation Ode* that he wrote for the crowning of Edward VII in 1901. The song's covert militarism, its claim of divine sanction for the Empire, and its promise of seemingly endless territorial expansion, gave it instant success as an imperialist anthem.

DEAR Land of Hope, thy hope is crowned.
  God make thee mightier yet!
On Sov'ran brows, beloved, renowned,
  Once more thy crown is set.
Thine equal laws, by Freedom gained,
  Have ruled thee well and long;
By Freedom gained, by Truth maintained,
  Thine Empire shall be strong.
    Land of Hope and Glory, Mother of the Free,
    How shall we extol thee, who are born of thee?
    Wider still and wider shall thy bounds be set;
    God, who made thee mighty, make thee mightier yet.

Thy fame is ancient as the days,
  As Ocean large and wide;
A pride that dares, and heeds not praise,
  A stern and silent pride:
Not that false joy that dreams content
  With what our sires have won;
The blood a hero sire hath spent
  Still nerves a hero son.
    Land of Hope and Glory, Mother of the Free,
    How shall we extol thee, who are born of thee?
    Wider still and wider shall thy bounds be set;
    God, who made thee mighty, make thee mightier yet.

ALGERNON CHARLES SWINBURNE

'THE FIRST OF JUNE', 1902

———

The Boer forces in South Africa surrendered unconditionally on
1 June 1902; in celebrating the British triumph, Swinburne
recalls Admiral Howe's naval victory over the French on The
Glorious First of June in 1794.

PEACE and war are one in proof of England's deathless praise.
    One divine day saw her foemen scattered on the sea
Far and fast as storm could speed: the same strong day of days
    Sees the imperial commonweal set friends and foemen free.
Save where freedom reigns, whose name is England, fraud and
        fear
    Grind and blind the face of men who look on her and lie:
Now may truth and pride in truth, whose seat of old was here,
    See them shamed and stricken blind and dumb as worms that
        die.
Even before our hallowed hawthorn-blossom pass and cease,
    Even as England shines and smiles at last upon the sun,
Comes the word that means for England more than passing peace,
    Peace with honour, peace with pride in righteous work well
        done.
Crowned with flowers the first of all the world and all the year,
Peace, whose name is one with honour born of war, is here.

FRANCIS THOMPSON

'CECIL RHODES', written 1902

Rescued from obscurity and opium addiction by the Roman Catholic writers Wilfrid and Alice Meynell, Thompson (1859–1907) established his reputation in 1893 with his first volume of poetry, which included his best-known work 'The Hound of Heaven'. Something of the mysticism and intensity of Thompson's religious verse is apparent, perhaps rather surprisingly, in this elegy on that most megalomaniac of empire-builders, Cecil Rhodes. Made vastly wealthy by his control of the British South Africa Company and the De Beers diamond mines, Rhodes founded Rhodesia and promoted the idea of a global Anglo-Saxon ascendancy, in pursuit of which he established the Rhodes Scholarships. His burial place in Zimbabwe's Matoppo Hills is referred to in the later part of the poem.

> THEY that mis-said
> This man yet living, praise him dead.
> And I too praise, yet not the baser things
> Wherewith the market and the tavern rings.
> Not that high things for gold,
> He held, were bought and sold,
> That statecraft's means approved are by the end;
> Not for all which commands
> The loud world's clapping hands,
> To which cheap press and cheaper patriots bend;
> But for the dreams,
> For those impossible gleams
> He half made possible; for that he was
> Visioner of vision in a most sordid day:
> This draws
> Back to me Song long alien and astray.
>
> In dreams what did he not,
> Wider than his wide deeds? In dreams he wrought
> What the old world's long livers must in act forego.
> From the Zambesi to the Limpopo
> He the many-languaged land
> Took with his large compacting hand
> And pressed into a nation: 'thwart the accurst

And lion-'larumed ways,
Where the lean-fingered Thirst
Wrings at the throat, and Famine strips the bone;
A tawny land, with sun at sullen gaze,
And all above a cope of heated stone;
He heard the shirted miner's rough halloo
Call up the mosquèd Cairene; harkened clear
The Cairene's far-off summons sounding through
The sea's long noises to the Capeman's ear.

He saw the Teuton and the Saxon grip
Hands round the warded world, and bid it rock,
While they did watch its cradle. Like a ship
It swung, whileas the cabined inmates slept,
Secure their peace was kept,
Such arms of warranty about them lock.
Ophir he saw, her long-ungazed-at gold,
Stirred from its deep
And often-centuried sleep,
Wink at the new Sun in an English hold;
England, from Afric's swarthy loins
Drawing fecundity,
Wax to the South and North,
To East and West increase her puissant goings-forth,
And strike young emperies, like coins,
In her own recent effigy.
He saw the three-branched Teuton hold the sides
Of the round world, and part it as a dish
Whereof to each his wish
The amity of the full feast decides.

So large his dreams, so little come to act!
Who must call on the cannon to compact
The hard Dutch-stubborned land,
Seditious even to such a potent hand;
Who grasped and held his Ophir: held, no less,
The Northern ways, but never lived to see
The wing-foot messages
Dart from the Delta to the Southern Sea;
Who, confident of gold,
A leaner on the statesman's arts
And the unmartial conquests of the marts,
Died with the sound of battle round him rolled,
And rumour of battle in all nations' hearts;

Dying, saw his life a thing
Of large beginnings; and for young
Hands yet untrained the harvesting,
Amid the iniquitous years if harvest sprung.

So in his death he sowed himself anew;
Cast his intents over the grave to strike
In the left world of livers living roots,
And, banyan-like,
From his one tree raise up a wood of shoots.
The indestructible intents which drew
Their sap from him
Thus, with a purpose grim,
Into strange lands and hostile yet he threw,
That there might be
From him throughout the earth posterity:
And so did he—
Like to a smouldering fire by wind-blasts swirled—
His dying embers strew to kindle all the world.

Yet not for this I praise
The ending of his strenuous days;
No, not alone that still
Beyond the grave stretched that imperial Will:
But that Death seems
To set the gateway wide to ampler dreams.
Yea, yet he dreams upon Matoppo hill,
The while the German and the Saxon see,
And seeing, wonder,
The spacious dreams take shape and be,
As at compulsion of his sleep thereunder.
Lo, young America at the Mother's knee,
Unlearning centuried hate,
For love's more blest extreme;
And this is in his dream,
And sure the dream is great.
Lo, Colonies on Colonies,
The furred Canadian and the digger's shirt,
To the one Mother's skirt
Cling, in the lore of Empire to be wise;
A hundred wheels a-turn
All to one end—that England's sons may learn

The glory of their sonship, the supreme
Worth that befits the heirs of such estate.
All these are in his dream,
And sure the dream is great.

So, to the last
A visionary vast,
The aspirant soul would have the body lie
Among the hills immovably exalt
As he above the crowd that haste and halt,
'Upon that hill which I
Called "View of All the World"'; to show thereby
That still his unappeasable desires
Beneath his feet surveyed the peoples and empires.
Dreams, haply of scant worth,
Bound by our little thumb-ring of an earth;
Yet an exalted thing
By the gross search for food and raimenting.
So in his own Matoppos, high, aloof,
The elements for roof,
Claiming his mountain kindred, and secure,
Within that sepulture
Stern like himself and unadorned,
From the loud multitude he ruled and scorned,
There let him cease from breath,—
Alone in crowded life, not lonelier in death.

Rudyard Kipling

'BOOTS', 1903

Published with other 'Service Songs' in *The Five Nations*, 'Boots' remarkably captures the hypnotic fatigue of the seemingly endless marches that, for the ordinary Victorian infantryman, was the main feature of colonial campaigns in Africa.

WE'RE foot—slog—slog—slog—sloggin' over Africa!
Foot—foot—foot—foot—sloggin' over Africa—
(Boots—boots—boots—boots—movin' up and down again!)
    There's no discharge in the war!

Seven—six—eleven—five—nine-an'-twenty mile to-day—
Four—eleven—seventeen—thirty-two the day before—
(Boots—boots—boots—boots—movin' up and down again!)
    There's no discharge in the war!

Don't—don't—don't—don't—look at what's in front of you.
(Boots—boots—boots—boots—movin' up an' down again);
Men—men—men—men—men go mad with watchin' 'em,
    An' there's no discharge in the war!

Try—try—try—try—to think o' something different—
Oh—my—God—keep—me from goin' lunatic!
(Boots—boots—boots—boots—movin' up an' down again!)
    There's no discharge in the war!

Count—count—count—count—the bullets in the bandoliers.
If—your—eyes—drop—they will get atop o' you—
(Boots—boots—boots—boots—movin' up and down again)—
    There's no discharge in the war!

We—can—stick—out—'unger, thirst, an' weariness,
But—not—not—not—not—the chronic sight of 'em—
Boots—boots—boots—boots—movin' up an' down again,
    An' there's no discharge in the war!

'Tain't—so—bad—by—day because o' company,
But—night—brings—long—strings—o' forty thousand million
Boots—boots—boots—boots—movin' up an' down again.
There's no discharge in the war!

I—'ave—marched—six—weeks in 'Ell an' certify
It—is—not—fire—devils—dark or anything,
But boots—boots—boots—boots—movin' up an' down again,
An' there's no discharge in the war!

WILLIAM WATSON

From *FOR ENGLAND*, 1904

The subtitle of the *For England* collection, *Poems written during Estrangement*, locates the contents in the period in which Watson was ostracized for his anti-imperialist stance towards the Boer War. Of the poems chosen here 'The True Imperialism' seeks to redirect British attention from aggrandisement abroad to the poverty and destitution of so much of the domestic population. The two sonnets refer directly to the war, the first ironically weighing the Boer cause against Britain's much-vaunted love of liberty, the second offering a nihilistic view of the slaughter. The epigrammatic 'Rome and Another' subverts the standard Edwardian comparison between the British and Roman empires.

'THE TRUE IMPERIALISM'

HERE, while the tide of conquest rolls
    Against the distant golden shore,
The starved and stunted human souls
    Are with us more and more.

Vain is your Science, vain your Art,
    Your triumphs and your glories vain,
To feed the hunger of their heart
    And famine of their brain.

Your savage deserts howling near,
    Your wastes of ignorance, vice, and shame,—
Is there no room for victories here,
    No field for deeds of fame?

Arise and conquer while ye can
    The foe that in your midst resides,
And build within the mind of Man
    The Empire that abides.

'THE ENEMY'

UNSKILLED in Letters, and in Arts unversed;
Ignorant of empire; bounded in their view
By the lone billowing veldt, where they upgrew
Amid great silences; a people nursed
Apart—the far-sown seed of them that erst
Not Alva's sword could tame: now blindly hurled
Against the march of the majestic world,
They fight and die, with dauntless bosoms curst.

Crazed, if you will; demented, not to yield
Ere all be lost!   And yet it seems to me
They fought as noblest Englishmen did use
To fight, for freedom; and no Briton he,
Who to such valour in a desperate field
A knightly salutation can refuse.

'THE SLAIN'

PARTNERS in silence, mates in noteless doom,
Peers in oblivion's commonalty merged;
Unto like deeds by differing mandates urged,
And equalled in the unrespective tomb;
Leal or perfidious, cruel or tender, whom
Precipitate fate hath of your frailties purged;
Whom duly the impartial winds have dirged,
In autumn or the glorying vernal bloom:
Already is your strife become as nought;
Idle the bullet's flight, the bayonet's thrust,
The senseless cannon's dull, unmeaning word;
Idle your feud; and all for which ye fought
To this arbitrament of loam referred,
And cold adjudication of the dust.

'ROME AND ANOTHER'

SHE asked for all things, and dominion such
    As never man had known,
The gods first gave; then lightly, touch by touch,
    O'erthrew her seven-hilled throne.

Imperial Power, that hungerest for the globe,
    Restrain thy conquering feet,
Lest the same Fates that spun thy purple robe
    Should weave thy winding-sheet.

ALFRED NOYES

From *DRAKE*, 1906–8

Noyes (1880–1958) belonged to that post-Tennysonian genera-
tion of English poets whose work was virtually untouched by the
advent of Modernism. In an active literary career that spanned
the first quarter of the twentieth century and included a period
as Professor of Modern English Literature at Princeton, his out-
put was both prolific and varied—lyrics, epic poems, ballads,
verse dramas—and he commanded a genuinely wide audience.
Drake was his first major popular success. The idea of an epic
poem based on the rise of Elizabethan sea power was put forward
by the historian J.A. Froude in *English Seamen of the Six-
teenth Century* (1895), and much of *Drake* draws on this source.
Unique to the poem, however, is the creation of the central
character himself. Noyes's Drake is both an adventurer and a
visionary whose heroic destiny is impelled by a prophetic—and
thoroughly paradoxical—dream of British naval power as the
agent and guarantor of a global empire of peace and freedom.

Having started on his voyage of circumnavigation, Drake tells
his crew about his dream of a future empire of the West; from
Book 2.

>   ... In that Golden World
> Which means much more to me than I can speak,
> Much more, much more than I can speak or breathe,
> Being, behind whatever name it bears—
> Earthly Paradise, Island of the Saints,
> Cathay, or Zipangu, or Hy Brasil—
> The eternal symbol of my soul's desire,
> A sacred country shining on the sea,
> That Vision without which, the wise king said,
> A people perishes; in that place of hope,
> That Tirn'an Og, that land of lasting youth,
> Where whosoever sails with me shall drink
> Fountains of immortality and dwell
> Beyond the fear of death for evermore,

There shall we see the dust of battle dance
Everywhere in the sunbeam of God's peace!
Oh, in the new Atlantis of my soul
There are no captives: there the wind blows free;
And, as in sleep, I have heard the marching song
Of mighty peoples rising in the West,
Wonderful cities that shall set their foot
Upon the throat of all old tyrannies;
And on the West wind I have heard a cry,
The shoreless cry of the prophetic sea
Heralding through that golden wilderness
The Soul whose path our task is to make straight,
Freedom, the last great Saviour of mankind.
I know not what I know: these are wild words,
Which as the sun draws out earth's morning mists
Over dim fields where careless cattle sleep,
Some visionary Light, unknown, afar,
Draws from my darkling soul. ...

Drake abandons his attempt to find the North East Passage and
lands on the Pacific coast of America to repair the *Golden Hynde*
before sailing again in pursuit of his vision of an English
Empire; from Book 6.

And when a fair wind rose again, there seemed
No hope of passage by that fabled way
Northward, and suddenly Drake put down his helm
And, with some wondrous purpose in his eyes,
Turned Southward once again, until he found
A lonely natural harbour on the coast
Near San Francisco, where the cliffs were white
Like those of England, and the soft soil teemed
With gold.   There they careened the *Golden Hynde*—
Her keel being thick with barnacles and weeds—
And built a fort and dockyard to refit
Their little wandering home, not half so large
As many a coasting barque to-day that scarce
Would cross the Channel, yet she had swept the seas
Of half the world, and even now prepared
For new adventures greater than them all.
And as the sound of chisel and hammer broke
The stillness of that shore, shy figures came,
Keen-faced and grave-eyed Indians, from the woods
To bow before the strange white-faced new-comers

[343]

As gods. Whereat the chaplain much aghast
Persuaded them with signs and broken words
And grunts that even Drake was but a man,
Whom none the less the savages would crown
With woven flowers and barbarous ritual
King of New Albion—so the seamen called
That land, remembering the white cliffs of home.
Much they implored, with many a sign and cry,
Which by the rescued slaves upon the prize
Were part interpreted, that Drake would stay
And rule them; and the vision of the great
Empire of Englishmen arose and flashed
A moment round them, on that lonely shore.
A small and weather-beaten band they stood,
Bronzed seamen by the laughing rescued slaves,
Ringed with gigantic loneliness and saw
An Empire that should liberate the world;
A Power before the lightning of whose arms
Darkness should die and all oppression cease;
A Federation of the strong and weak,
Whereby the weak were strengthened and the strong
Made stronger in the increasing good of all;
A gathering up of one another's loads;
A turning of the wasteful rage of war
To accomplish large and fruitful tasks of peace,
Even as the strength of some great stream is turned
To grind the corn for bread.   E'en thus on England
That splendour dawned which those in dreams foresaw
And saw not with their living eyes, but thou,
England, mayst lift up eyes at last and see,
Who, like that angel of the Apocalypse
Hast set one foot upon thy sea-girt isle,
The other upon the waters, and canst raise
Now, if thou wilt, above the assembled nations,
The trumpet of deliverance to thy lips.

———

At last their task was done, the *Golden Hynde*
Undocked, her white wings hoisted; and away
Westward they swiftly glided from that shore
Where, with a wild lament, their Indian friends,
Knee-deep i' the creaming foam, all stood at gaze,
Like men that for one moment in their lives
Have seen a mighty drama cross their path
And played upon the stage of vast events

[344]

Knowing, henceforward, all their life is nought.
But Westward sped the little *Golden Hynde*
Across the uncharted ocean, with no guide
But that great homing cry of all their hearts. ...

Walsingham and Drake persuade Elizabeth to authorize the Cadiz expedition. Walsingham, reassuring the Queen as to the loyalty of English Catholics, foresees a world revitalized by Christian faith, and Drake describes his vision of an English maritime empire as the divinely ordained vehicle of that faith; from Book 10.

         " 'Fore God,"
Cried Walsingham, "my Queen, you do them wrong!
There is another Rome—not this of Spain
Which lurks to pluck the world back into darkness
And stab it there for gold. There is a City
Whose eyes are tow'rd the morning; on whose heights
Blazes the Cross of Christ above the world;
A Rome that shall wage warfare yet for God
In the dark days to come, a Rome whose thought
Shall march with our humanity and be proud
To cast old creeds like seed into the ground,
Watch the strange shoots and foster the new flower
Of faiths we know not yet. Is this a dream?
I speak as one by knighthood bound to speak;
For even this day—and my heart burns with it—
I heard the Catholic gentlemen of England
Speaking in grave assembly. At one breath
Of peril to our island, why, their swords
Leapt from their scabbards, and their cry went up
To split the heavens—*God save our English Queen!*"
Even as he spake there passed the rushing gleam
Of torches once again, and as they stood
Silently listening, all the winds ran wild
With clamouring bells, and a great cry went up—
God save Elizabeth, our English Queen!

"I'll vouch for some two hundred Catholic throats
Among that thosand," whispered Walsingham
Eagerly, with his eyes on the Queen's face.
then, seeing it brighten, fervently he cried,
Pressing the swift advantage home, "O, Madam,
The heart of England now is all on fire!

[345]

We are one people, as we never have been
In all our history, all prepared to die
Around your throne. Madam, you are beloved
As never yet was English king or queen!"
She looked at him, the tears in her keen eyes
Glittered—"And I am very proud," she said,
"But if our enemies command the world,
And we have one small island and no more ..."
She ceased; and Drake, in a strange voice, hoarse and low,
Trembling with passion deeper than all speech,
Cried out—"No more than the great ocean-sea
Which makes the enemies' coast our frontier now;
No more than that great Empire of the deep
Which rolls from Pole to Pole, washing the world
With thunder, that great Empire whose command
This day is yours to take. Hear me, my Queen,
This is a dream, a new dream, but a true;
For mightier days are dawning on the world
Than heart of man hath known. If England hold
The sea, she holds the hundred thousand gates
That open to futurity. She holds
The highway of all ages. Argosies
Of unknown glory set their sails this day
For England out of ports beyond the stars.
Ay, on the sacred seas we ne'er shall know
They hoist their sails this day by peaceful quays,
Great gleaming wharves i' the perfect City of God,
If she but claim her heritage."
                              He ceased;
And the deep dream of that new realm, the sea,
Through all the soul of Gloriana surged
A moment, then with splendid eyes that filled
With fire of sunsets far away, she cried
(Faith making her a child, yet queenlier still)
"Yea, claim it thou for me!"

ALFRED NOYES

In a characteristically Edwardian blend of patriotism and religiosity, this poem from *Forty Singing Seamen* images the common people of Britain as united in the service of an empire which, however inscrutably, is part of a divine plan.

WHO are the Empire-builders?   They
   Whose desperate arrogance demands
A self-reflecting power to sway
   A hundred little selfless lands?
Lord God of battles, ere we bow
   To these and to their soulless lust,
Let fall Thy thunders on us now
   And strike us equal to the dust.

Before the stars in heaven were made
   Our great Commander led us forth;
And now the embattled lines are laid
   To East, to West, to South, to North;
According as of old He planned
   We take our station in the field,
Nor dare to dream we understand
   The splendour of the swords we wield.

We know not what the Soul intends
   That lives and moves behind our deeds;
We wheel and march to glorious ends
   Beyond the common soldier's needs:
And some are raised to high rewards,
   And some by regiments are hurled
To die upon the opposing swords
   And sleep—forgotten by the world.

And not where navies churn the foam,
   Nor called to fields of fierce emprize,
In many a country cottage-home
   The Empire-builder lives and dies:
Or through the roaring streets he goes
   A lean and weary City slave,
The conqueror of a thousand foes
   Who walks, unheeded, to his grave.

Leaders unknown of hopes forlorn
  Go past us in the daily mart,
With many a shadowy crown of thorn
  And many a kingly broken heart:
Though England's banner overhead
  Ever the secret signal flew,
We only see its Cross is red
  As children see the skies are blue.

For all are Empire-builders here,
  Whose hearts are true to heaven and home
And, year by slow revolving year,
  Fulfil the duties as they come;
So simple seems the task, and yet
  Many for this are crucified;
Ay, and their brother-men forget
  The simple wounds in palm and side.

But he that to his home is true,
  Where'er the tides of power may flow,
Has built a kingdom great and new
  Which Time nor Fate shall overthrow.
These are the Empire-builders, these
  Annex where none shall say them nay
Beyond the world's uncharted seas
  Realms that can never pass away.

JOHN MILTON HAYES

'THE GREEN EYE OF THE YELLOW GOD', 1911

―――――

An actor, music-hall turn, and occasional writer, Jacky Hayes (*fl.* 1910–1930) composed this most celebrated—and most parodied—of all dramatic recitations in just five hours. It was made famous by Bransby Williams, whose heart-stopping renditions made him the *doyen* of the music-hall monologue in the early twentieth century. The ingredients of the poem—romance, vengeful orientals, forbidden riches—all played their part in the popular construction of the imperial East, and were successfully used in fiction by Wilkie Collins and Conan Doyle, among others.

THERE'S a one-eyed yellow idol to the north of Khatmandu,
There's a little marble cross below the town;
There's a broken-hearted woman tends the grave of Mad Carew,
And the Yellow God forever gazes down.

He was known as "Mad Carew" by the subs at Khatmandu,
He was hotter than they felt inclined to tell;
But for all his foolish pranks, he was worshipped in the ranks,
And the Colonel's daughter smiled on him as well.

He had loved her all along, with a passion of the strong,
The fact that she loved him was plain to all.
She was nearly twenty-one and arrangements had begun
To celebrate her birthday with a ball.

He wrote to ask what present she would like from Mad Carew;
They met next day as he dismissed a squad;
And jestingly she told him then that nothing else would do
But the green eye of the little Yellow God.

On the night before the dance, Mad Carew seemed in a trance,
And they chaffed him as they puffed at their cigars;
But for once he failed to smile, and he sat alone awhile,
Then went out into the night beneath the stars.

He returned before the dawn, with his shirt and tunic torn,
. And a gash across his temple dripping red;
He was patched up right away, and he slept through all the day,
And the Colonel's daughter watched beside his bed.

He woke at last and asked if they could send his tunic through;
She brought it, and he thanked her with a nod;
He bade her search the pocket saying, "That's from Mad Carew,"
And she found the little green eye of the god.

She upbraided poor Carew in the way that women do,
Though both her eyes were strangely hot and wet;
But she wouldn't take the stone and Mad Carew was left alone
With the jewel that he'd chanced his life to get.

When the ball was at its height, on that still and tropic night,
She thought of him and hastened to his room;
As she crossed the barrack square she could hear the dreamy air
Of a waltz tune softly stealing thro' the gloom.

His door was open wide, with silver moonlight shining through;
The place was wet and slipp'ry where she trod;
An ugly knife lay buried in the heart of Mad Carew,
'Twas the "Vengeance of the Little Yellow God."

There's a one-eyed yellow idol to the north of Khatmandu,
There's a little marble cross below the town;
There's a broken-hearted woman tends the grave of Mad Carew,
And the Yellow God forever gazes down.

ALFRED NOYES

'THE HEART OF CANADA', written 1912

Despite British rhetoric about imperial solidarity, the colonies of white settlement consistently refused to make any more than minimal defence provision, leaving almost all the naval and military cost of the Empire to be borne by the mother country. This situation changed marginally in the years immediately before the Great War, and in this somewhat hysterical poem Noyes greets the decision of the Canadian government in 1912 to make a contribution to the imperial navy. By 1918 Canada had built one cruiser and two destroyers.

BECAUSE her heart is all too proud
   —Canada! Canada! fair young Canada—
To breathe the might of her love aloud,
   Be quick, O Motherland!
Because her soul is wholly free
   —Canada kneels, thy daughter, Canada—
England, look in her eyes and see,
   Honour and understand.

Because her pride at thy masthead shines,
   *—Canada! Canada!—*queenly Canada
Bows with all her breathing pines,
   All her fragrant firs.
Because our isle is little and old
   *—Canada! Canada!—*young-eyed Canada
Gives thee, Mother, her hands to hold,
   And makes thy glory hers.

Because thy Fleet is hers for aye,
   *—Canada! Canada!—*clear-souled Canada,
Ere the war-cloud roll this way,
   Bids the world beware.
Her heart, her soul, her sword are thine
   —Thine the guns, the guns of Canada!—
The ships are foaming into line,
   And Canada will be there.

WILFRED SCAWEN BLUNT

From 'QUATRAINS OF LIFE', 1914

In this extract from the retrospective poem written towards the
end of his long life, Blunt revisits the subject matter of 'The
Wind and the Whirlwind' and again regrets the defeat of Arabi
Pasha's forces, attributing to them a piety that he contrasts with
the lower-class coarseness of the British soldiery.

I saw it, and I blushed for my Man's race,
And once again when in the foremost place
   Of human tyranny its latest born
Stood threatening conquest with an English face.

Chief of the sons of Japhet he, with hand
Hard on the nations of the sea and land,
   Intolerant of all, tongues, customs, creeds,
Too dull to spare, too proud to understand.

I saw them shrink abashed before his might,
Like tropic birds before the sparrow's flight.
   The world was poorer when they fled.　But he
Deemed he had done "God" service and "his right."

I saw it and I heard it and I rose
With the clear vision of a seer that knows.
   I had a message to the powers of wrong
And counted not the number of my foes.

I stood forth in the strength of my soul's rage
And spoke my word of truth to a lewd age.
   It was the first blow struck in that mad war,
My last farewell to my fair hermitage.

O God of many battles!　Thou that art
Strong to withstand when warriors close and part,
   That art or wast the Lord of the right cause!
How has thy hand grown feeble in its smart!

How are the vassals of thy power to-day
Set in rebellion mastering the fray!
   Blaspheming Thee they smite with tongues obscene,
While these Thy saints lie slaughtered where they pray.

How is the cauldron of thy wrath the deepest,
Cold on its stones? No fire for it thou heapest.
   Thou in the old time wert a jealous God.
Thieves have dishonoured Thee. And lo, Thou sleepest!

Between the camps I passed in the still night,
The breath of heaven how pure, the stars how bright.
   On either hand the life impetuous flowed
Waiting the morrow which should crown the fight.

How did they greet it? With what voice, what word,
What mood of preparation for the sword?
   On this side and on that a chaunt was borne
Faint on the night-wind from each hostile horde.

Here lay the camps. The sound from one rose clear,
A single voice through the thrilled listening air.
   "There is no God but God," it cried aloud.
"Arise, ye faithful, 'tis your hour of prayer."

And from the other? Hark the ignoble chorus,
Strains of the music halls, the slums before us.
   Let our last thought be as our lives were there,
Drink and debauchery! The drabs adore us.

And these were proved the victors on that morrow,
And those the vanquished, fools, beneath war's harrow.
   And the world laughed applauding what was done,
And if the angels wept none heard their sorrow.

Harwood E. Steele

'THE FLAT-IRON
(H.M. FLAT-BOTTOMED RIVER GUNBOATS)', 1914

Steele was a minor writer on military topics whose only collection of poetry, *Cleared for Action*, produced on the eve of the Great War, attempted to do for the Empire's navy what Kipling's poetry had done for the army, and in much the same style. Though far less accomplished than Kipling's, Steele's verse has a certain vigour, as in this account of the practicalities of gunboat diplomacy.

In charge o' a sub. or a midshipman wi' a thing they calls a crew,
Aflying the Ensign at the stern the same as the real ships do,
She goes around in a Tropical stream wi' a foot o' wash below,
To teach the lesson a *ship* can teach wherever a *boat* can go.

> So please don't laugh at the Flat-iron—
> It's not wot a gent would do.
> The pore little puffin' Flat-iron,
> She never did nought to you!
> She's a good little ship, the Flat-iron,
> At doin' wot she's to do.
> So please don't laugh at the Flat-iron,
> The Flat-iron, the sub. an' the crew!

Whenever Somebody o' So-an'-so 'as started to play the goat,
Along comes a man in an ol' canoe to talk to an 'At-an'-Coat,
An' the 'At-an'-Coat, 'e sends for the sub. an' gives 'im
> instructions trite,
An' the sub. goes back an' the steam blows off, an' the Flat-iron
> leaves that night.

They crosses the bar wi' an inch to spare, an' they steers by the
> trees ashore,
An' the man oo came in the ol' canoe, 'e lies on the cabin floor;
An' 'e's sick as ever a man can be, disgraceful to be seen,
While the sub. 'angs on to the rail an' laughs when the Flat-iron
> takes it green!

They gets to the mouth o' the So-an'-so, where the sea an' the
    river meet,
An' the Flat-iron spins in the current's grip an' the sub. falls off
    'is feet;
An' she goes aground on the bloomin' bank, an' she's landed, 'igh
    an' dry,
Till they all get out an' push 'er off, when the second tide
    comes by!

Then off she goes like a bloomin' lord atrailin' 'is bloomin' train,
A dozen times they run 'er ashore an' back 'er off again;
An' at last they come where they want to come an' they stops
    where the foe can see,
An' the sub. goes off, as the steam blows off, to call on the
    Tweedle-dee.

The sub. 'e calls on the Tweedle-dee an' 'e tells 'im wot 'e
    should—
That someone will spank the Somebody if the Somebody won't be
    good;
An' the Tweedle-dee says that 'e *won't* be good, an' the sub. 'e
    drinks 'is tea,
An' 'e tells 'im all that 'e's goin' to do to the 'ouse of' the
    Tweedle-dee.

The sub. goes back to the Flat-iron then, for 'e's tired o' 'is
    country's foes,
An' that impudent Somebody's on the shore, 'is fingers up 'is nose;
An' the crew they jumps at the little thing that the sub. 'e calls
    a gun—
The thing that you train wi' the Flat-iron's wheel an' jams when
    the fight is won.

The crew, they shoot wi' the pea-shooter, an' the Flat-iron waltzes
    round;
They scare all the birds in the wavin' palms, an' they scare all the
    beasts on the ground;
They play Aunt Sally wi' Somebody an' Somebody tells 'em plain,
'E's ready to do as 'e ought to do an' the sub. goes ashore again.

The Somebody kisses the sub.'s left cheek, an' the Tweedle-dee
    kisses the right,
An' everyone praises their noble selves, an' nobody wants to fight;
So the sub. 'e carries them both aboard an' they all are friends
    again,
An' the sub. makes both o' them awful drunk on a case o' the
    best champagne!

So that is the way that the thing is done whenever the trouble
    comes,
An' that is the way that 'e settles things wi' never a roll o'
    drums—
The sub. 'e goes wi' 'is Flat-iron an' 'is bottles o' best champagne,
An' the Somebody drinks wi' the Tweedle-dee an' they all are
    friends again!

    So please don't laugh at the Flat-iron—
      The Flat-iron that knows wot to do,
    When trouble's in wait for the Flat-iron
      An' trouble's in wait for the crew,
    An' the King, oo's the boss o' the Flat-iron,
      Is in for a shindy or two.
    Then give a good cheer for the Flat-iron,
      The Flat-iron, the sub. an' the crew—Hoo! Hoo!—
    The Flat-iron, the sub. an' the crew!

Lawrence Eastwood

'THE ANSWER OF THE ANZACS', 1916

———

Patriotic songs and monologues became a standard part of the
music-hall repertoire during the Great War, though few were
concerned in any but a general way with the Empire, or with the
huge contribution made by colonial troops. This monologue, by
an author who seems not to have written regularly for the halls,
is an exception. The ANZACs (the Australian and New Zealand
Army Corps) suffered particularly heavily in the botched Galli-
poli campaign of 1915; here, the British lion, battling against
the German eagle, welcomes her imperial cubs to the European
theatre of war.

THERE was once a mother Lion,
   And she stood on Dover cliffs,
Where the water gags and washes,
   Where the salt the Sea-Horse sniffs.
And she growled: 'The clouds look angry,
   They'll burst in storm today—
And all my cubs are distant,
   Twelve thousand miles away.'
And mother stood there all alone,
   And mother *meant* to stay,
Though all her cubs were distant,
   Twelve thousand miles away.
Then rose a mighty eagle,
   And it screeched at Dover cliffs,
Where the water wags and washes,
   Where the salt the Sea-Horse sniffs.
'I'll break you, mother lion,
   Though you're mighty proud today,
Don't count upon your cubs, my dear,
   Kids don't turn out that way.'
Still mother faced the storm alone,
   For *that* was mother's way.
But her cubs were calling to her—
   Twelve thousand miles away.
Then hove in sight a mighty fleet,
   That made for Dover cliffs—

Where the water wags and washes,
　Where the salt the Sea-Horse sniffs.
And from that mighty fleet there sprang
　The 'Anzacs' in array—
A hundred thousand cubs
　From twelve thousand miles away.
And mother locked them to her breast,
　Then thundered 'cross the bay—
'My cubs are all around me,
　They're by my side today;
You've blundered, master eagle,
　And your blunder's deep and vast;
For mother England's mighty cubs
　Will bring you down—*at last!*'

BILLY BENNETT

From 'MANDALAY', 1929

After the First World War, in which he was decorated for gallantry, Bennett (*fl.* 1918–35) became a music-hall star, first as 'The Trench Comedian', then with the billing 'Almost a Gentleman'. He specialized in wildly unlikely parodies of popular poems and dramatic monologues, many of them spoofing the patriotic and uplifting sentiments of the originals. In this characteristically surreal example he burlesques Kipling's 'Mandalay'—and with it much of the supposed glamour of the Orient. Like most of Bennett's monologues, verses could be added almost at random.

By an old whitewashed Pagoda
   Looking eastward to the west
There's a Burma girl, from Bermondsey,
   Sits in a sparrow's nest.

She's as pretty as a picture,
   Though she lost one eye, they say,
Through the black hole of Calcutta—
   Perhaps the keyhole of Bombay!

Look as far as you can see, boy;
   Look a little further, son,
For that Burma girl is burning—
   Stick a fork in, see if she's done.

Oh, there's not a drop of water
   In that waste of desert land,
And the soldiers' tongues are hanging out
   And trailing in the sand.

Oh, they're hanging out like carpets,
   And you'll hear the natives say
Mr. Drage has laid the lino
   On the road to Mandalay!

As the temple bells are ringing
  Comes a soldier from his hut.
Will he be in time for service?
  No, too late, the canteen's shut!

There's a pub three miles behind us
  And we've passed it on the way;
Come you back, you British soldiers,
  There's a Scotsman wants to pay!

See, the desert moon is rising,
  For the golden sun has dropped,
And the Burma girl is sleeping—
  Sleeping sleeps she never slopped.

She is lying on an ant hill;
  Soon the ants come out to play;
Then she wakes and finds she's bitten—
  On the road to Mandalay!

ALAN SANDERS

'TOMMY OUT EAST', 1932

———

Sanders is an obscure figure who wrote pieces for music-hall performance between the world wars. Apart from the occasional patriotic demonstration, British working-class people never showed much interest in the Empire, though they provided the great bulk of the regular army and navy who helped keep it in being. This cockney monologue—undoubtedly closer to authentic proletarian feeling than the Kipling poems on which it is modelled—expresses the tedium and homesickness that typified colonial soldiering for other ranks. Pointedly, the poem's sentimental longing for home is not for some notion of England, but for Seven Dials, a tough working-class enclave in central London.

I am baked and I am thirsty, in this blarsted burnin' sun,
  For the sand's got in my system, and it's damned near spoilt
    my gun.
But our blue-eyed baby captain, who is learnin' 'ard to swear,
  Says we're 'oldin' up the Empire, though we're far from
    Leicester Square.
I believes him when 'e says it, but at times I wish I knew
  That a little 'ome I thinks of, in the Dials—where I grew,
Were just a trifle nearer, so that I could go and see
  What my mother is a-doin'—if she's thinkin' 'long o' me.
For it's marchin', and it's fightin' and it's 'ard I give my word
  To keep yer face a-smilin' when they've given yer 'the bird',
But when murky day is over, and we gets the 'LIGHTS OUT'
    clear,
  I can 'ear the call of London, and I dream I'm tastin' beer.
I've got a gal in Shoreditch—'ere's 'er photo next me 'eart—
  And Gawd, I wonder if she's gone and left me in the cart.
For this waitin' game don't suit 'er; she says all soldiers flirt,
  Just as if she couldn't trust me with another bit o' skirt!
The rosy East ain't rosy like them writers 'ave you think.
  And if you should 'ave a 'beano', well, they shoves yer into
    'clink'.

With the Temples and Pagodas all a-roastin' in the sun,
    You can 'ave the blinkin' blindin' East—give me 'Ampstead
    'Eath for fun!
Oh, we're 'oldin' up the Empire, though we're distant from the
    smoke,
    And the sun beats down in glory, 'nuff to burn up any bloke.
But it's night-time when I feels as if I'd copped out unawares
    'Cos my 'eart's in Seven Dials, in my 'ome up many stairs!

Noël Coward

'MAD DOGS AND ENGLISHMEN', 1934

Dramatist, composer, and brilliantly inventive lyricist, Coward (1899–1973) enjoyed a glamorously successful career in theatre and revue from the 1920s through to the 1960s. In this famous song from *Words and Music*, Coward mocks the obstinate Englishness that helped maintain colonial superiority in the Empire.

In tropical climes there are certain times of day
When all the citizens retire
To tear their clothes off and perspire.
It's one of those rules that the greatest fools obey,
Because the sun is much too sultry
And one must avoid its ultry-violet ray.

Papalaka papalaka papalaka boo
Papalaka papalaka papalaka boo,
Digariga digariga digariga doo,
Digariga digariga digariga doo.

The natives grieve when the white men leave their huts,
Because they're obviously definitely nuts!

Mad dogs and Englishmen
Go out in the midday sun,
The Japanese don't care to.
The Chinese wouldn't dare to,
Hindoos and Argentines sleep firmly from twelve to one.
But Englishmen detest a siesta.
In the Philippines
There are lovely screens
To protect you from the glare.
In the Malay States
There are hats like plates
Which the Britishers won't wear.
At twelve noon
The natives swoon
And no further work is done.
But mad dogs and Englishmen
Go out in the midday sun.

It's such a surprise for the Eastern eyes to see
That though the English are effete,
They're quite impervious to heat,
When the white man rides every native hides in glee,
Because the simple creatures hope he
Will impale his solar topee on a tree.

    Bolyboly bolyboly bolyboly baa,
    Bolyboly bolyboly bolyboly baa,
    Habaninny habaninny habaninny haa,
    Habaninny habaninny habaninny haa.

It seems such a shame
When the English claim
The earth
That they give rise to such hilarity and mirth.

Mad dogs and Englishmen
Go out in the midday sun.
The toughest Burmese bandit
Can never understand it.
In Rangoon the heat of noon
Is just what the natives shun.
They put their Scotch or Rye down
And lie down.
In a jungle town
Where the sun beats down
To the rage of man and beast
The English garb
Of the English sahib
Merely gets a bit more creased.
In Bangkok
At twelve o'clock
They foam at the mouth and run,
But mad dogs and Englishmen
Go out in the midday sun.

Mad dogs and Englishmen
Go out in the midday sun.
The smallest Malay rabbit
Deplores this stupid habit.
In Hongkong
They strike a gong
And fire off a noonday gun

To reprimand each inmate
Who's in late.
In the mangrove swamps
Where the python romps
There is peace from twelve till two.
Even caribous
Lie around and snooze,
For there's nothing else to do.
In Bengal
To move at all
Is seldom, if ever done,
But mad dogs and Englishmen
Go out in the midday sun.

JOHN MASEFIELD

'AUSTRALIA', 1936

Masefield (1878–1967) belonged to the same generation of poets as Noyes, and was similarly prolific. He made his reputation with seafaring ballads and with a number of long, supposedly realist narrative poems; he also wrote plays, novels, and prose works on the First World War. Masefield's poetry enjoyed wide popularity, his *Collected Poems* of 1923 selling over 200,000 copies. He became Poet Laureate in 1930. Despite his nautical enthusiasms, he did not share Noyes's explicitly imperialist concerns, but this relatively late poem records personal responses to a visit to Australia and catches something of the sense of national renewal that the British often felt was exemplified by the colonies of white settlement.

> WHEN the North Lander saw the rose in blossom,
> He thought the bush bore fire, and knelt and prayed.
> When first the desert woman saw the sea,
> She cried, "O under God, the day and night."
>
> We have but language for the starry Heaven,
> And words for continents and emperors.
> I have but images within my heart
> And words with which to make those images
> Form in the minds of others, and, alas,
> You are too wonderful and beautiful,
> I cannot tell the marvel of your land,
> But can be happy with my memories.
>
> I think at first of cities bright with flowers,
> Flowers for everybody, everywhere;
> Then of a grass unlike the English turf,
> "Buffalo grass," you called it, tough and springy;
> Then of the birds, the exquisite blue wrens,
> The kookaburras laughing in the fig-tree,
> The whip birds slashing in the rainy glen,
> The blue and scarlet parrots rushing past,
> And black swans on the lake at Woolongoon.
> Yet of the birds the black-backed magpie seems
> The very soul of the Australian scene.

Often in early morning I would hear him
In strange, sweet song, now like to jingling glasses,
Now piping, now like flutes, but always telling
Of morning coming over the world's rim.

Then I remember how upon the hill,
Among the gumtrees, on the holiday,
The car sped past a sunny group of children,
And on the instant as we hurried past,
I heard a little girl cry, "There's John Masefield,"
And knew upon the instant what a power
A language has to give a fellowship
Over the distances of earth and sea.

Next, I remember how the forest stood;
Mile after mile of giant gums, blue-gray,
Glen after glen, blue-gray; peak after peak;
With blackened rampikes from old forest fires,
And bones of dead gums, white as skeletons,
And silence everywhere, not to be broken,
Save by the water in the gully talking.

Then, the great spaces like the Berkshire downs;
Mile after mile, with clumps upon the skyline
Of gumtrees which at distance looked like beech;
The wind-swept, rolling plain, dotted with sheep;
The station buildings here and there: few men,
Perhaps two children upon pony back,
Turning a mob of cattle, or the slow,
Part staggering figures of two sundowners,
Bent underneath the long rolls of their blueys,
Silently moving to a camping-place.

Next, as it were a river of bright flowers
In Earth's most lovely garden, and great rain
Ceasing above a multitude, and sun
Struggling through cloud, and lighting up the scene
Of splendid horses going to the post.

Then in the quagmire of the course, the thunder
Of the great race's passing, with surmise
From all those thousands, of which rider led;
Nothing but distant, flitting, coloured caps,
Shewed in a bunch along the rail; then, lo,
They swerved into the Straight, the great horse leading.

He bore topweight; the going was a bog;
He strode at ease, ahead, his ears still cocked.
Had he been called-upon he could have won
By half-a-mile, it seemed: his image stays
Forever in my mind as one of Power
That achieves easily while Weakness strives.

Next, I remember all the sun-swept, wind-swept
Hills of the pasture up above the brook;
No fence in sight; the cattle in small groups
Moving and grazing in the same direction,
And all the landscape stretching on and on,
To unknown mountains, forty miles away,
Where sheep and dogs and cattle, all gone wild,
Ran in the range, men said, and dingoes throve.

There was an ancient tree outside the station,
Which marked (they said) an English convict's grave.
He swallowed stolen jewels and so died.
Often I hope that that free space and light
Have freed him to the lovely universe,
So that he rides upon the wind there, singing
For joy that the old iron of his sins
Is snapped in pieces from his fettered soul.

Always above these memories is the sense
Of charming people, ever kind and thoughtful;
Most generous in thought, in word, in deed,
And faithful in their kindness to the end.
The mind is glad with many memories
Of kind things done and uttered by the race,
Earth's newest race of men, whose bodies' beauty
Surpasses all the peoples of the world;
Whose grace and care and generosity
Though never thanked, can never be forgotten.
A marvellous kind people, beautiful.

I shut my eyes and hear the magpies utter
Their magical, sweet cry like jingling glass,
And see the barren with the whited bones
Of gumtrees stretching to the flood-water,
Where black swans straddle in a line, like men
Pretending to be swans. Beyond the flood
There are the shearing sheds, where men of Anzac,
The shearers about whom the ballads tell,

Wonderful men whose fame this country treasures,
Strip off the fleeces from the sheep as though
Each fleece were but a woolly coat unbuttoned.

And many many other memories come,
Of cities fairer than our country holds;
Of waters gushing among blue-gray gums;
Or mighty pastures, each with lonely horsemen
Loping the morning, singing as they go;
Of beaches where the sun-tanned dare the sharks;
Or bush, the same for miles, all feathery-dim,
Each fathom of it green-gray, feathery-dim,
(Distinct, yet indistinct, almost like seaweed),
Where thirst has killed her hundreds, and will kill.

But among all these memories I hear
From gumtrees dead or blossoming, the magpies,
With that strange song so moving and so sweet,
The very voice of that far distant land,
So sweet that all who hear it must be moved
To hear it once again before they die.

NOËL COWARD

'I WONDER WHAT HAPPENED TO HIM', c.1944

Written during the Second World War while Coward was in India entertaining the British forces, this song parodies retired Indian army officers—frequently satirized as 'Colonel Blimp'—still obsessed with the trivial gossip of the regimental mess. The song subsequently featured in the revue *Sigh No More*.

The India that one read about
And may have been misled about
In one respect has kept itself intact.
Though 'Pukka Sahib' traditions may have cracked
And thinned
The good old Indian army's still a fact.
That famous monumental man
The Officer and Gentleman
Still lives and breathes and functions from Bombay to Katmandu.
At any moment one can glimpse
Matured or embryonic 'Blimps'
Vivaciously speculating as to what became of who.
Though Eastern sounds may fascinate your ear
When West meets West you're always sure to hear—

Whatever became of old Bagot?
I haven't seen him for a year.
Is it true that young Forbes had to marry that Faggot
He met in the Vale of Kashmir?
Have you had any news
Of that chap in the 'Blues',
Was it Prosser or Pyecroft or Pym?
He was stationed in Simla, or was it Bengal?
I know he got tight at a ball in Nepal
And wrote several four-letter words on the wall.
I wonder what happened to him!

Whatever became of old Shelley?
Is it true that young Briggs was cashiered
For riding quite nude on a push-bike through Delhi
The day the new Viceroy appeared?
Have you had any word
Of that bloke in the 'Third',

COWARD (*c.*1944)

Was it Southerby, Sedgwick or Sim?
They had him thrown out of the club in Bombay
For, apart from his mess bills exceeding his pay,
He took to pig-sticking in *quite* the wrong way.
I wonder what happened to him!

One must admit that by and large
Upholders of the British Raj
Don't shine in conversation as a breed.
Though Indian army officers can read
A bit
Their verbal wit—has rather run to seed.
Their splendid insularity
And roguish jocularity
Was echoing through when Victoria was Queen.
In restaurants and dining-cars,
In messes, clubs and hotel bars
They try to maintain tradition in the way it's always been.
Though worlds may change and nations disappear
Above the shrieking chaos you will hear—

Whatever became of old Tucker?
Have you heard any word of young Mills
Who ruptured himself at the end of a chukka
And had to be sent to the hills?
They say that young Lees
Had a go of 'D.T.s'
And his hopes of promotion are slim.
According to Stubbs, who's a bit of a louse,
The silly young blighter went out on a 'souse',
And took two old tarts into Government House.
I wonder what happened to him!

Whatever became of old Keeling?
I hear that he got back from France
And frightened three nuns in a train in Darjeeling
By stripping and waving his lance!
D'you remember Munroe,
In the P.A.V.O.?
He was tallish and mentally dim.
That talk of heredity can't be quite true,
He was dropped on his head by his ayah at two,
I presume that by now he'll have reached G.H.Q.
I'm sure that's what happened to him!

Whatever became of old Archie?
I hear he departed this life
After rounding up ten sacred cows in Karachi
To welcome the Governor's wife.
D'you remember young Phipps
Who had *very* large hips
And whose waist was excessively slim?
Well, it seems that some doctor in Grosvenor Square
Gave him hormone injections for growing his hair
And he grew something here, and he grew something there.
I wonder what happened to her—him?

WYSTAN HUGH AUDEN

'PARTITION', 1948

———

Auden (1907–73) was the leading poet of the generation that followed Eliot, the socialist stance of much of his work, particularly in the 1930s, in marked contrast to the right-wing position of the older Modernists. Auden largely abandoned political poetry after the Second World War, but here he comments on the expediency that determined the partition of India and Pakistan in the last days of the Raj: hundreds of thousands of people died in the violence that ensued.

Unbiased at least he was when he arrived on his mission.
Having never set eyes on this land he was called to partition
Between two peoples fanatically at odds,
With their different diets and incompatible gods.
'Time', they had briefed him in London, 'is short. It's too late
For mutual reconciliation or rational debate;
The only solution now lies in separation.
The Viceroy thinks, as you see from his letter,
That the less you are seen in his company the better.
So we've arranged to provide you with other accommodation.
We can give you four judges, two Moslem and two Hindu,
To consult with, but the final decision must rest with you.'

Shut up in a lonely mansion, with police night and day
Patrolling the gardens to keep assassins away,
He got down to work, to the task of settling the fate
Of millions. The maps at his disposal were out of date
And the Census Returns almost certainly incorrect.
But there was no time to check them, no time to inspect
Contested areas. The weather was frightfully hot.
And a bout of dysentery kept him constantly on the trot.
But in seven weeks it was done, the frontiers decided,
A continent for better or worse divided.

The next day he sailed for England, where he quickly forged
The case, as a good lawyer must. Return he would not.
Afraid, as he told his Club, that he might get shot.

STEVIE SMITH

'THE JUNGLE HUSBAND', 1957

Smith (1902–71) was a remarkably independent poet, with a flair
for the unexpected. This poem takes the form of a letter from a
husband absent on a big-game hunting expedition.

Dearest Evelyn, I often think of you
Out with the guns in the jungle stew
Yesterday I hittapotamus
I put the measurements down for you but they got lost in the fuss
It's not a good thing to drink out here
You know, I've practically given it up dear.
Tomorrow I am going alone a long way
Into the jungle. It is all gray
But green on top
Only sometimes when a tree has fallen
The sun comes down plop, it is quite appalling.
You never want to go in a jungle pool
In the hot sun, it would be the act of a fool
Because it's always full of anacondas, Evelyn, not looking ill-fed
I'll say. So no more now, from your loving husband, Wilfred.

JON STALLWORTHY

'AN ODE FOR TRAFALGAR DAY', 1965

Stallworthy (b. 1935) is well known as both poet and scholar, particularly of the literature of the First World War. This even-handed poem looks at the Empire through the eyes of Admiral Nelson, whose statue dominates Trafalgar Square.

As I was crossing Trafalgar Square
whose but the Admiral's shadow hand
should tap my shoulder. At my ear:
'You Sir, stay-at-home citizen
poet, here's more use for your pen
than picking scabs. Tell them in England
this: when first I stuck my head in the air,

'winched from a cockpit's tar and blood
to my crow's nest over London, I
looked down on a singular crowd
moving with the confident swell
of the sea. As it rose and fell
every pulse in the estuary
carried them quayward, carried them seaward.

'Box-wallah, missionary, clerk,
lancer, planter, I saw them all
Linked like the waves on the waves embark.
Their eyes looked out—as yours look in—
to harbour names on the cabin-
trunks carrying topees to Bengal,
maxims or gospels to lighten a dark

'continent. Blatant as the flag
they went out under were the bright
abstractions nailed to every mast.
Sharpshooters since have riddled most
and buried an empire in their rags—
scrivener, do you dare to write
a little 'e' in the epilogue

'to an empire that spread its wings
wider than Rome? They are folded,
you say, with the maps and flags; awnings
and verandahs overrun
by impis of the ant; sun-
downers sunk, and the planters' blood
turned tea or siphoned into rubber saplings.

'My one eye reports that their roads
remain, their laws, their language
seeing all winds. They were no gods
from harnessed clouds, as the islanders
thought them, nor were they monsters
but men, as you stooped over your page
and you and you and these wind-driven crowds

'are and are not. For you have lost
their rhythm, the pulse of the sea
in their salt blood. Your heart has missed
the beat of centuries, its channels
silted to their source. The muscles
of the will stricken by distrophy
dishonour those that bareback rode the crest

'of untamed seas. Acknowledge
their energy. If you condemn
their violence in a violent age
speak of their courage. Mock their pride
when, having built as well, in as wide
a compass, you have none. Tell them
in England this.'
          And a pigeon sealed the page.

PHILIP LARKIN

'HOMAGE TO A GOVERNMENT', written 1968

Although Larkin (1922–85) was generally regarded as the most accomplished of the so-called 'New Movement' poets of the 1950s, his output was limited and he remained detatched from contemporary literary and cultural developments, writing very little after 1970. Politically and socially reactionary, he was increasingly disenchanted by postwar and postcolonial Britain. In this poem—unusually explicit for Larkin—he attacks Harold Wilson's socialist government of the late 1960s for its decision to accelerate British withdrawal from what then remained of the Empire.

Next year we are to bring the soldiers home
For lack of money, and it is all right.
Places they guarded, or kept orderly,
Must guard themselves, and keep themselves orderly.
We want the money for ourselves at home
Instead of working. And this is all right.

It's hard to say who wanted it to happen,
But now it's been decided nobody minds.
The places are a long way off, not here,
Which is all right, and from what we hear
The soldiers there only made trouble happen.
Next year we shall be easier in our minds.

Next year we shall be living in a country
That brought its soldiers home for lack of money.
The statues will be standing in the same
Tree-muffled squares, and look nearly the same.
Our children will not know it's a different country.
All we can hope to leave them now is money.

FRED D'AGUIAR

'AT THE GRAVE OF THE UNKNOWN AFRICAN',
1993

D'Aguiar was born in London in 1960, grew up in Guyana, and returned to Britain where he has become known as a poet and playwright. This poem is taken from *British Subjects* (1993).

1

Two round, cocoa faces, carved on whitewashed headstone
protect your grave against hellfire and brimstone.

Those cherubs with puffed cheeks, as if chewing gum,
signal how you got here and where you came from.

More than two and a half centuries after your death,
the barefaced fact that you're unnamed feels like defeat.

I got here via White Ladies Road and Black Boy's Hill,
clues lost in these lopsided stones that Henbury's vandal

helps to the ground and Henbury's conservationist
tries to rectify, cleaning the vandal's pissy love-nest.

African slave without a name, I'd call this home
by now. Would you? Your unknown soldier's tomb

stands for shipload after shipload that docked,
unloaded, watered, scrubbed, exercised and restocked

thousands more souls for sale in Bristol's port;
cab drivers speak of it all with yesterday's hurt.

The good conservationist calls it her three hundred year war;
those raids, deals, deceit and capture (a sore still raw).

St Paul's, Toxteth, Brixton, Tiger Bay and Handsworth:
petrol bombs flower in the middle of roads, a sudden growth

at the feet of police lines longer than any cricket pitch.
African slave, your namelessness is the wick and petrol mix.

Each generation catches the one fever love can't appease;
nor Molotov cocktails, nor when they embrace in a peace

far from that three-named, two-bit vandal and conservationist
binning beer cans, condoms and headstones in big puzzle-pieces.

2

Stop there black Englishman before you tell a bigger lie.
You mean me well by what you say but I can't stand idly by.

The vandal who keeps coming and does what he calls fucks
on the cool gravestones, also pillages and wrecks.

If he knew not so much my name but what happened to Africans,
he'd maybe put in an hour or two collecting his Heinekens;

like the good old conservationist, who's earned her column
inch, who you knock, who I love without knowing her name.

The dead can't write, nor can we sing (nor can most living).
Our ears (if you can call them ears) make no good listening.

Say what happened to me and countless like me, all anon.
Say it urgently. Mean times may bring back the water cannon.

I died young, but to age as a slave would have been worse.
What can you call me? Mohammed. Homer. Hannibal. Jesus.

Would it be too much to have them all? What are couples up to
when one reclines on the stones and is ridden by the other?

Will our talk excite the vandal? He woz ere, *like you are now,*
armed with a knife, I could see trouble on his creased brow,

love-trouble, not for some girl but for this village.
I share his love and would have let him spoil my image,

if it wasn't for his blade in the shadow of the church wall
taking me back to my capture and long sail to Bristol,

then my sale on Black Boy's Hill and disease ending my days:
I sent a rumble up to his sole; he scooted, shocked and dazed.

Here the sentence is the wait and the weight is the sentence.
I've had enough of a parish where the congregation can't sing.

Take me where the hymns sound like a fountain-washed canary,
and the beer-swilling, condom wielding vandal of Henbury,

reclines on the stones and the conservationist mounts him,
and in my crumbly ears there's only the sound of them sinning.

BIBLIOGRAPHY

1. General works

C.A. Bayly (ed.) *Atlas of the British Empire*. London: Hamlyn, 1989.

Cynthia Fansler Behrman, *Victorian Myths of the Sea*. Ohio: Ohio University Press, 1977.

Patrick Brantlinger, *The Rule of Darkness. British Literature and Imperialism 1830–1914*. Ithaca: Cornell University Press, 1988.

M.E. Chamberlain, *The Scramble for Africa*. London: Longman, 1974.

Linda Colley, *Britons. Forging the Nation 1707–1837*. London: Pimlico, 1992.

Lance E. Davis and Robert A. Huttenback, *Mammon and the Pursuit of Empire. The Economics of British Imperialism*. Cambridge: Cambridge University Press, 1988.

Paul Gilroy, *Small Acts. Thoughts on the Politics of Black Culture*. London: Serpent's Tail, 1993.

Martin Green, *Dreams of Adventure, Deeds of Empire*. New York: Basic Books, 1977.

Christopher Hibbert, *The Great Mutiny. India 1857*. Harmondsworth: Allen Lane, 1978.

E.J. Hobsbawm, *The Age of Empire*. London: Weidenfeld and Nicolson, 1987.

Peter Hulme, *Colonial Encounters. Europe and the Native Caribbean 1492–1797*. London: Methuen, 1986.

M. Hulse, D. Kennedy and D. Morley (eds), *The New Poetry*. London: Bloodaxe, 1993.

John Lucas, *England and Englishness. Ideas of Nationhood in English Poetry 1688–1900*. London: The Hogarth Press, 1990.

John M. Mackenzie (ed.), *Imperialism and Popular Culture*. Manchester: Manchester University Press, 1986.

J.A. Mangan, *The Games Ethic and Imperialism. Aspects of the Diffusion of an Ideal*. Harmondsworth: Viking, 1986.

Bill Pearson, *Rifled Sanctuaries. Some Views of the Pacific Islands in Western Literature to 1900*. Auckland: Auckland University Press, 1984.

Bernard Porter, *The Lion's Share. A Short History of British Imperialism, 1850–1983*. London: Longman, 1975; 2nd edition, 1984.

Edward Said, *Culture and Imperialism*. London: Chatto and Windus, 1993.

Edward Said, *Orientalism*. New York: Pantheon Books, 1978.

Surendra Nath Sen, *Eighteen Fifty-Seven*. Calcutta: Ministry of Information, 1957.

Wylie Sypher, *Guinea's Captive Kings. British Anti-Slavery Literature of the Eighteenth Century*. New York: Octagon Books, 1942.

Joanna Trollope, *Britannia's Daughters. Women of the British Empire*. London: Cresset Women's Voices, 1983.

James Walvin, *Black Ivory. A History of British Slavery*. Cambridge, Mass.: Harvard University Press, 1992.

2. Anthologies of poetry from the former British Empire

The Penguin Book of Canadian Verse, edited by Ralph Gustafson. Harmondsworth: Penguin, 1958; revised edition, 1967.

The Penguin Book of New Zealand Verse, edited by Alan Curnow. Harmondsworth: Penguin, 1960.

The Penguin Book of Australian Poetry, edited by Harry Heseltine. Harmondsworth: Penguin, 1972.

Poems of Black Africa, edited by Wole Soyinka. London: Heinemann, 1975.

The Penguin Book of Caribbean Verse in English, edited by Paula Burnett. Harmondsworth: Penguin, 1986.

The New Oxford Book of Irish Verse, edited by Thomas Kinsella. Oxford: Oxford University Press, 1986.

The Penguin Book of South African Verse, edited by Stephen Gray. Harmondsworth: Penguin, 1989.

3. Anthologies of poetry used in this collection

The Bentley Ballads, comprising the Tipperary Hall Ballads, now first republished from 'Bentley's Miscellany', edited by John Sheehan. London: Richard Bentley, 1846.

Australian Ballads and Rhymes; Poems inspired by Life and Scenery in Australia and New Zealand, selected and edited by Douglas B.W. Sladen. London: Walter Scott, 1888.

Ballads of the Brave. Poems of Chivalry, Enterprise, Courage and Constancy, edited by Frederick Langbridge. London: Methuen, 1889; 4th edition, 1911.

Lyra Heroica: A Book of Verse for Boys, edited by W.E. Henley. New York: Scribners, 1891; London: David Nutt, 1892.

A Book of Heroic Verse, edited by Arthur Burrell. London: J.M. Dent, 1910.

Mount Helicon. A School Anthology of Verse. London: Edward Arnold, 1922.

The Book of Comic and Dramatic Monologues, edited by Michael Marshall. London: Hamish Hamilton, 1981.

The New Oxford Book of Eighteenth-Century Verse, edited by Roger Lonsdale. Oxford: Oxford University Press, 1985.

Eighteenth-Century Women Poets, edited by Roger Lonsdale. Oxford: Oxford University Press, 1989.

4. Individual poets used in this collection

The Poems of William Allingham, edited by John Hewitt. Dublin: Dolmen Press, 1967.

Collected Poems of W.H. Auden, edited by Edward Mendelson. London: Faber and Faber, 1976.

Lyrical Poems, by Alfred Austin. London: Macmillan, 1891.

The History of Methodism, or the Wesleyan Centenary, A Poem, in Twelve Books, by George Beard. London: J.C. Beard and Simpkin, Marshall, 1840.

The Works of Aphra Behn, edited by Janet Todd. Vol. 1, London: William Pickering, 1992.

The Modern Traveller, by Hilaire Belloc. London: Edward Arnold, 1898.

The Poems of William Blake, edited by W.H. Stevenson. London: Longman, 1972.

The Poetical Works of Wilfrid Scawen Blunt. 2 vols, London: Macmillan, 1914.

The Complete Poetical Works of Robert Buchanan. 2 vols, London: Chatto and Windus, 1901.

The Poetical Works of Thomas Campbell, edited by W. Alfred Hill. London: George Bell, 1875.

The Poems of George Chapman, edited by Phyllis Brooks Bartlett. New York: Russell and Russell, 1962.

The Poems of Arthur Hugh Clough, edited by F.L. Mulhauser. Oxford: Clarendon Press, 1974.

The Poems of Eliza Cook. 4 vols, London: Simpkin, Marshall, 1853.

The Lyrics of Noël Coward. London: Heinemann, 1965.

The Complete Poetical Works of William Cowper, edited by H.S. Milford. London: Oxford University Press, 1907.

British Subjects, by Fred D'Aguiar. London: Bloodaxe, 1993.

The Works of Michael Drayton, edited by J. William Hebel. 5 vols, Oxford: Shakespeare Head Press, 1932–3.

The Poems of John Dryden, edited by James Kinsley. 4 vols, Oxford: Clarendon Press, 1958.

The Complete Poems of Thomas Hardy, edited by James Gibson. London: Macmillan, 1976.

The Poetical Works of Reginald Heber. London: John Murray, 1841.

[383]

The Works of Mrs Hemans. 7 vols, Edinburgh: Blackwood and Sons, 1839.
The Works of W.E. Henley. 7 vols, *Poems*, Vols. 1–2, London: David Nutt, 1908.
The Works of Thomas Hood, Comic and Serious, in Prose and Verse, edited by his son [Thomas Hood]. 7 vols, London: Moxon, 1862–3.
The Collected Poems of A.E. Housman. London: Jonathan Cape, 1939.
Poems by Charles Kingsley. 2 vols, London: Macmillan, 1884.
Rudyard Kipling's Verse. Inclusive Edition, 1885–1918. 3 vols, London: Hodder and Stoughton, 1920.
The Poetical Works of Andrew Lang, edited by Leonora Lang. 4 vols, London: Longman, 1923.
High Windows, by Philip Larkin. London: Faber and Faber, 1974.
Verses Written in India, by Sir Alfred Lyall. London: Kegan Paul, Trench, Trübner, 1889.
The Poetical Works of George Macdonald. 2 vols, London: Chatto and Windus, 1893.
Poetic Gems. Selected from the Works of W. MacGonagall. First printed 1890, London: Duckworth, 1953.
The Poetical Works of Charles Mackay. London: Frederick Warne, 1870.
The Poems and Letters of Andrew Marvell, edited by H.M. Margoliouth. 2 vols, Oxford: Clarendon Press, 1927.
The Collected Poems of John Masefield. London: Heinemann, 1938.
My Lyrical Life, by Gerald Massey. 2 vols, London: Kegan Paul, Trench, 1869.
The Poetical Works of James Montgomery, collected by himself. 4 vols, London: Longman, 1841.
The Works of Sir Lewis Morris. London: Kegan Paul, Trench, Trübner, 1907.
Collected Poems 1897–1907, by Henry Newbolt. London: Nelson, 1907.
The Collected Poems of Alfred Noyes. 4 vols, Edinburgh and London: Blackwood and Sons, 1927–9.
The Poems of Alexander Pope, edited by John Butt. London: Methuen, 1963.
The Poetical Works of Samuel Rogers. London: Moxon, 1856.
The Poetical Works of Christina Georgina Rossetti, edited by William Michael Rossetti. London: Macmillan, 1904.
Democratic Sonnets, by William Michael Rossetti. London: A. Rivers, 1907.
The Battle of the Bays, by Owen Seaman. London: John Lane, 1896.
The Poetical Works of Anna Seward, edited by Walter Scott. 3 vols, Edinburgh: James Ballantyne, 1810.
Ballads and Poems, by George R. Sims. London: John P. Fuller, 1883.
The Collected Poems of Stevie Smith. Harmondsworth: Allen Lane, 1975.

The Poems of Robert Southey, edited by M.H. Fitzgerald. London: Oxford University Press, 1909.

Epilogue to an Empire, by Jon Stallworthy. London: Chatto and Windus, 1986.

Cleared for Action, by Harwood E. Steele. London: T. Fisher Unwin, 1914.

The Poems of Algernon Charles Swinburne. 6 vols, London: Chatto and Windus, 1912.

The Poems of Tennyson, edited by Christopher Ricks. 3 vols, London: Longman, 1969.

The Works of Francis Thompson. 3 vols, London: Burns and Oates, 1913.

James Thomson. Liberty, The Castle of Indolence, and Other Poems, edited by James Sambrook. Oxford: Clarendon Press, 1986.

The Plays of James Thomson. A Critical Edition, edited by John C. Greene. New York and London: Garland Publishing, 1987.

James Thomson. The Seasons, edited by James Sambrook. Oxford: Clarendon Press, 1981.

Poems by Richard Chevenix Trench, Archbishop of Dublin, Collected and Arranged Anew. London: Macmillan, 1865.

The Poems of Sir William Watson. London: George Harrap, 1936.

The Complete Works of Oscar Wilde. London: Collins, 1966.

The Poetical Works of William Wordsworth, edited by Ernest de Selincourt and Helen Darbishire. 5 vols, Oxford University Press, 1940–9.

Lays of Ind, by 'Aliph Cheem' [Walter Yeldham]. Bombay and London: W. Thacker, 1881.

ACKNOWLEDGEMENTS

We would like to thank the Exeter students who followed our course on Literature and Imperialism, from which the idea of this anthology first derived. For practical help, advice on particular poems and writers, and for much useful discussion, our thanks are due to Richard Bradbury, Inga Bryden, Richard Crangle, David Evans, Nick Groom, Greg Harper, Su Jarwood, Peter Quartermaine, and Teresa and David Sladen.

The cover illustrations show two early twentieth century sets of song cards from the collection of Richard Crangle.

The editors gratefully acknowledge permission to reproduce copyright poems in this book.

W.H. AUDEN: 'Partition', published in *Collected Poems of W.H. Auden*, Faber and Faber, 1976. © 1976 by W.H. Auden. Reprinted by permission of Faber and Faber Ltd, and Random House Inc. New York.

HILAIRE BELLOC: *The Modern Traveller*, published by Edward Arnold, 1898. Reprinted by permission of Peters Fraser & Dunlop.

NOËL COWARD: 'I Wonder What Happened to Him', © 1945 The Estate of Noël Coward; 'Mad Dogs and Englishmen', © 1932 The Estate of Noël Coward, published in *The Lyrics of Noël Coward*, Heinemann, 1965. Reprinted by permission of Michael Imison Playwrights Ltd 28 Almeida Street, London N1 1TD.

FRED D'AGUIAR: 'At the Grave of the Unknown African', published in *British Subjects*, by Fred D'Aguiar, Bloodaxe Books, 1993. Reprinted by permission of Bloodaxe Books Ltd.

THOMAS HARDY: 'Embarcation (*Southampton Docks: October 1899*)', 'Departure (*Southampton Docks: October 1899*)', 'The Going of the Battery. Wives' Lament (*November 2, 1899*)', 'A Wife in London (*December 1899*)', 'Drummer Hodge', from 'War Poems', 1899–1900, published in *The Complete Poems of Thomas Hardy*, edited by James Gibson, © 1976, Macmillan London Ltd. Reprinted with the permission of Macmillan General Books, and Simon & Schuster, New York.

ACKNOWLEDGEMENTS

A.E. Housman: 'Lancer', 'Astronomy', published in *The Collected Poems of A.E. Housman*, Jonathan Cape, 1939. Reprinted by permission of The Society of Authors as the literary representative of the Estate of A.E. Housman, and Henry Holt and Co., Inc., New York. Copyright 1939, 1940 by Holt Rinehart and Winston, Inc. Copyright © 1967 by Robert E. Symons. Reprinted by permission of Henry Holt and Co., Inc.

Rudyard Kipling: 'The Story of Uriah', 'Arithmetic on the Frontier', 'The Widow at Windsor', 'Mandalay', 'Shillin' a Day', 'A Song of the English', 'Recessional', 'The White Man's Burden', 'Boots', published in *Rudyard Kipling's Verse, Inclusive Edition, 1885–1918*, published by Hodder and Stoughton, 1920. Reprinted by permission of A.P. Watt Ltd.

Philip Larkin: 'Homage to a Government', published in *High Windows*, by Philip Larkin, Faber and Faber, 1974. Copyright © 1974 by Philip Larkin. Reprinted by permission of Faber and Faber Ltd, and Farrar, Straus & Giroux Inc., New York.

John Masefield: 'Australia', published in *The Collected Poems of John Masefield*, Heinemann, 1938. Reprinted by permission of The Society of Authors as the literary representative of the Estate of John Masefield.

Henry Newbolt: 'Vitaï Lampada', 'He Fell Among Thieves', 'April on Waggon Hill', 'The Only Son', published in *Collected Poems of Henry Newbolt*, Nelson, 1907.

Alfred Noyes: 'The Empire Builders', 'The Heart of Canada', lines from *Drake* Books 2, 6, and 10, published in *The Collected Poems of Alfred Noyes*, Blackwood and Sons, 1927–9. Reprinted by permission of Mr Hugh Noyes.

Stevie Smith: 'The Jungle Husband', published in *The Collected Poems of Stevie Smith*, Harmondsworth: Allen Lane, 1975. Reprinted by permission of Mr James MacGibbon.

Jon Stallworthy: 'An Ode for Trafalgar Day', from 'The Anzac Sonata', published in *Epilogue to an Empire*, Chatto and Windus, 1986. Reprinted by permission of Random House UK Ltd.

William Watson: 'England and Her Colonies', 'How Weary is Our Heart!'; 'The Enemy', 'The Slain', 'Rome and Another', 'The True Imperialism', from *For England. Poems written during Estrangement*: published in *The Poems of Sir William Watson*, George Harrap, 1936.

Every effort has been made to trace copyright holders, but in a few cases this has proved impossible. The publishers would be interested to hear from any copyright holders not here acknowledged.

Chris Brooks and Peter Faulkner
August 1996